Comics and Language

COMICS and LANGUAGE

Reimagining Critical Discourse on the Form

Hannah Miodrag

University Press of Mississippi / Jackson

www.upress.state.ms.us

The University Press of Mississippi is a member
of the Association of American University Presses.

Copyright © 2013 by University Press of Mississippi
All rights reserved
Manufactured in the United States of America

First printing 2013
∞
Library of Congress Cataloging-in-Publication Data

Miodrag, Hannah.
Comics and language : reimagining critical discourse on the form / Hannah Miodrag.
pages cm
Includes bibliographical references and index.
ISBN 978-1-61703-804-4 (cloth : alk. paper) — ISBN 978-1-61703-805-1 (ebook)
1. Comic books, strips, etc.—Criticism, Textual. 2. Graphic novels—History and criticism. 3. Comic books, strips, etc.—Authorship. 4. Discourse analysis, Literary. I. Title.
PN6714.M56 2013
741.5'9—dc23   2013003471

British Library Cataloging-in-Publication Data available

For David

Contents

Comics and Language

Introduction

The term "comics" has come to be used, within the Anglophone industry, as a non-count noun that collectively refers to the drawn strip medium's various subcategories. It subsumes, but is not reducible to: children's comic books, which first took off when newspaper strips were sectioned into supplements, and which were increasingly aimed at a juvenile audience from the early twentieth century; classic genre serials, popularly associated with the superhero Golden Age that kicked off in the 1930s; the unruly underground comix of the 1960s counterculture; adult graphic novels, which began to gain cultural currency in the 1980s; and a host of other subsets of format, content, and target audience that continue to develop and expand. It is broadly agreed that the form began to cohere into what is currently recognized as comics in the early nineteenth century, particularly with the work of Swiss teacher Rodolphe Töpffer (Chute 2008: 455, Beaty 2007: 21).

The coalescing of the conventions and practices by which we now identify the form was, of course, a gradual process, and the modern medium can count the likes of eighteenth-century satirical caricatures, such as William Hogarth's series, and the strip narratives that appeared in popular prints of the sixteenth and seventeenth centuries as its antecedents. Some critics go so far as to include such artifacts as the Bayeux Tapestry and cave paintings under the banner of comics (McCloud 2000: 201), though most concur that "this kind of historical extrapolation is dubious in its logic, and often used to 'justify' comics by association with more culturally-respected forms" (Sabin 1993: 13). Despite efforts to argue otherwise, there is simply no traceable lineage from today's *Beano* back to medieval stained glass windows.[1]

Though the form itself has a long history, comics scholarship has been slower to develop, only emerging as a coherent discipline within Anglophone academia over the past twenty to thirty years. (European comics criticism, particularly in Francophone circles where comics, not incidentally, enjoy a better popular reputation, predates Anglophone scholarship by several decades [McQuillan 2005: 7–13].) Throughout its evolution, the field has been pervaded by the sort of "justificatory" strategies that lead critics into dating the medium's genesis at the very dawn of civilization, or adopting the plural form as a universal label so as to avoid the light-hearted, jokey connotations of the singular "comic." Comics scholarship has been riddled with "status anxiety" (Hatfield 2005: xii), and it may well be the case that the comics form is widely perceived as inherently low-brow, more readily associated, in the popular imagination, with *The Beano* and men in tights than with (to pick some diverse examples at random) the politically engaged New Journalism of Sue Coe, dark and dreamlike defamiliarization of Peter Blegvad, or the Tarkovsky-esque narrative styl-ings of Lorenzo Mattotti. However, the "belaboured alternately defensive and celebratory prose" (Chute 2006: 1,018) with which comics scholars have often attempted to combat this poor repute does little to improve the standing of either the medium or scholarly interest in it. Comics critics too often extol the virtues of the form to the hilt, "championing [their] interest in comics with the aggressive attitudes of the fan [becoming] carried away into exaggerated statements of faith, if only to overcome a certain embar-rassment [they] may still feel [themselves]" (Eco cited in Christiansen & Magnussen 2000: 20).[2] Critics have tended to overreact to perceived slights against the medium, often at the expense of responding analyti-cally to the exigencies of the corpus itself. There is a growing sense that "it's probably time to let go of that strain of earnest defensiveness" (Wolk 2007: 67), but the formal approaches to comics dominating current criti-cism remain the result of this very stance, and this book seeks to address the problems endemic in this defensively inspired formalist framework.

The origins of comics scholarship partially lie with the ascendency of cultural studies (Sabin 1993: 92, Christiansen & Magnussen 2000: 18, Heer & Worcester 2009: xi). The field has consequently been imbued with dem-ocratic leanings, strongly bound up with a suspicion of both the distinc-tion between high and low culture, at the bottom of which heap comics traditionally ended up, and the authority of academic institutions histori-cally implicated in maintaining that hierarchy. But the Anglophone field is also widely acknowledged to have received its jumpstart from practi-tioner-theorists (Baetens 2001: 147, Whitlock 2006: 966, Lent 2010: 23). It was "non-scholarly researchers – critics, practitioners, journalists, and avocational researchers – whose work, in fact, laid much of the ground-work on which scholars now stand" (Troutman 2010: 437). This legacy has had significant implications for the field. Current scholarship owes much to these trailblazers and their work provides an immensely valuable basis for academic study, but it has tended to be "removed from the schol-arly traditions with which it might best intersect" (Groensteen 2006: viii).

Though this seminal work cannot be dismissed, it has often been theoreti-cally unsophisticated. Comics scholarship continues to wrestle with the task of balancing due deference to this practice-oriented strain of com-mentary with a duty to correct its theoretical errors and omissions.

It has been suggested that, particularly within the arena of the Bowling Green State University hub and *Journal of Popular Culture*, a counter-culture atmosphere is fostered where "results can be described more as a celebration of popular culture than as methodological and theoretical new thinking" (Christiansen & Magnussen 2000: 20). These practices "reflect the conscious and conscientious ambivalence the Popular Culture Asso-ciation historically bears to the academy in general" (Troutman 2010: 437), and within the field of comics studies this feeds into the parallel propen-sity of practitioner-critics to sidestep the theoretical traditions and dis-courses that might usefully inform their otherwise insightful observations and commentary. The result of this twin inheritance is "a kind of hesitancy or even resistance on the part of comics scholars to participate fully in the modes of academic writing and research" (Troutman 2010: 433). Even academic proponents of the field can neglect the relevant source theory, abandoning scholarly rigor in favor of respectful repetition. The state of Anglophone comics criticism's consolidation period resonates strongly with James Elkins's recent assessment of visual studies: "As a new field, visual culture has a nature [*sic*] propensity to search for founding texts and ideas, but theorists and critics can do themselves a disfavor by anchoring their work to those authors and ideas, especially where the directions of the new scholarship diverge from their sources" (Elkins 2003: 101).

Comics scholars' adoption and perpetuation of popular generaliza-tions, suppositions, and suggestions that the academic has a professional duty to engage with and challenge (in a way the expert pundit does not) does little to assist the ongoing sophistication of the field as a demanding discipline.

Given comics' struggle against blanket dismissal beside elite cultural forms, it is perhaps understandable that critics are reluctant to embrace what might be charged with being another kind of intellectual snobbery. The cross-pollination of the field with practitioners and academics does not foster the kind of discourse that conscientiously speaks to and posi-tions itself within ongoing scholarly practices. Art Spiegelman notes, of reactions to his own commentary on his work, that "academics were hap-pier with idiot-savant cartoonists," suggesting burgeoning scholarship enables an exclusion as "only now that this jargon has been perfected, is it possible for everybody who's not in the club to be an idiot-savant, because they're never going to understand the framing device which the criticism is" (cited in Witek 2008: 218). Ivan Brunetti makes similar reference to academics "condescendingly" bracketing off "practitioners" under that dissociating label (2006: 7), implicitly protesting the colonization of the field by scholastically minded latecomers. Scholarly critics' capitulation to this sort of inverted snobbery, facilitated by cultural studies' open, democratic agenda, and exacerbated by an underlying fear that "everyone else thinks what they do is kind of trashy and disreputable" (Wolk 2007: 67), can work to derail scrupulous academic vigilance. It too often results in "an argument delivered from the defensive couch, a discourse addressed not to an audience of informed and sympathetic colleagues but to an imperfectly imagined hangman's jury of deans, intra- and extra-disciplinary experts, the editors and readers of the *Comics Journal*, and the people who write book reviews on Amazon.com, all of these divergent discursive expectations and often contradictory intellectual goals" (Witek 2008: 219).

The novelist and essayist Curtis White points out that "from a philosopher's perspective, one of the sure signs that there's no thinking going on [in a particular discourse] is that there is never a context for what they do. They are never thinking in the context of other thinkers. They are never reading, considering, interpreting what someone else has thought as a point of departure for what they think. It's all *ex nihilo*, as if ideas just burst in your head like an aneurysm" (White 2007: 79).

This charge resonates with the situation Elkins alludes to within visual studies, where critics use foundational works as a springboard without dealing with the wider established theory that could inform it. Within Anglophone comics criticism, the core *ex nihilo* text from which much subsequent theory has issued is Scott McCloud's *Understanding Comics* (1993). McCloud is widely cited as the founding father of the field, and though it is sometimes acknowledged that he is a distinctly "second-rate theoretician" (Baetens 2003: np), reverent allegiance to his seminal primer has more consistently seen it "elevate[d] [. . .] to the status of holy writ" (Harvey 2009: 25). McCloud himself defends his uncontextualized speculations, stating "my academic aspirations stemmed from a conviction that not every work of theory could be built on other works of theory. I was convinced that useful discourse often started with direct observation, logic and a horde of semi-educated guesses" (cited in Witek 2008: 219). Convinced as McCloud may be, and influential as *Understanding Comics* has proven, given the staggering multi-disciplinarity of comics studies, it is vital that critics are responsive to relevant scholarly contexts if they are to engage in genuinely new thinking. The diversity of approaches to comics (variously treated as cultural, educational, literary, political, geographical, or socio-historical artifacts) means that robust, constructive theory must address itself to an established set of issues and questions it seeks to further and enrich, or risk instituting an enthusiastic but under-informed celebration of comics as the standard critical practice.

In the spirit of countering this tendency, this book anchors itself in literary and linguistic theory, addressing the sometimes over-general use comics criticism makes of these discourses. This is an arena in which the defensiveness that drives so much critical work on comics is most ripe. The comics form is (usually) a mixed one, so the characteristics of words and images, and the ways they operate in conjunction, are pertinent issues for anyone concerned with its structural mechanisms. But the usage of semiotic theory to illuminate these issues is shot through with an anxiety about the relative status of images versus words. Comics criticism participates in a historic rivalry between art forms, or "war of signs" (Mitchell 1986: 47), that has seen their relative attributes, virtues, and capabilities long debated. Comics critics are frequently keen to champion the efficacy and worth of images. A perceived "privileged status often accorded to narratives in linguistic media" (Walsh 2006: 860) leads to earnest insistence that "pictorial language seems as capable as words of communicating ideas" (Beronä 2001: 19); that "drawing, as a system, is not necessarily less true than other systems of representation" (Chute 2006: 1,017); and that before literacy extended beyond the privileged (read "elitist") classes, "pictures were an effective way to communicate information" (Versaci 2008: 7). Notwithstanding the shortcomings of an approach to an art form that views words and images as functionalist vessels for information, anxiety about the value of images leads critics into dubious theoretical territory. Understandably keen to state the parity of words and images, critics too often overstate this equal validity as outright equivalence.

This practice runs throughout the critical literature. It is variously stated that the distinction between words and images is "an arbitrary separation" (Eisner 1985: 13); that "from the point of view of semiotics theory, images and words are equivalent entities [. . .] perceived in much the same way" (Varnum & Gibbons 2001: xi); and that snobbery about visual narrative forms such as comics is "reinforced by assumptions about essential 'differences' between communication by text and communication by images" (Hatfield 2005: 32), with those artfully placed scare quotes seeking to unsettle any such assumptions the reader might be harboring. One does not need an extensive knowledge of semiotic theory in order to question this flattening of distinctions, but Anglophone critics typically invoke it in a very generalized way, positing all signifying practices as broadly similar instances of signs standing in for things, ordered by codes and conventions. In order to catch all semiological practices within a general science of signs (this general science was a hypothetical postulate for Ferdinand de Saussure [1983: 16] and had still not transpired according to Barthes, writing in the 1960s [1967: 9], or Mitchell, in the 1980s [1986: 54]; both these latter critics see semiotics' linguistic basis as a stumbling block to wider application), the initial linguistic model can only be invoked in a rather generalized, even vague, way in order to be applicable to the diverse modes of language, images, and the comics form. Such vagueness leads to an advancement of neither semiotic theory itself, nor the discipline that purports to utilize it. The distinction lies in the details, but heeding these specificities little serves the assertions of communicative parity that are routinely made via claims that any difference between visual and verbal is spurious to begin with.

Differences do exist and they are crucial to understanding the distinct ways words and images are deployed and perceived within comics. To begin with, language is built from a limited set of discrete minimal units, while visual signification, as I will go on to demonstrate, is continuous and infinitely gradated. Language is based around "a finite number of characters [. . .] and the gaps between them are empty; there are no intermediate characters between "a" and "d" that have any function in the system, whereas the dense system provides for the introduction of an infinite number of meaningful new marks into the symbol" (Mitchell 1986: 68). That is to say, the distinctions between language's limited set of distinctive sounds are binary either/or distinctions: there is no functional midpoint between "cat" and "cad," though the lines and curves that make up a drawing of a cat may be adjusted in myriad subtle ways with no definitive cutoff point determining when that sign has become a different sign. Language is founded on the principle of double articulation with a small fixed number of phonemes (distinctive phonic units) that make up a limited pool of morphemes (minimal significant units, for example, basic words such as "like" or "lady," or semantic fragments such as "un-" that can be combined to form more complex words such as "unladylike"), which can then be combined in infinite variation to create phrases, sentences, and texts.

It is not possible to find minimally significant units within visual images:

The image is syntactically and semantically dense in that no mark may be isolated as a unique, distinctive character (like a letter of an alphabet) [. . . .] Its meaning depends rather on its relations with all the other marks in the dense, continuous field. A particular spot of paint might be read as the highlight on Mona Lisa's nose, but that spot achieves its significance in the specific system of pictorial relations to which it belongs, not as a uniquely differentiated character that might be transferred to some other canvas. (Mitchell 1986: 66)

Umberto Eco posits a comparable example of a semicircle and dot that, in a drawing of a human face, might represent a smile and eye, while the exact same forms within a depiction of a bowl of fruit might signify a banana and grape seed (Eco 1976: 215). Unlike the morpheme "lady," which contributes the same significance to the larger units "ladylike" and "unladylike" (or even phrases such as "green with envy" or "green around the gills," whose figurative significance is latent in the usual meaning of "green," and is drawn out and anchored by its context), the continuous and dense field of visual images proves much more manipulable.

Linguistic signs are, furthermore, arbitrary. The relationship between signifier and signified is purely conventional, based on knowledge. Visual signs are (certainly more often) motivated, with some logical relationship existing between a sign's form and its significance. Pictures look like the thing they represent, and though there are codes regulating the relationship between signifier and signified, it is not always necessary to have prior knowledge of a particular sign in order to work out what it represents in the way that it is with arbitrary words, whose signifier-signified association must simply be learnt. This enables a degree of freedom for images, whose potential deducibility, stemming from that motivated relationship between form and meaning, means signs need not be preexistent and already familiar in order to be functional. We may be able to interpret a visual form we have never seen before, but we cannot work out the meaning of a verbal signifier whose significance we have not already learnt: we can deduce the significance of "unladylike" only if we are already familiar with each of its arbitrary constituent units. As such, visual signification is less constrained than language by a preexistent *langue*—the abstract differential system of language that all instances of *parole* (particular utterances) are obliged to comply with in order to be functionally meaningful. Whereas individual words have an abstract, conventional meaning that recurs when they are used in different contexts, the spot of paint on the Mona Lisa's nose, or Eco's semicircle, are imbued with significance by their place within a particular context—and before then, do not have a fixed significance. As has been asserted of cinema, visual signification "is *parole* and not *langue*" (Mitchell 2009: 119).

The key distinctions this book maintains are: arbitrariness and motivation; differing levels of constraint by a preexistent *langue*; double articulation and constitution in minimal units, as distinct from continuity and density. It will also touch on the issues of language's dual graphic-phonic form and the radical heterogeneity of visual signification, which subsumes an array of different codes such as size, color, texture, and location, very different to language's finite pool of like units. This rather cursory summary will be fleshed out in the ensuing discussion, through which a more attentive use of source theory will help demonstrate not only that these differences exist, but that they are pertinent to our understanding of how each semiotic mode generates the specific effects it does. Supportive close readings from a range of texts illustrate the ways in which an understanding of the mixed medium's operations in fact depends on addressing the different ways words and images work. The texts used are drawn from a range of comics formats and periods. The emphasis will be on more recent and, in particular, more "arty" or experimental comics, but these have been selected purely as they best clarify the points raised about comics' formal makeup, which apply to comics in general and not only the formally innovative texts that best facilitate an explication of these points.

The ongoing anxiety about the supposed hierarchy of words and images means that comics are habitually defended against the benchmark of language and literature. If images—or even the comics form itself—can be argued to work just like verbal language, then comics must be as good as "proper books." As such, "the dominant thread in the scholarly study of comic books has always been the literary and textual" (Beaty 2007: 8).[3] It has become near automatic to class comics as a literary form (Meskin 2009: 219, Wolk 2007: 14, Chute 2008), a kind of writing (Raeburn 2004: 17, Hatfield 2005: 33), or, most habitually, as a language itself.[4] The defensive root of this tendency, and extent to which it has become a mechanical move, are both exemplified by Charles Hatfield's self-defeating claims (made on the very same page) that "recent insistence on comics-as-reading seems designed to counter a long-lived tradition of professional writing that links comics with illiteracy" and that, nevertheless, "my bedrock claim [is] that comic art is a form of *writing*" (Hatfield 2005: 33). Comics criticism has coalesced around the critical models of language, reading, and literature. However, the dominant usage of these models is theoretically impoverished. Semiotics is used to obliterate pertinent distinctions and ideas of literariness imprecisely synonymized with narrative. Both critical models are invoked in service of aggrandizing the visual mode and comics form to the perceived privileged position of the verbal. Though not convinced these discourses are the only—or even best—available, and without room to fully espouse the possibility of using cinema as a closer structural kin (which has, at any rate, frequently been addressed elsewhere), this book expressly challenges the specific *use* that is routinely made of linguistic and literary theory, seeking an adjusted critical framework that is better attuned to the specificities of the visual and verbal modes. The aim is to minimize the defensiveness that can so often be found underpinning the dominant approach to comics' formal structure, and also to challenge the deleterious habit of using "language" as the "vernacular" "for what should properly be called 'symbol systems'" (Mitchell 1994: 349). In doing this, the revised framework does not aspire to "rehabilitate" comics beside the supposedly hallowed benchmark of other semiotic modes or art forms, but instead aims at incorporating the more consistent and established critical standards of adjacent scholarly disciplines.

The book tackles three particular problematic aspects of the linguistic model as it is currently used. Each section in turn is further subdivided, examining these three core issues from different but related angles. Part One addresses "Language in Comics," and is deliberately skewed towards linguistic content in an attempt to redress a common insistence that comics visual content must always—definitively—control the narrative and dominate the text. It is common for critics to assert that there must necessarily be "a preponderance of image over text" (Kunzle 1973: 2), and to suggest that where words undertake too much of the narrative burden, the very classification of a work is compromised. So keen can critics be to champion the power, efficacy, and importance of the visual, that they display an "almost universal" fear that words might somehow take over or conquer comics' images, an anxiety Dylan Horrocks terms "logophobia" (2001: 5). It is not difficult to find examples refuting the notion that words are always the ancillary extra to primary images within comics, but this section particularly aims to show how we lose out on an appreciation of literary language in comics if we refuse to recognize its *potential* centrality. Comics frequently incorporate highly literary writing, and Part One, focusing on three different authors in turn, looks at how those specific features of language (its arbitrariness, constitution in minimal units, and constraint by the *langue*) in fact enable the precise literary tricks these texts accomplish. This section also looks at how text is read in comics, considering the verbally generated effects garnered by fragmenting text across comics' delimited panels, subframes, and speech balloons, and arranging these over a two-dimensional page surface. The purpose of this first part is to examine linguistic content, highlighting language's distinct semiotic features, but also showing how the comics form can deploy words in its own specific ways.

Part Two operates under the banner "Comics as Language," addressing two key aspects of the postulation that the medium's practices and devices are structured like a verbal symbol system. Typically, claims that comics possess a comparable "grammar, syntax and punctuation" (Sabin 1993: 9, Kunzle 1990: 349) are not quantified or explained. Such statements are so pervasive as to have attained the veneer of accepted fact, though attempts to enumerate how the features of comics replicate these linguistic properties vary immensely.[5] The first chapter in this section deals with the suggestion that, because visual and verbal interact, they become an inextricable blend that can therefore be framed as a unified language in itself; a suggestion I refute, by showing that distinctions between the two modes and their operations persist, even when they are drawn into collaborative play. The next two chapters address the question of sequentiality and the proposition that panels are semiotic units whose signifieds are units of story time, which are articulated in texts like linguistic units in longer phrases. I do not extensively address the elliptical nature of stories told through sequences of panels here, because the issue of how story content is delivered seems more a question of *narrative theory* than one of language or symbol system. Rather than the marshaling of story content, these chapters instead discuss the privileging of sequentiality within the current critical framework. This emphasis proves to be a mistaken move, for what truly distinguishes comics from other narratives is the *simultaneity* of narrative segments on the two-dimensional page, which is incidental in prose and does not occur with film's temporally progressing shots. Rather than the structural definition it is often claimed to be, sequentiality can be better explained as a kind of realism principle, a tendency, not an absolute, which can be altered, reinvented, or even discarded, in ways language can be seen to resist.

The third and final part considers the framing of visual signification in terms of language. "Images as Language" in part addresses comics' images and cartooning specifically, following on from and furthering the discussion of comics as a kind of language. It also provides parallel arguments to those made in Part One, examining visual signification's continuousness, motivation, and flexibility, and showing how these features are as instrumental to its operations as language's contrasting characteristics are shown to be. A challenge is also raised to the very idea of a semiotic, language-based approach to images by examining the aesthetic visual style of comics artwork. By adopting the methodology of the art-historian's formal analysis, it can be implicitly demonstrated that semiotics does not provide an effective framework for analyzing visual art beyond its functional and reductive "message." Part Three also considers how comics systematically organize smaller constituent units into a coherent, larger whole, expanding on the issue of comics as language, but specifically looking at the page as a delimited unit, and thus at the possible linguistic structures organizing the page as an integrated image. While something must be conceded to the idea that some aspects of comics function as a symbol system, ultimately it will be shown that, as this system is motivated and non-minimal, it differs in crucial ways from verbal language.

The central thrust of this book is to demonstrate via close analysis of both texts and source theory the precise differences between the visual and verbal modes, which are habitually swept aside, seemingly for defensive reasons. It aims to show that *adjusting* the language-based model is necessary to make it appropriate for assessing visual images. Such an adjustment renders semiotics a useful tool for explicating the mechanics of the mixed medium, in terms of both its use of words and images, and its own devices and signifying practices. I focus on formalism because it is precisely in the conception of comics' formal structures that the field's greatest critical weak spots lie, more so than the plethora of sociological/ political/historical/readership-centered approaches to comics that have developed in conjunction. Of course, strong theorizations of comics do exist, and the challenges raised here should not be read as an outright dismissal of the decades of diverse scholarship that have presaged the rise of the field as a recognized academic discipline. But, particularly where formalist approaches are concerned, critical standards remain distinctly patchy and there exists a real problem with adequately distinguishing between conceptually sound criticism and less carefully considered offerings. This difficulty needs to be addressed as comics criticism becomes ever more widely recognized within academia, if the field is to shake off any last vestiges of that denigrated status with which so many critics have been concerned. I do not aim to dismiss so much as alter and augment existing conceptions of comics' structure and workings, to yield a modified framework that is more theoretically precise and more closely attuned to the scholarly discourses that inform it. The defensive reaction against the art form's "poor relation" status that has often sought to aggrandize both visual images and the comics form, if it is indeed necessary in the first place (is the Sistine Chapel ceiling really considered inferior to *Great Expectations*?), is ill-served by a vague and generalized use of theory that does little to bolster the perceived seriousness of either the art form or its study. As a discipline, comics criticism is gaining ground in the academic sphere, in both prevalence and esteem. It is therefore all the more imperative that the field's proponents finally abandon those core tenets that characterized the discipline's awkward adolescence, ensuring comics studies is instituted not as a vague and general pulp of piecemeal theory, celebratory criticism, and a denial of hierarchies that is extrapolated to a lack of discernment, but as a more consistently serious and rigorous discipline whose only necessary defense is that it self-evidently merits inclusion.

PART ONE
Language in Comics

Chapter One

Arbitrary Minimal Units in *Krazy Kat*

Comics critics' default justification for asserting that comics are a literary form is that, like prose fiction, they tell stories. Time and again, "themes, plots, and characterisations" (Lombard et al. 1999: 23) are emphasized in discussions of comics' literary properties. Their parity with verbal literary forms is couched in terms of generic *narrative* attributes or, even more diffusely, as lying in such sweeping artistic values as being "creative, original, well-structured, and unified" (Meskin 2009: 220). George Herriman's *Krazy Kat* ran in the newspapers of William Randolph Hearst from 1913 to 1944, its core plot repeated day after day: mouse throws brick at cat; dog arrests mouse. Few critics would argue that complex "literary" themes may be found in this repetitive riffing, and in the case of Herriman, it has been said that critical attention is usually devoted to his "peerless drawing skills, while his writing tends to be scanted" (Heer 2008: 7). Herriman's writing is, in fact, often referred to, though the general critical tendency to downplay linguistic content risks a scandalous neglect of the precise mechanics of his dazzlingly virtuoso writing. In his brief analysis of Herriman's linguistic ingenuity, Jeet Heer compares his writing style to the "exhibitionist speechifying" of the carnival barkers, newspapers hawkers, sports announcers and traveling salesmen of his day, men who profited by a "glib and copious tongue" (2008: 8). Certainly, Herriman was a master of grandiloquent garrulousness, as evidenced by the sales pitch: "It will nectarize every nick in your neck and starch a shirt – lend lilt and loquacity to every line of your language – raise a mess of muscle that'll toss a ton with tidiness – burnish your buttons, buzzers and badges – and put a kamel's kick in your katnip – and now the sultan will pass among you with this elixir of the elite – potation of potentates – nobles' nippage" (Herriman 2006: 13).

Herriman's literariness does not lie in his ability to construct a story, nor can any comics' narrative content be used as evidence for their *literary* prowess. Indeed, "A ballet can be a narrative. A hospital chart can be a narrative. A stock-market report can be a narrative" (Lewis 2010: 77). But none of these things are literature, and though comics' narratives can be constructed in highly artistic ways, a text's *literariness* lies in the formal features of its language, not the fact it happens to communicate a story. Due to the supposed hierarchy between words and images, critics place a great deal of emphasis on communicative serviceability. French critic Thierry Groensteen objects to this "all too functionalist conception of the story in images" (2009b: 126), which privileges the utilitarian information value of pictures. Protesting against those earnest explanations that pictures are "as capable as words of communicating ideas," Groensteen advocates an approach that "restore[s] to the image its true semantic richness (and the arising emotional dimension), that the reduction to a linguistic statement corresponding to its immediate narrative 'message' tends to mechanically overshadow" (2009b: 121). This "mechanical reduction" aptly characterizes what Anglophone comics critics have often tended to make of semiotics in general, and the relationship of this problem to semantically rich images will be addressed in due course. What Herriman's work in particular highlights is the corresponding problem of treating textual content this way, emphasizing story information rather than the language-specific formal features of literary writing.

Critics' ongoing preoccupation with the idea that pictures must *definitively* tell the bulk of the story (Horrocks 2001: 5, Meskin 2007: 369) demonstrates the way words as well as pictures are treated as vehicles of a message whose aesthetic qualities, the "emotional force and presence that cannot be entirely reduced to meaning" (Petersen 2009: 165), are neglected. According to the customary formulation of literature as storytelling (which rather perversely aligns narratology with literature, though no comics critic would credit the assumption that prose literature is the default narrative form), Herriman's repetitive and ridiculous micro-plot hardly warrants literary analysis. However, a more exacting characterization of literary writing is found in Jonathan Culler's assertion that though "literature is clearly a form of communication, it is cut off from the immediate pragmatic purposes which simplify other sign situations" (1981: 35). This viewpoint echoes Groensteen's assertion that the artistic contribution of comics' visual element "cannot be evaluated in terms of information" (2009b: 126). Once we abandon the general critical reluctance to focus on verbal content, it soon becomes clear that Herriman's text is intensely poetic, aesthetically rich, and inventively comical; and it is this, rather than the pragmatic communication value of his writing, that presents the most convincing case for comics' potential literariness. Herriman

1.1 George Herriman, *Krazy & Ignatz: 1937–1938*, ed. by Bill Blackbeard
(Seattle: Fantagraphics, 2006), p. 31 (original publication date 16 May 1937).

possessed "a poet's ability to have fun with words" (Heer 2008: 9). His
strips are less concerned with the utilitarian conveyance of a message
that critics' preoccupation with story and themes over-emphasizes, and
more with a playful treatment of the formal surface features of language.
Words proliferate, not in service of conveying more meaning, but for their
own aesthetic sake. His manipulation of linguistic possibilities took many

forms and an exemplary grain of just about all of them can be found in the strip above (Fig. 1.1).

Krazy Kat, an endearing dolt of indeterminate gender, watches the performance of a "tide rupp wokka," termed by his more ornately eloquent acquaintance, Ignatz Mouse, a "funambulist." The high-flown formalism is typical, as is Krazy's mildly bemused, heavily phoneticized response: "Poddin', was that rimmok a lengwidge – or wot?" In Ignatz's response, "I said funambulist – a term better fitted to qualify so apt an artist – plain language, but in a higher plane," Herriman pulls off several of his favorite tricks. The high register his characters so often favor is evidenced by the ceremonially decorous vocabulary, with the slightly anomalous use of "qualify" to signify naming or describing sounding convincingly grandiose. The self-consciously literary feeling generated by this lofty tone is complemented by the alliteration of "so apt an artist," a habitual device that tends to lend a gently silly singsong air even as it emphasizes the lyrical elegance of these elevated constructions. Alliteration plays off words' sound qualities, and Herriman has a keen ear for language's potential musicality. Homophones, homonyms, and synonyms are particularly beloved, exploiting the excess of signification that "is always a threat to order" (Lecercle 1985: 95) in language. "[P]lain language" is here neatly subverted by the "higher plane" which aurally echoes its counterpart and baffles the cat with terminology that is anything but plain. Language's graphic and phonic forms are made to duel with one another here, and are further exploited by Herriman through the vague and mangled phonetic formulations of Krazy Kat—who, in this strip, parrots Ignatz's term as "finnembillisk." Krazy is often befuddled by language. This confusion manifests itself in the transposing of approximate syllables to create a kind of colloquial pidgin dialect (such as "poddin" for "pardon," "diffint" for "different") and in the explicit perplexity that is expressed here. The cat is frequently stumped by language's slipperiness, wrong-footed by illogicalities such as homophones, and language's continual refusal to follow its own rules.

These features form the core threads of Herriman's giddy volubility: the slipperiness of language and its proliferations of meaning; the graphic-phonic forms and ways their refusal to absolutely concur can be used to great effect; and the different registers language can be organized into, on which Herriman draws. The aim, in appraising these in turn, is to demonstrate how vital these specific features of language are to its literary effects. These effects show how wrong critics are to sideline language in comics, and suppress the peculiarities of different signifying systems in service of proving their equality. This chapter will also take a very brief look at how Herriman's delirious poetry reflects a twin "visual loopiness" (Wolk 2007: 355) as, obviously, comics can never be comprehensively grasped by looking at only linguistic content. But the tacit agenda in deliberately sidelining visual (and thematic) content in favor of linguistic, is to illustrate how comics might truly be approached as literature, and to present a more convincing argument than has previously been achieved for their literary potential.

The first point of inquiry concerns language's minimal units. Herriman plays with the articulations that divide the temporal stream of sound into discrete linguistic units. Humorous misformulations are generally uttered by Krazy who, for example, consoles dog and mouse, both suffering acute indigestion, that "annie ho, it's a cute illment" (Herriman 2006: 43). The joke here derives from drawing the divisions that separate words in different places. Herriman makes a game out of this with the tale of Sir William Bee, taking the innocent word "bumble" and drawing out the hidden morpheme that is integrated into a multi-syllable, minimally significant unit. Those first three letters act as a phoneme here, though when taken alone they have their own separate significance: Sir William, for a social misdemeanor, is dubbed "bum" by the Queen, and henceforth is "To society 'Sir William Bee', To his peers, 'Bill Bee' – And to the world today 'Bum-Bill Bee'" (Herriman 2008: 47). This joke works by finding a smaller significant unit within the minimal unit "bumble" and artificially segregating its two phonemes by transmuting the non-significant "-ble" ending into "Bill," cheekily freeing up the other, which happens to have its own meaning.

Beyond this playful approach to the articulation of units, Herriman coins words that depend on recognized morphemes for ungrammatical but clearly decipherable significance. Heer has pointed out that "it's easy enough to classify [Herriman] as a nonsense poet," but that "he usually doesn't make words up however much he might twist them around" (2008: 7–8). Indeed, Nonsense-like as Herriman often sounds, his linguistic constructions are free from the "snarks" and "dongs" of true Nonsense poets like Lewis Carroll and Edward Lear. He is not, however, hemmed in by "correct" linguistic constructions, operating instead at the edges of what is permitted by the linguistic system. Exemplary is Officer Pupp's pronouncement on the pot plant he stumbles across: "A potted 'cactus' – what a waste of pottage – and when such pretty posy plants like peonies, petunias and pansies are pleading for potment" (Herriman 2007: 18). This takes the morpheme "pot" and creates from it two verbal nouns, both of which refer to "the state of being potted." No such words exist (or, at least, they do not attach to the significance they are given here according to any dictionary), but in this utterance, they make perfect sense.

Such examples illustrate Jean-Jacques Lecercle's assertion that, paradoxically, "what lies outside language is still within language" (1985: 88). Lecercle claims that the unruly, unsystematic "outside" of language—which he terms *délire*—is in fact integral to constituting the orderly, systematic "inside." He avers that every rule of grammar draws a border between what can and cannot be said, but notes that "there are linguistic values, which distinguish correct or "normal" language from *délire*, and yet the rejected elements play a part in the constitution of linguistic values" (Lecercle 1985: 89). That is to say, that which belongs to the system is defined in relation to what lies outside it. The very incorrectness of certain linguistic utterances ("potment") plays a part in drawing the frontier between these misconstructions and correct language ("potted"). Herriman shows that the border between sayable and unsayable can be crossed: the word "potment" does not exist according to the dictionary, and "pottage" here takes on a very different meaning, but though both are recognizably linguistically incorrect, they *can* be said and *can* be invested with significance. The relationship between the elements inside and outside of language, which here each draw the same morpheme into correct and incorrect constructions, enables the non- or extralinguistic phrase to signify nonetheless. However, its significance incorporates misarticulation. The sense of these coinages depends on the differentiation of correct and incorrect, and in playing with this frontier in a way that foregrounds its existence, Herriman here exemplifies "an utterance that, at the very moment it plays havoc with language, acknowledges the domination of the rules it transgresses" (Lecercle 1985: 55). In recognizing that a rule has been broken, we must also acknowledge the existence of the rule being flouted.

Herriman does not exemplify Lecercle's concept of radically disruptive *délire*, but rather compares with the benign Nonsense of Lewis Carroll, in which "frontiers are temporarily forgotten" (Lecercle 1985: 78). Lecercle identifies an opposition in language between "the dictionary" (language as an abstract, systematic tool of communication) and "the scream" (language as a material, individual expression of the passions, instincts, and drives of the body). True *délire* is sense-devouring, "raucous, violent, full of consonants and unpronounceable sounds, of screams and hoarse whispers" (Lecercle 1985: 41). Herriman's language-play, like Carroll's, "belongs to the surface, it abides by all the rules and conventions, it is highly grammatical and engages in games (e.g. the portmanteau words) which do not threaten, but on the contrary reinforce it" (Lecercle 1985: 41). Herriman's games, though seemingly anarchic and wilful, in fact sustain sense and order. Words that are not quite words are given meaning, and their linguistic value—their very literary effectiveness—is in part gleaned from the sense that they violate the rules of the linguistic system, which are thus tacitly reinforced. In Herriman's coinages, morphemes that are constitutive parts of the linguistic system lend meaning to linguistic constructions not instituted into that system, creating a pseudo-Nonsense effect that is at once playful, expressive, and highly literary.

Examples abound of this creative coinage of words from the *langue*'s permitted morphemes. The oft repeated "jailment" (Herriman 2008: 35) makes a noun from the verb "to jail," a word describing not an action but a quantifiable thing that the cop "administer[s]" (Herriman 2006: 24), and whose syntactic construction adds to the illustrious tone. Similarly, "how I unadmire him" (Herriman 2008: 48) ventures a logical, but unapproved combination of units, while "a lot of foolishment" (Herriman 2007: 100) makes noun from adjective. These violations of the system bear witness to the existence of the very rules they break: "The flouting of linguistic and literary conventions by which literary works bring about a renewal of perception testifies to the importance of a system of conventions as the basis of literary signification" (Lecercle 1985: 37). The institution of a linguistic rule presupposes that the rule can be broken, but this flouting in turn testifies to the existence of that rule, which sanctifies or denies the utterance that conforms with or flouts it. As discussed in the introduction, visual signification is far freer, not only to use signs out of context but also to form signs anew (as we shall see in Chapter Seven). Herriman adroitly demonstrates here that it is *possible* also to coin new sign forms in language, but the rules that designate the coinages as "outside" the linguistic system are precisely what lend his writing its off-the-wall flavor. Indeed, everywhere in Herriman's writing the jubilant ingenuity of his gymnastic inventiveness is derived from the sense he is in breach of established rules. It is the very palpable authority of those temporarily discarded rules that makes his writing sound so wildly colorful.

The sense of gleefully eccentric creativity within Herriman's writing is furthered by the false aggrandizement of words alluded to above. Herriman plays with language's minimal units by lengthening them, turning them into more elaborate terms, but ones not actually recognized as belonging to the linguistic system. The "-age" ending is appended to words at will, as when Officer Pupp declares that Ignatz's "sinful tossage of bricks" could be dealt with by "more tappage of this smacker" (his truncheon), embellishing the two units "toss" and "tap" with the orotund-sounding ending. This lackadaisical approach to grammar creates ornate words from simple ones, but elsewhere, as operated by Krazy Kat, conjures up guileless, yet expressive formulations. Noting that Officer Pupp is "bitzy injoyin' himself," the cat decides "I'll go fine Ignatz Mice an' made myself injoyfil, too" (Herriman 2006: 12). With "tossage" and "tappage," a recognizable suffix is applied in ways the *langue* does not recognize. The remit of the grammatical rule is extended to augment words to which it cannot correctly be applied. Krazy, on the other hand, obliterates these rules. Hanging on to the central morpheme "joy," the cat layers up indiscriminate grammatical constructions, mashing together "enjoy" and "joyful" to create "injoyfil," which alludes to the approximately equivalent sense of "fill" and "full" and misspells according to the cat's peculiar phonetics as usual.

Minimal units are demonstrably integral to the operations of the linguistic system. Critics such as Groensteen question those who insist on the necessity of identifying minimal units for any signifying system (2009a: 2). This is a valid challenge insofar as there exist systems, such as visual images, which refute this prescription, as they demonstrably do not decompose into meaningful minimal units. However, it would be an error to extend this refutation into a denial of the relevance of minimal units to the operations of a system that is so constituted: language's constitution in discrete, repeatable morphemes explains how the above examples generate the effects they do. So too is visual signification's analogical nature relevant to its dynamics. Attempts have been made by some comics critics, such as Guy Gauthier, to artificially select "lines or groups of lines, spots or groups of spots, and to locate for each signifier thus determined, a precise signified" (Groensteen 2006: 3). Such efforts[1] fail in the face of Eco's semicircle/dot example, which proves that, though forms can be isolated within the visual continuum, "as soon as they are detected, they seem to dissolve again" (Eco 1976: 215), relying as they do on the surrounding context to imbue them with a "precise signified." Verbal signifiers, on the other hand, are separable units whose association with a signified preexists their evocation in a particular context. However, the effect of deploying these signs in different contexts challenges the naive empiricism suggested by critics' aforementioned tendency to characterize signs as vehicles for ideas.

In Herriman's language game, the simplistic idea that any "precise" or fixed meaning can be found even for language's minimal units is challenged. Possible meanings proliferate "behind" (for want of a better word) the sign-forms that stand in for them, as in Krazy's excited comment about his/her new-planted corn: "Now, I will have korn bread, korn mill mutch, korn poems, korn plestas, korn kopias" (Herriman 2008: 64). Here, signifier starts to come unstuck from signified. The "corn" of "cornucopia" and "corn plaster" is rather different from that of "corn bread" or "corn pone."² The humor here is derived from the repetition of the same minimal unit across a range of larger units, each of which appeals to a different aspect of that word's cluster of significance. The varying repetition of "korn" shows exactly how a word's context affects its meaning. Unlike the semicircle that is *made* into a smile or banana, the context of a word merely *anchors* its meaning in a particular utterance. The joke here is generated by the juxtaposition of several semantic units that put "corn" to work in different ways. The "corn" of "corn bread" echoes in "corn plaster," exposing the cluster of potential significance that proliferates behind a single unit. The context in which a word is used would usually mask this cluster of potential meanings, making obvious which pre-associated meaning was relevant in a given instance of *parole*. It is important to stress that this is a *pre*-association. Herriman does not *make* corn plaster somehow mean corn bread; what he does through repetition of the minimal unit "corn" is show that this word already appeals to a cluster of significance prior to its multiple invocation here. By repeating the word in different juxtaposed phrases, Herriman draws out the alternative meanings latent in that word, which each phrase taken alone would effectively anchor.

Everywhere this minimal unit game is played, there is a certain unsticking of signifier and signified. Misarticulated words retain the ghost of their original sense, even as we infer a different meaning from their misarticulation (for example, we can still decipher "bumble" hovering somewhere in "Bum-Bill"). Where basic units ("tap," "toss") are lengthened by appendages that do not properly belong to them, sense comes unstuck from the linguistic system, with nonsense utterances making perfect, comically amplified sense. This pulling apart of signifier and signified again compares with Lecercle's *délire*: at the precise point such an utterance appears to nonsensically flout rules, it bears witness to the authority of the rule being transgressed. The quirkiness of Herriman's language, the humor of its proliferations, is effectively bestowed by the very rules violated. Though language's structural rules prove easy to breach, the sustained sense that they *are being* breached points to the existence of an organizing system that enables this sort of disruptive communication.

Herriman's punning use of homonyms fractures signifiers, betraying the various meanings that can potentially lie "behind" them. This is done with sustained silliness in the strip in which the repeated cry "Duck!" (Herriman 2006: 77) causes the jumpy cop to duck for cover, only to be revealed as a call for the attention of the duck, Mrs. Kwakk Wakk. Here, words signify more than they are intended or assumed to, pointing in multiple directions and baffling the attempts of those who seek in them a single unequivocal signified. Herriman rides roughshod over the simplistic view that signifier and signified operate on a "one to one relationship that has, in fact, never existed except in the fantasies of linguists" (Lecercle 1985: 89). This is exemplified by the humorous repetition of "corn" that rhizomatically runs away with its speaker, but there is a flipside to this proliferation of meanings in the proliferation of words Herriman so relishes.

Signifiers may point in multiple directions at once, but in Herriman's hands language too proliferates, as he gleefully allows himself to get carried away with words. The most mundane of actions are subject to verbose over-description, as when a caption intones, "Ignatz Mouse enters a status of acute and arrant visibility," with the next panel declaiming, "And in this panel Officer Pupp pops into perceptibility, exuding an aura of law and order" (Fig. 1.2). The absolute redundancy of this information makes a mockery of the idea that the pertinent critical point is that pictures can say things "as well as words" or which of the two carries the burden of the narrative. The picture *says* next to nothing, its informational content is negligible, and the words do not add to or even describe the pictures but wordily *repeat* their self-evident manifestation of the figures of mouse and dog. This effusive enjoyment of words for their own sake embodies one critic's description of Herriman as "word-drunk" (Wolk 2007: 355). The enjoyment of this strip lies not in the story that is so redundantly over-explicated, but in the verbose revelry in language, whose value as hard information this strip's narration text explicitly mocks. However, this protracted over-explanation, daftly poetic as it is, is not the real opposite of that proliferation of meaning "behind" words. Herriman achieves that countermove instead through the use of tautology, which sees words proliferate in place of a meaning.

Throughout *Krazy Kat*, signifiers mushroom in prolix effusion. Descriptions of the strip's embryonic plot propagate: mouse will "baste your bonny bean with a brick" (Herriman 2008: 53); mouse enjoys "the delight of denting that cat's dome" (Herriman 2006: 45); cop declares brick "will not kiss his noble brow" (Herriman 2007: 90); mouse recalls

Krazy Kat　　　　By Herriman

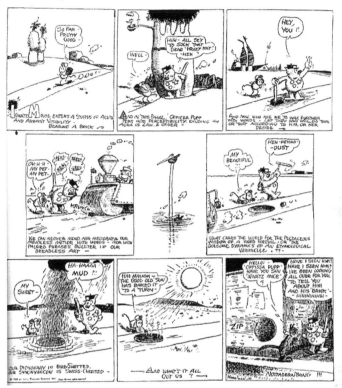

1.2 George Herriman, *Krazy & Ignatz: 1925–1926*, ed. by Bill Blackbeard (Seattle: Fantagraphics, 2002), p. 75 (original publication date 7 March 1926).

how he "impose[d] smitage" (Herriman 2006: 56) on cat, how "a brick [was] creased over that quaint cabeza" (Herriman 2006: 22). In a splendid episode of redundant repetition, Ignatz describes to Officer Pupp what has befallen the unconscious cat. The extreme tautology of the report (playfully alphabetic)—"Assault, battery, calamity, damage, evil, fracas, grief, harm and injury"—grows funnier as Ignatz verbally reiterates further atrocities and elucidates each verbal statement with a physical repetition of the described action, incriminating himself, but affording another go at violently smiting the cat as he does so. Repetitious chains, such as "in this style, this manner – sic, so – thus – was a brick creased over that quaint cabeza" (Herriman 2006: 22), take part in riot of mimicry, with synonyms propagating in excess of the information being conveyed. Krazy's

own garbled attempts to grasp language's slippery proliferations are fertile
ground for the incorporation of confused tautology, as s/he layers his/her
own colloquial descriptions on top of more high-flown formulations that
assert the same thing. A character congratulates, "Well done, 'K' you are an
apt pupil" and is superfluously advised, "Also, I'm a smott 'kett' – rimemba
that" (Herriman 2008: 37). Queues of synonyms line up in characters'
utterances to repetitively reinforce their meaning. Tautologies abound
when Officer Pupp gives Krazy a white flag to wave, advising, "No enemy,
no foe, no nemesis will fail to give you mercy" (Herriman 2006: 93); and
when Ignatz, with characteristic alliteration, comments to a supine Officer
Pupp, "You seem to have given way to rest and repose . . . does no purport of purpose, plan or project perturb your peace and poise?" (Herriman
2007: 89). These synonymic lineups are not concerned with communicating content. Rather the layering up of signifiers for their own wordy sake
takes precedence over the presumed conveyance of meaning.

Herriman's use of synonyms in particular reveals something important about language. When Officer Pupp rhetorically asks, "You peruse a
book, Krazy?" only to be corrected, "No, I yem riddin it" (Herriman 2006:
67), Herriman reveals the necessarily *approximate* nature of synonyms,
through which they risk "ambiguity [and] equivocation" (Lecercle 1985:
37). Though, "we speak [. . .] of various ways of saying 'the same thing'"
(Culler 1981: 40), Herriman's fertile lists of redundant words reveal a certain duplicity in language, exposing and drolly challenging our Western
logo-centrism: "the rationality which treats meanings as concepts or logical representations that it is the function of signs to express" (Culler 1981:
40). Such a viewpoint is much in evidence in many comics critics' utilitarian conceptions of sign function. Herriman's use of language begs the
question of how so many words—richly rhyming, playing different linguistic music, evoking different registers—can ever be thought to be saying the *same* thing. This is underlined by a sort of anti-synonymic move
that insists on the specificity of words. Asked for assistance with the cross-
word puzzle "a four-letter word, meaning to 'incarcerate,'" Mrs. Kwakk
Wakk responds, "if it only had four letters, it couldn't mean to 'incarcerate'" (Herriman 2007: 31). This is pretty irrefutable, and Herriman cannot resist adding a confused cat asking "wots a 'leven-letta woid mins to
'jail,'" splicing still further signifiers in place of signified with the culmi-
nating words spoken from inside the prominently labeled jail: "The word
'kop' – is G-A-O-L – pronounced JALE." Signifiers multiply, each pointing
toward the same signified, yet saying something different. Ultimately none

of these labels can claim to grasp the thing they all purport to stand in for. In this, Herriman obliquely mocks the very idea that language expresses concepts for us by placing diverse multiplying signifiers in place of the same general idea. One's "foe" is at once the same, and yet not quite the same, as one's "enemy," the same but not quite the same as one's "nemesis," and these proliferating labels only ever offer an approximation.

The insistence on language's specificity and literalness is a counterpoint to Herriman's use of synonyms and tautology, nodding at the differential relationships between signs at their ability to *approximate* each other, but also at their refusal to *equate* with any other sign. Herriman shows that this proliferation is possible on each side of the signifier-signified relationship, and in doing so unsettles the notion that the divisions in the temporal flux of sound, which articulate discrete morphemes, ever comfortably adjoin with concepts that categorize the flux of experience into differentiated meanings. By embedding individuated signs in multiple utterances, he further shows how context can also work to pull apart the signifier and signified, complicating the relationship between form and meaning. When Krazy responds to the auctioneer's repeated cry of "Do I hear . . . ?" with the befuddled literalism "I dun't hear nuddin', do you?" (Herriman 2007: 48), Herriman shows how this conventionalized phrase has its own function in discourse, beyond its literal signification. The phrase as a unit conveys its own meaning, quite apart from the sum of the meanings of each word in it: the auctioneer's "do I hear" does not actually ask what can be heard. It has been said that "the pragmatic aspects of language have been regarded as being 'outside the language'" (Aijmer 1996: 29), but this example shows this not to be the case. The phrase signifies against its own literal meaning precisely because it has entered the *langue*: it exemplifies what Barthes calls "the 'glottic' version of the syntagm" (1967: 62), a collection of individual signs that is "felt and handled as a unit" (Aijmer 1996: 1). Herriman handles this "glottic" phrase in a way that again reaches out to a cluster of pre-associated meaning, enabling these ready-made signs to function both literally and as an idiomatic discursive unit—and has a great deal of fun with making them do both at the same time in exchanges such as this one.

It is perhaps rather po-faced to view Herriman's language games through the lens of structural semiotics, for their *raison d'être* is purely and simply their delightful, ingenious silliness. However, in pulling off these dextrous turns so well, Herriman inadvertently presents critics with an excellent case for examining comics' use of verbal language, and *against* the sort of simplistic conceptions of the linguistic system that underpin so much Anglophone comics criticism. There is a giddy willfulness to misunderstand in the zeugmatic reply Krazy gives to Officer Pupp's question, "Am I cutting fair?": "You sim to be cuttin' a mellin" (Herriman 2007: 16). However, the linguistic incompetence that guilelessly carries the sentence in the opposite direction to that (obviously) intended serves as another in the string of examples listed above, which underscore just how easy it is for signifier and signified to come unstuck.

The fractures Herriman creates between signifier and signified, the proliferation of words on the one side and meanings on the other, all refute the logocentrism of critics such as McCloud, who see "language as the conduit through which meaning is transmitted from the speaker to the audience" (Horrocks 2001: 6). According to this prevalent conception of signification as a vehicle for meaning, "The challenge of discourse is to smuggle your idea (or signal) through to the listener as clearly as possible – i.e. with as little interference (noise) from the medium as possible" (Horrocks 2001: 3). For Herriman, this "noise" is half the fun. He revels in language's refusal to behave as speakers expect. By showing that even correct language can be used for the dereliction of sense, Herriman continually and comically undermines the idea of language as a functional vehicle for ideas. His habit of placing words, particularly nouns, in inverted commas implicitly questions the idea that words label things, while he frequently mocks the irrationalities of grammar and spelling, for example, through the baffled cat's puzzling over "why cell ain't sell and sell ain't cell", and how "houses ain't hice an' mouses is mice" (Herriman 2006: 57). Language cannot be grasped and wielded as a tool, for meaning constantly evades speakers. Comics critics' efforts to argue that pictures can communicate "as well as" words fall flat in the face of a cartoonist like Herriman, for whom language's very slipperiness enables the sense-disrupting games that make his work—and his *language* in particular—so delicious.

Herriman makes extensive use of the surface "noise" language generates, which gets in the way of communication yet lends these cartoons their irresistible musicality. The cat's confusion over the inconsistencies of grammatical rules grows even more acute when faced with illogical spelling patterns. Krazy is particularly perturbed by the name of a passing wren, entreating, "Yetz, yetz – I know – but how about the 'wubbil-wu' – what's that for?" (Herriman 2007: 115). Receiving no adequate answer (what indeed is it *for?*), Krazy concludes "dun't make no cents to me – must be boid lengwitch", with the broadly homophonic "cents" and wrenched phonetics of "boid lengwitch" flagging up just how futile it is to seek agreement between language's written and spoken forms. The cat is further assaulted by a hasty roll call of Robert Rabbit, Ronald Rat, and Robin Redbreast, all dashing past engaged in "running a race with that 'wren.'" This refusal of written and spoken forms to agree peaks when Krazy asks Ignatz, "If I tole you a 'wren' was 'wrunning' a 'wrace' – would you billiv me?" Ignatz's unfazed assent hammers home the fact that the disjunction that perplexes the cat is inscribed only on the written version of this utterance. When spoken aloud, the graphic dissonance of "but would it be 'wright'?" and "Of course – quite right" is masked by aural agreement. The cat is left utterly bamboozled after a second exchange with the wren, in which he restores to the "w" its phonic effect, commenting "well I won the race"—which sends the cat into a frenzied blur of agitation.

Herriman is very much attuned to language's built-in quirks, and he frequently pitches graphic and phonic inconsistencies against each other in the form of homophones. Homophones provide another avenue of proliferation, utilizing both the disparities between language's two forms, and also appealing to the signifier's "proliferating life of its own," allowing a sign's material surface to signify "in excess of the signified it is supposed to bear" (Lecercle 1985: 108). *Krazy Kat*'s jousting remains on the safe, sense-sustaining side of nonsense. These dalliances with contraventions of sense give the impression of a disregard for boundaries, but all their drollery is drawn from a very palpable sense of that transgression, effectively nodding at the ascendancy of the rules they make a show of temporarily forgetting. Homophones encourage a proliferation of both signifiers and signifieds around surface similarities, further fracturing the articulations in the continuum of sound into multiple *graphic* signifiers. For example, when Officer Pupp tells Krazy to "peek if it 'piques' your curiosity" (Herriman (2008: 73) he creates a sort of pun, with the two distinct letter patterns and their respective signifieds both echoing in the shared sound pattern. The repetitious agreement of "an' so it did, sow it did, sew it did" (Herriman 2008: 68) grafts a multitude of signs together into a homophonic heap, and disrupts its own sense of assent by inserting slippery soundalikes into an apparently recurring phrase. The punning exchange "what ho, 'sweetums'" and "what hoe yourself, you rake," which leads Krazy to conclude the speakers are "eggriculturists" (Herriman 2007: 41), mines the flourishing chain of associations set off by this phonic mimicry. These homophonic turns unstick language's dual forms, unsettling the conception of signifiers as orderly articulations of temporal sound by splicing into each multiple, graphically distinct signs. Herriman carries this poetic attention to sound qualities beyond the puns and contradictory spellings the *langue* asserts are "correct," and choreographs a mischievous tango between graphic and phonic forms, disregarding the "frequently analysed [. . .] prescriptively taught [. . .] meticulously policed" written form (Kress & van Leeuwen 1996: 34) and allowing language's talkative surface to speak for itself.

Comics have a strong tradition of "non-standard or distorted vocabulary, phrasing and spelling" (Hatfield 2005: 34). The form's concern with the difference between spoken and written language is by no means unique; the established tradition of vernacular literature, from Mark Twain's *Huckleberry Finn* (1884) to James Kelman's Booker prize-winning *How Late It Was, How Late* (1994), has sought to emulate speech, though comics' heavy reliance on dialogue makes this a particularly pertinent consideration. *Krazy Kat* both explicitly references and makes tacit use of the discrepancies between "correct" and phonetic spelling. The insistent use of the latter breaches language's rules at its surface level, and continually threatens to derail the sense of what we read. The "tallow-whoa" (Herriman 2008: 34) that issues from Krazy's car horn half *reads* as a barely coherent restraining call, but is recognizable via phonic similarity as the rallying cry, "tally-ho." The real joke lies in the approximation of the *sound* of these words, which draws into association the divergent meanings with which each phrase is pre-associated. There is a simultaneous association of sound and dissociation of meaning at work here, brought together by a breach of linguistic rules, the precise sense of which once again depends on the tangible illegitimacy of this rebellious phrase-making. Here, we see how Herriman achieves this as much through surface "noise" as through the semantic proliferations examined above. Beyond colloquialisms and accented pronunciation, Herriman exploits the potential musicality of language, drawing its surface into play with meaning. In the chiming, onomatopoeic lilt of "the lingling gling of a bell" (Herriman 2007: 1996), Herriman plays the role of the poet according to Lecercle, "reminding us that sense and nonsense are inseparable, that the signifier has a proliferating life of its own, always in excess of the signified it is supposed to bear" (Lecercle 1985: 108). Surface here becomes significant, and the noisy interference of the medium is made to participate in the effect of the message.

Herriman's fondness for alliteration has already been mentioned, and indeed is hard to avoid, so habitual is this device. Its continual trumpeting adds to the general feeling of frantic poetry, and lends a mannered air to Herriman's ostentatiously lofty constructions. Determined use of alliteration constrains the vocabulary available for use in any given sentence, and Herriman is forced to employ some fairly outlandish terminology in order to comply with his self-imposed sound patterns. This contributes to the remarkable prolixity of Herriman's characters, for a kind of rambling bombast is made necessary when words are selected as much for their constituent sounds as for the sense they suggest. In turn, this furthers the sense of a proliferation of language, as in the caption "A brace of 'Coconino County's' most masterful minds meet in mutual maunder" (Herriman 2007: 28). Little of informational import is *communicated* here (both picture alone and ensuing action will tell us that characters are gathered in collaborative rumination), but a mouthful of eloquently exotic signifiers nonetheless queues up to verbalize it with profligate superfluity.

Like the grammatical contortions examined earlier, *Krazy Kat's* alliterative echoes have a tendency towards aggrandizement. The excessive consonance of the tagline "'Joe Stork' purveyor of progeny to prince and proletarian" (Herriman 2008: 46) is rendered funny in its formality. So too the half rhyme of phrases such as "no more undue ado," "the odor of odium" (Herriman 2007: 17), and the aforementioned "aura of law and order" draw attention to their own affectation. At the same time, more insistent, urgent rhymes such as "there was a heap of sleep in that jug [of ether]" (Herriman 2008: 32) draw out a faintly preposterous nursery-rhyme quality, which clashes with the consistent loftiness of register the high-flown grammar and grand vocabulary help to create. This undermining is part of Herriman's deliberate jest. Language's innate surface melodies are exploited partly for their own sake, but additionally the gleeful extravagance of these singsong sounds exposes the exaggerated swagger of the register, rendering it ridiculous in its overblown magnificence. *Krazy Kat* utilizes a range of linguistic registers. Herriman's linguistic prowess allows him to masterfully intermingle high, Biblical, arcane, formal, and other registers, even deftly constructing the cat's phonically mangled mishandling of these registers, and thus comically subverting their grandeur.

If register is the organization of language into socially situated usage practices, then there is a sense in which Herriman "unsticks" these associations. Placing these lofty locutions in what looks for all the world like a classic "funny animal" comic appears to breach rules whose tangibility must again be acknowledged if the reader is indeed able to recognize that they have been breached. Herriman mixes registers in ways that provoke our expectations, ramping up the humor through a collision of high and low. There is something jarringly incongruous in the closing colloquialism of the dog's musing, "I'll bet myself a wager evil lurks in that noodle" (Herriman 2006: 24). The register is not only misplaced and finally disrupted, but its grammar slightly contorted: one does not bet a wager; in *making* a wager one already bets. This utterance is undone by its own wordiness. The use of too many words subtly undercuts the very grandeur its protracted syntax aims to invoke. The verboseness of the likes of "it will render you a quantity of safety" verges on garbled rather than eloquent in its prolixity.

Though register is often subverted in this way, Herriman also displays affection for unreconstructed archaisms. The ceremonial-sounding admonishment "have done with gammer" (Herriman 2008: 37) and the alternative "have done with yammer" (Herriman 2007: 17) both crop up frequently. Interestingly, the former noun is recognized by the OED as an archaic term for "old woman," though Heer describes the term as deriving from old whaler jargon for friendly or inconsequential conversation, but without citation (2008: 9). In the case of the similarly antiquated and frequently exhumed "don't fash yourself so" (Herriman 2008: 54), meaning to fret or worry, Heer and the OED agree on the term's meaning and early modern Scottish roots. These obsolete phrases support the often arcane feeling of the register, which frequently flows into mellifluous, cod-Shakespearean utterances such as: "At times the dislike I bear that officious oaf well-nigh consumes me – he engenders a burning ire within me" (Herriman 2006: 44). Hardly erupting with the professed anger, Ignatz's words here are intensely poetic, with just a hint of that subversive alliteration sparkling through in "officious oaf."

The cat's idiosyncratic delivery makes a farce of the elevated registers s/he attempts to emulate. Though it mimics the loquacious tautology of mouse and dog, the declaration "Now will I skwench my thirtz – wed my witzil – mersin my poached lips" (Herriman 2006: 80) comes out of the cat's mouth sounding like baby-talk—albeit rather ambitious baby-talk. The antediluvian flavor of the grammatical inversion "will I" is elsewhere mirrored by the arcane phrases rendered in this childish tongue: "hiddatidda and yunn – I will folla" (Herriman 2002: 99). Krazy's peculiar phonetic flurry is the most obviously vernacular voice of any of the characters. It is evocative in places of a Deep South drawl, though elsewhere distorted to the point of incoherence by mispronunciations and vaguely approximate phonetics. In the cat's exaggerated accent, Herriman transposes the loosest of equivalent syllable sounds to render words in such a way that challenges the reader to make sense of them:

My kittil of soup is werra dry,
My kendil has gone out,
My krimm has toined to chizz,
The dippest pott of the dipp blue sea is where I otta be.
  (Herriman 2007: 69)

There is a recognizable hint of an accented vowel sound in "toined," "kit-til," and "pott," but the foreshortened vowel of "chizz" and cutesy, childish "werra" seem to invent ways of pronouncing words entirely special to Krazy. The consistent twinning of identifiably authentic and invented aspects in producing this lively voice adds to the gentle loopiness of the strip as a whole. The reader is forced into a mental recitation of these often mystifying spellings in order to hear what actual words stand behind the wrenched phonics of "movillis – stipenditz – killotzil" (Herriman 2008: 68). Here as nowhere else does Herriman present us with language "as garbled by the human tongue" (Heer 2008: 8), swapping actual for loosely similar syllables in order to create echoes of the cat's words unrecognizable in their written form. Occasionally Herriman goes beyond this—in echoing Ignatz's reference to "Mr Confucius" as "Mr Konfusion" (Herriman 2007: 30), Krazy lights on the most similar-sounding word available to him/her in order to ape another, unfamiliar term. Similarly, s/he replaces the bona fide "Thursday" for the intended 'thirsty' (Herriman 2006: 80), mistaking aurally similar words, and yet again managing to signify beyond the actual signifier s/he employs, so that the sense of the phrase persists, but with an anarchic feeling of disruption at its core.

The flipside of this syllabic wrenching is the use of eye dialect, where words are written in such a way that their pronunciation is not altered, but an impression of accented speech is given graphically. This is a recognizable convention and signifies dialect through writing dialogue in non-standard ways, even though this non-standard *written* form presents no audible aberration from standard English. The most obvious example in *Krazy Kat* is the unruly insertion of "k" in place of "c," which doesn't change the actual sound of the word being spoken, but has a noticeable effect on the way we read it. Persistent references to "the kwaint konfines of Kokonino Kounty" (Herriman 2007: 36) read as if they take an active part in the musical delirium of these strips, but any sense of accent or dialect is entirely down to the graphic form and not the spoken phrase it represents. An example of true eye dialect lies at the end of the phrase "no rissin a-tall" (Herriman 2002: 37), in which the written version looks odd, as if misspoken, when in fact the suggestion of a pause that places the "t" at the start of the second syllable rather than the end of first, better represents the way we actually pronounce the phrase. Ultimately, the effect of these examples is similar. They layer on additional encouragement to approach the dialogue as being elaborately mannered and accented.

These accented, mispronounced, and otherwise aurally slippery constructions are almost exclusively the preserve of Krazy. This peculiar expressive style and his/her overt linguistic confusion come together in conjuring up the cat's winsome but rather dunderheaded persona. Heer writes that "Herriman liked to be consistent with the diction he gave his characters, using words to define their personalities" (2008: 9), which is true to a certain extent. The cat's almost idiot savant-like character depends hugely on its way of talking, though this has more to do with the enunciative (or rather "pronunciative") aspects of diction than it has with the choice of words. The cat is capable of the same highfalutin register consistently employed by Ignatz and, to a lesser extent, Officer Pupp, but linguistic mismanagement and madcap phonetics lend Krazy's delivery an aura of doltish, unwitting logic. In encountering the self-professed "equatorial bear" (Herriman 2006: 27), the cat perfectly mimics the elevated, tautological prolixity that is the preserve of the other, more linguistically adept characters: from dog or mouse the comment "the mark of the polar regions is all over your form, shape and figure" would exemplify Herriman's grandly arcane and dignified register. However, this impression is transformed into something between charming and childish when Krazy solemnly intones, "The mokk of the polo rijjins is all ova your fomm, shape and figga." Despite the elevated tone, the cat is left sounding somewhat feather-brained, as if struggling with language in the form of these high-flown sentences which his/her artless delivery shows s/he cannot quite comfortably wield.

Herriman is a master of language and an impishly inventive manipulator of features specific to the linguistic system. Under his deft guidance, minimal units are transposed into ungrammatical but *logically* correct formulations and extended in order to further elevate an already elaborate register. Herriman exploits his readers' logocentric tendencies, relying on the fact that we treat language as a conveyor of our chosen meanings and then mischievously unpeeling signifier-signified associations. He layers multiple meanings onto sign forms via homonyms, homophones, and puns, and hedonistically allows himself to get carried away with tautological profusions that see strings of not-quite equivalent synonyms proliferate in place of a simple meaning. Herriman relishes words for their own sake, for their rich variety, and not solely for what they "say." He has a keen ear for the acoustic surface of language, and exploits the system's dual graphic-phonic form both for its screwball inconsistencies and for the impressionistic auditory effects of those surface sounds. Through the use of distorted phoneticisms alongside adroitly handled vocabulary and syntax, Herriman also makes much sport of linguistic registers. By mixing and mispronouncing registers, Herriman consistently destabilizes them, though merely constructing these eminent circumlocutions in the first place seems somewhat subversive, given the frivolous escapades they narrate. It is the very out-of-place quality of the lofty register, as much as its perversion through misuse, that makes it seem so riotously, ludicrously inspired.

The impression produced by Herriman's linguistic horseplay depends for its effect upon the very language rules it flouts. To this end, it belongs to the "tame and respectable" (Lecercle 1985: 106) category of wordplay, in which Lecercle places Lewis Carroll. Unlike the destructive *délire* that devours sense, Herriman's language game "belongs to the surface, it abides by all the rules and conventions, it is highly grammatical and engages in games (e.g., portmanteau words) that do not threaten [the linguistic system], but on the contrary reinforce it." Herriman's phrases parade an air of hectic, rambling novelty, not through their nonsensicality, but through their precisely structured, disciplined choreographing of language's ordering principles. Linguistic rules are made to work for Herriman's ends, insofar as he appears rebelliously to disregard them, while actually relying on them to make perfect expressive and evocative sense in ways that seem to temporarily disrupt, but never really challenge, the organization of the linguistic system. It is an oversight to fail to attend to what Herriman pulls off with language, and eliding the specifics of the linguistic system that enable this exploitation of its operations ultimately does comics criticism no favors.

There is no suggestion here that visual signification is not capable of its own beguiling effects, nor that it cannot reproduce its own version of some of the effects examined here. Demonstrably, it does not consist in those minimally significant units that Herriman uses as building blocks in his games of sense and nonsense. Nor can visual signification emulate the playoff between graphic and phonic forms that is possible in language. Arguably, visual signification is organized into registers in a similar way to language, though it is equally arguable that these registers, not so socially enforced as the rules of language on which we are dependent for primary communication, are less finely tuned and prescribed. It is therefore reasonable to suggest that dextrous, deliberate subversions of these less-established registers might be harder to pull off. Later it will be shown just how pictures' own peculiar features, their analogical nature, motivation, infinite possible forms, and (comparative) lack of (enforced) usage rules enable them to signify in ways that the discrete, finite, double-articulated, arbitrary, and rule-bound language system cannot. These two systems might well be able to replicate each other's basic "message" to convey describable information "as well as" each other, but attempts to equate the effects they can generate misrepresent both—and potentially impoverish our understanding of them.

This chapter cannot pretend to have comprehensively evaluated the *Krazy Kat* cartoons by looking only at their use of language, for there is a corresponding visual lunacy running through these works. We get a taste of this in the strip below (Fig. 1.3) in which the cat's contortions and the hammy, staged poses of the dog, along with the oddly mutating background formations, operate like that anti-literal "do I hear" discussed above. These images signify according to the standard conventions that organize iconic signs. Unlike, say, abstract images, they are easily interpretable with clear and accessible signifieds: we can clearly "read" the cat peeking out from under the propped up tent of his/her book; plainly recognize the circus pavilion-like shape of the distant mountains in the last panel of the third row. But, like the phrase "do I hear," which in practice signifies against its own face value, these images do not tell us quite what they first appear to. We know not to infer from these panels that cat and dog are engaged in purposeful acrobatics during this conversation: the excitable peeking and squirming instead adds to the exaggerated, suspenseful thrill of the cat's retelling of the book's plot.

Similarly, we can deduce that these panels do not literally indicate that Coconino County exists in a bizarre state of geographic flux, but assimilate these signifiers into the madcap impression given by the strip as a whole and interpret it accordingly. Crucially, though, where we *recognize* the idiomatic, non-literal "do I hear," and know by instituted convention that it does not actually ask the question it appears to pose, we *intuitively* interpret these visual images, deducing that these off-the-wall representations are as intentionally ludicrous as Herriman's custom-defying language. Where the auctioneer's phrase has become conventionalized and

1.3 George Herriman, *Krazy & Ignatz: 1937–1938*, ed. by Bill Blackbeard (Seattle: Fantagraphics, 2006), p. 22 (original publication date 14 March 1937).

has entered the linguistic system as a signifying unit itself that we read with prior knowledge of its ready-made associations, the atypical significance of these visual forms must be interpreted, its *lack* of conventional significance recognized, and its implied connotations worked out anew. Broadly similar affects thus draw on distinctive systemic operations to generate the effect they do.

To neglect language in comics, to fail to pay truly *literary* attention to these strips, is to overlook a fundamental aspect of the imaginative magic of *Krazy Kat*. The analysis carried out here necessarily passes up the captivating delights of Herriman's pictures and deft use of the comics form: from the deranged geometries of his desert landscapes, to his erratically shaded sky and orange peel moon; from his pioneering use of the two-dimensional page surface, to his self-conscious attention to the sequential strip format. The purpose of this chapter has been to restore some semblance of balance, by looking at that aspect of comics which has not only habitually been ignored, but whose importance is even denied by comics critics intent on defending and elevating the importance of visual signification—both in relation to comics' narrative economy, and besides the presumed benchmark of verbal signification in general. If comics really are to be considered as a form of literature, then plotline alone (certainly in the case of a cartoonist like Herriman) is insufficient to ascertain a text's credentials. Only by looking at language can critics attest to comics' literary potential, and such an analysis proves Herriman to be a virtuoso *writer*. Even if we acknowledge that it is rather reductive to view comics as a subcategory of prose literature, from which it is as manifestly distinct as other narrative forms such as cinema or opera, the verbal ingenuity of an artist like Herriman remains central to the impact of his works. Thus, critics can acknowledge the specificity of the comics art form and yet still pay adequate attention to language, enabling them to demonstrate the deeply arresting *literary* turns that can be carried out within this very distinctive medium.

Chapter 2

Langue, Parole, and Constraint in the Cartoons of Lynda Barry

Lynda Barry's cartoons possess the kind of strong characterizations, poignant plots, and grim themes that resonate with Anglophone comics critics' content-focused criteria for literariness. However, like Herriman, her work is ill-served by a conception of the form that sidelines textual content, and ignores the truly literary formal features of language. Barry's cartoons further undermine assertions about the primary role of images in conveying narrative information. Frequently, words are indispensable to the sense of her strips, as in the example below (Fig. 2.1). The pictures provide context here, with the narration tellingly detached from the parallel visual strand to create a sense of disconnection between the dancing figure and narrator who pronounces over her. The fragmentation into panels adroitly paces the strip, lending the final twist into jaded despondency a climatic emphasis: the tonally seamless textual flow is broken into rhythmically consistent chunks, or lexias,[1] the last of which pulls the rug out from under both the reader and—prophetically—the oblivious twirling youngster. But though the visual apparatus is undeniably significant, it is the words that fill in all the details of this scenario. This particular comic strip depends absolutely on its linguistic content.

Throughout her typically text-heavy strips, Barry's lively literary language also showcases a particular feature of the linguistic system that further differentiates it from visual signification, namely the fact that language is constrained by a *langue.* Language "is always an inheritance" (Saussure 1983: 71), an abstract differential system and set of combinatory rules that precede speakers, and which they must learn and follow. Language cannot be made up as we go along: its arbitrary nature necessitates that all users abide by its established conventions in order for it to be functional. The relative freedom of visual signification, in counterpoint to this, will be fully explicated in Chapter Seven, but here, along with furthering the arguments that language can be central in comics and that literary

41

2.1 Lynda Barry, "All Different," *The! Greatest! Of! Marlys!* (Seattle: Sasquatch, 2000), np.

analyses must look at formal qualities not content, the aim is to demonstrate the extent to which users of language are indeed constrained by it.

Attempts have been made by critics to emphasize the prevalence and conventionalization of visual signification, positioning it as a rule-bound system whose pervasiveness is coming to rival language. With one eye perceptibly on the primacy of language as a communicative tool, critics variously claim that "ours is an increasingly symbol-oriented culture" (McCloud 1993: 58); that we are witnessing a "growing use of icons" (Beronä 2001: 19); and that the balance of power between word and image "seems to be shifting in favour of the image" (Varnum & Gibbons 2001: ix). Some, such as the comics critic and cognitive psychologist Neil Cohn, go so far as to suggest "comics are the *parole* of the visual *langue*" (Cohn 2005: 241). The visual semioticians Gunther Kress and Theo van

Leeuwen, who share much with comics critics' attempts to frame visual signification in linguistic terms, mirror this move in ascribing to media as multifaceted and dense as television a *langue* of which every program is *parole* (1996: 9). In the latter case in particular, the proposed *langue* seems to constitute a set of common practices and devices more than a differentially valuated system of like units, and, as we shall come to see, the fact that a medium possesses "its own signifying codes and practices" (Hatfield 2005: 33) does not equate to it being constrained by a *langue*. Other critics tacitly acknowledge that visual signification is *parole* but not *langue*, in protesting the assumption that all systems must have a *langue* (Groensteen 2006: 7). As stated in relation to minimal units, this is a reasonable challenge insofar as there exist systems, such as visual signification, which we shall see have no *langue*. However, the existence or not of a preexistent *langue* has considerable implications for the operation of a system so constituted. This chapter aims to show the impact of this constitution on language users and demonstrate that, while the *langue* does not necessarily provide a model for understanding all symbol systems, it remains a vitally relevant feature of the specific system of language.

The role played by the *langue* distinguishes visual and verbal as, respectively, a system in which signs are *made* and a system in which signs are *used*. In language, speakers are always reusing preexistent signs, whereas visual signification affords scope for creating new ones. Kress and van Leeuwen, who go into more depth than has often been characteristic of comics critics in rejecting word/image distinctions, actually showcase the implications of this difference in attempting to deny it. They cite a child describing the steep hill he is struggling to climb as a "heavy hill" (Kress & van Leeuwen 1996: 9), a peculiar phrase that has much in common with the sprightly idiosyncrasies of Barry's child characters. Kress and van Leeuwen claim this expression demolishes the distinction between arbitrary signs, which have "meaning by decree"—and motivated signs, which are made and whose forms and context together imbue them with meaning (1996: 8). In their analysis, the boy in question *makes* a sign when he uses "heavy" to stand in for *"significant effort,"* and *"significant effort"* to denote *"climbing a steep slope"* (1996: 13). But this assessment utterly overlooks precisely what makes this highly original utterance so very quotable: the boy does not *create* the sound/letter pattern "heavy"; it already existed, and so did its decreed association with the connotations of effort, burden, and laboriousness. That the boy *used* these connotations, but did not invoke the traditional denotation, does not make this a new sign made,

but a conventionalized sign used in a new way—a way that is functionally meaningful and highly expressive, but also recognizably unorthodox.
Here, as in Herriman, the sense that a rule is being broken attests to the
existence of the rule that precedes this particular utterance. The meaning
of "heavy" in "heavy hill" may diverge from the instituted standard, yet it is
also richly redolent of that divergence, its very significance bound up with
the unusualness of such a usage.

This sort of engaging and childish misuse of language is the hallmark of
Barry's strips. Particularly inspired manglings include: "he is a gentle person and this is a juvenile delinquency world" (Barry 1999: 2); "the hot dogs
were very e.coli" (Barry 2000: np); and "I very stupid idiotly admitted to
Marlys I love him" (Barry 2002b: np). Such eccentric phraseology recalls
the ambitiously erudite missteps of Daisy Ashford in *The Young Visiters*
(1919). It exemplifies the "rupture with the ordinary regime of language"
that for Gerard Genette (1993: 12) characterizes literature, yet is furthermore highly suggestive of the unsteady grappling with linguistic rules that
goes along with language acquisition. What we see in Barry's strips are
children in the process of inheriting language, and though this paves the
way for much endearing linguistic eccentricity, there is a sense that this
imaginative rule-bending can only go so far. For Herriman, rules are the
props for linguistic capering, but in Barry's strips, though characters frequently parry with boundaries, they are just as often hemmed in by them.

As has already been asserted in relation to Herriman, our very
awareness of misarticulation testifies to the dominance of the rules of
the *langue*. Without those rules, we would have no sense of *mis*use as
such. However, the way language constrains speakers goes further than
an instituted norm that designates non-conforming utterances as being
outside the system. Language not only constrains speakers, but constitutes them, influencing the very way we see, relate to, and participate in
the world. Post-structuralism, which Barry's characters' struggles often
dramatize, offers a counterview to logocentrism, suggesting that rather
than language reflecting and conveying preexistent concepts and ideas, it
is in fact inherited language that bequeaths to us the differential categories through which we classify, define, and come to understand the flux of
experience. That is to say, "we learn a 'pre-given' language or languages,
grow up speaking it or them, and are therefore committed to the meanings that language carries" (Kitching 2008: 47). The most ready concrete
evidence for this theory is the difficulty of translating certain concepts
from one language to another: different languages do not always divide up

the world in corresponding ways, and it is not always possible to express the concepts afforded by one language in another. Similarly illustrative is the spectrum of colors, which we know to be a continuum yet which we segment through language, perceiving colors as belonging to a particular grouping that is linguistically picked out. Thus, we can see how humans "make sense of what we experience through our senses by subsuming it under linguistic categories. Though *sensations* may be of particulars, *perception* involves classifying experiences under universal categories, the majority of which will be derived from or enshrined in language" (Tallis 1995: 50).

Post-structuralism goes so far as to suggest that all "human identity and subjectivity has been socially constructed" (Kitching 2008: 9). Our sense of self and entire cognizance of the world we inhabit are dependent on language, through which we differentiate experience and give it meaning. Despite comics criticism's ongoing attempt to describe comics and the visual according to a linguistic model—and assert the import and efficacy of visual communication—the implication of the verbal system in constructing the world around us is not extended likewise. No one claims that identity and subjectivity are constructed through visual communication as they are suggested to be by verbal discourse. In Barry's cartoons, language is often seen to influence the way an understanding of the world is constructed: her work highlights the manifold implications of language's *langue/parole* foundation, demonstrates our inheritance of the system, and addresses the social imperative involved in language's usage and its role in organizing how we comprehend the world.

Barry's inventively off-kilter deployment of language is comparable, in some ways, to Herriman's, but it is peculiarly expressive of children's acquisition of language. Like Krazy et al., Barry's characters logically extend grammatical rules to words to which they would not normally apply. One character describes some dubious hot curlers that "put out a burningish extension cordly smell" (Barry 2002c: np). Elsewhere, zombie costumes are planned that entail "our hair [. . .] looking insane asylum" (Barry 2002d: np). Similarly, the word "cannery" is used as an adjective, designating the children of employees at this down-at-heel workplace as a kind of pariah class, so that one can *be* cannery; it is something that one *is* (Barry 2002e: np). These vivid misconstructions are strongly suggestive of the error-strewn process of learning language. As Steven Pinker points out, the over-application of grammar rules, particularly to exceptional cases, is a recognized stage in the process (1994: 268–77). Kress and van Leeuwen seem to make use of *social* semiotics specifically in order to dispense with the contrast, evidenced by these resourcefully expressive oddities, between signs used and signs made. They briskly explain that "in social semiotics [*sic*] the sign is not a pre-existing conjunction of a signifier and a signified, a ready-made sign to be recognized, chosen and used as it is" (Kress & van Leeuwen 1996: 8), which allows them to focus on signs-in-context while ignoring the relationship of event to system. However, just like their own "heavy hill" example, the sense generated by these particular contextualized utterances very much depends on their differential relationship to the decreed standards of the *langue*.

In attempting to flatten the distinction between signs made and used, Kress and van Leeuwen insist that: "Availability is not the issue. Children, like adults, make their own resources of representation. They are not "acquired," but made by the individual sign-maker" (Kress & van Leeuwen 1996: 9). Such assertions are simply not borne out by Barry's writing. There is a palpably *childlike* flavor to the questionable employment of "abolished" in the hypothetical proposition "if you go [away to live with imagined, glamorous 'real parents'], you can never see none of us guys again. We are abolished from you" (Barry 2003a: np). The word "abolished" is not *made* here, but its invocation in slightly the wrong way is evocatively characteristic of the precocious yet naive speaker, Marlys, who has most definitely *acquired* an impressive vocabulary but is obviously still in the process of acquiring the knowledge of how to use it. Comparable is the solemn pronouncement that the character Freddie has "certain mental disorders known as emotional problems" (Barry 1999: 2). Though broadly synonymous in literal terms, only the latter phrase is softened by recognizability, carrying the connotations of an established, official psychotherapeutic term—unlike the unfamiliar and hence blunt-sounding "mental disorders." The failure of these kids to discern the difference between a fully instituted word or phrase and a semantically similar one is highly suggestive of language acquisition, with nuances of connotation and literal denotation not always being grasped. The imperative to use language in ways that have been communally established is implicit here: though characters patently struggle to wield these tools correctly, they have recourse to none but the *available* language as best they understand it.

In Barry's work, language misuse does not always palpably flout a specific convention. The use of "insane asylum" and "cannery" as adjectives are of the neat, orderly Herriman type, but often her verbal eccentricities do not transgress a *particular* rule. In this way, Barry's language can be more free-flowing than Herriman's, whose unorthodoxy is always very strictly and precisely contorted. Krazy and company perpetrate *mis*-order, rather than *dis*order, as opposed to Barry's characters' more childishly haphazard grasping at approximate meanings, which are often inadvertently vividly expressive. "Donna's Mouth" features a friend whose "tragic bad habit" is a compulsion to bite everything that falls into her hands. Having allowed her to hold a treasured doll, the narrator reports that on looking over, "There's sudden wads of Tressy hair sticking out of Donna's mouth" (Barry 2000: np). The jumbled syntax is almost impressionistic: "Suddenly there are wads" would not convey nearly so well as "there's sudden wads" the sense that, while no one was looking, this hair sprouted of its own accord and without warning. It is the application of "sudden" to the wads of hair themselves that best conveys the impulsive swiftness of the action. Where the adverb "suddenly" would draw attention to the actual transference of hair into mouth, the abrupt presence of "sudden wads" elides the action that was missed.

Similar is the tale of "The Most Remembery Vacuum," bought cheap from a yard sale, which emits a piercing noise and choking smell when used. On discovering decomposing hamster bodies in its motor, "Mom tweezered out the tragic chunks but the haunting fumes and screaming stayed" (Barry 2000: np). The phrase "tweezered out the tragic chunks" particularly piles much vivid significance into a very small space, the few choice words conveying something delicate, mournful, and horribly, tangibly fetid all at once. The word "haunting" also becomes richly significant, redolent equally of the literal haunting of dead hamsters, the distracting, troubling pungency of the odor, and the way it lingers in the room resistant even to "Lysol, Pinesol, and Spic 'n' Span." Highly evocative, these phrases are odd, quirky, and unfamiliar, without actually breaking any one specific rule.

Without using language rules as boundary lines to be nimbly hopped over, as Herriman does, Barry nonetheless has recourse to set conventions from which her speaker's utterances are differentiated. Not only are these utterances discrepantly related to the recognized rules of the *langue*, but they are also pitted against more localized conventions, particularly standardized and authoritative "adult" registers. Childish attempts to mimic these grown-up ways of talking are often charmingly off-beam. Frequently, words are utilized in ways that go very subtly against the grain, with adult phrases put conspicuously in the mouths of children. In "Gum of Mystery," an "unknown juvenile delinquent" puts chewing gum under the arms of people's coats in the school cloakroom, prompting the child narrator to parrot the rather unnatural exclamation, "What a bad citizen" (Barry 2000: np). This is followed by a series of slight non sequiturs in a disciplinary classroom pow-wow on "why gum is insulting," which concludes it is "rude" and "disturbing" (Barry 2000: np). The oversimplified phrasing, presumably used for the children's benefit, leads to some slightly anomalous expressions that claim that gum itself—inanimate matter—is somehow capable of being "insulting" and "disturbing," rather than the use to which it is being put.

A comparable example of unpredictable mimicry can be found in Marlys's retort "that's what they all say" (Barry 2000: np) to her elder sister's explanation of why her overenthusiastic plant experiment is destined to go awry. The instituted phrase is used anything but literally here: no one else has offered comment of any kind, and the expression is deployed purely in its function as a rebuff, not for what it literally signifies. The opposite is true of the story parroted by the character Arna, when she pretends a borrowed dog is her own. Having been told by the real owner that her pet is "named for Agnes Moorhead, a rather distant cousin of mine – not that she'd stoop to admit it," Arna approximately repeats the story as: "Agnes. After my disturbed cousin. Not that she'd squat down and admit it" (Barry 2001: np). It is hard not to fall for the way the idiomatic "stoop down" goes through a very literal translation into "squat down." Characters are everywhere seen to be *repeating* language, *using* a system that is both preexistent and communal. In Barry's hands, the fact that speakers so often get it wrong is utilized to subtly allude to the necessity of using language correctly in order to enter social discourse. Where Herriman plays with linguistic rules, enacting meticulous subversions that tie language in knots, Barry's characters seem to take aim and miss the mark. Doing so frequently entails hitting on accidental eloquence, but the grim realism that infuses her strips often threatens to clamp down on childish inventiveness. Social constraint looms large, and the necessity of using language according to discursive conventions is a major theme.

Though Barry's strips do deal with the strictures of the linguistic system itself, frequently the evident constraints are situated in particular social settings. The registers of the schoolroom are particularly pertinent for these child characters, and overzealous creativity is often expressly frowned on. In an essay, Arna constructs an elaborate metaphor that likens the body's makeup of cells, tissues, and organs to a sweetshop, but scores poorly. Marlys crushingly explains, "Tolja it was too creative for her. I could tell from how excited you were when you wrote it", and the teacher's comment, "Please stick to the material in the book" (Barry 2007a: np), confirms that this unbridled inspiration cannot expect to be rewarded: the acceptable utterances are fixed in advance. Elsewhere, the telling question, "Are we getting graded on this or is it creative?" (Barry 1990: 60), is proposed by a teenager obviously better versed in the limitations social situations place on speakers. Creativity is permissible at particular times, but at others must be carefully reigned in, and only the appropriate utterances recited.

As in *Krazy Kat,* language's dual form creates difficulties: Arna fails to explain to champion speller Marlys how "'C' and 'K' are mad because they both are in 'stick' but 'K' can't be in 'drastic'" and that "'K' also hates 'N' because 'K' has to be silent like 'know'" (Barry 2002: np). The way language is experienced is personal, subjective, and individual, but to use it publically necessitates using it in collectively recognized ways. Arna further elucidates that "homonyms make the letters take sides. The 'W' in 'won' declares war on the 'E' in 'one'. In my pencil they battle all the way to the paper. 'E' conquers 'W' and I write 'W' just to make 'E' mad. I get a 'D' on the test" (Barry 2002: np).

There is humor in the way the final letter 'D' acts as a signifier, unlike the meaningless and problematically inconsistent letters that make up words. Here we see just how arbitrary are the rules that govern language: words—and letters—signify only what they are communally recognized to signify, and the imperative to comply with these conventions goes beyond social registers. Communication itself is reliant on learning to use language as others do. To participate in social discourse as a speaking subject, it is necessary to learn to operate within the accepted and recognized confines of this communal inherited system.

As mentioned above, the imperative to use language in particular ways is more than a question of wielding the appropriate register in a given situation or negotiating the standards of authoritative adult-speak. Language is, far more fundamentally, a means of relating to the world and participating in it: it is "a way of being in the world" (Auster 1988a: 123). As speaking subjects, we are dependent on language for our most banal and perennial communicative needs. Language's arbitrary nature makes it paramount that, in order to succeed, we use it in ways that are communally ratified. Post-structural theory avers that human subjectivity and selfhood are constructed through language, and, hence, we only exist as social beings through an obligatory complicity with the rules of language. Moreover, since language does not reflect concepts that exist prior to or external to the symbolic system, the ordered, meaningful reality that is constructed through it is in fact the only reality we can comprehend. Because language's signs are meaningful only in relation to each other, language is said to be a closed system: its signs refer only to other signs in the system, and not to any graspable external reality. Thus, everything we think we know and understand about the world around us is in fact an effect of the linguistic system itself. Language is "the field in which we construct meaning" (Horrocks 2001: 6).

In playing at the edges of the linguistic system, Barry's characters demonstrate what is at stake in failing to use language in agreed ways. Where Herriman's characters play with, but always keep very near to, the ratified, conventionalized boundaries of the *langue*, characters such as Freddie risk running too far from recognizable language, particularly in the dark sequence of strips that focus on his status as a social outcast. The musically inventive jive-talk unleashed towards the end of *The Freddie Stories* strays perilously close to outright gibberish. Utterances such as the description of Freddie's mother bursting in high-dudgeon into the principal's office to collect him after misbehavior teeter on the brink of intelligibility: "Mamu came in shrieky-babu, very screamy-sabu" (Barry 1999: 99). The syllables of "mamu" might be close enough to "ma" or "mama" to be coherent without out the framing context that elucidates this strange phraseology, but the "babu" and "sabu" suffixes hazard at being *sounds* rather than words.

Freddie's voluble mutiny strays toward a more extreme linguistic insubordination than Herriman's organized unruliness. This is "material language [...] unsystematic, a series of noises, private to individual speakers, not meant to promote communication" (Lecercle 1985: 44). Though vivaciously exuberant, this outlandish song-speak does not comply with any sort of collective contract that might guarantee meaning. The likes of "I'm chi-chi-ba-nana baba!" (Barry 1990: 100) or "Baby-baba-rocka-shaggy-mama-baba-saba-sister-brother-baba-doctor-shaggy-backa-baba-bubba-baby-boo" (Barry 1990: 92) do not fit into the differential system of signs through which meaning is constructed. Full of phonemes but light on morphemes, these vocal pantomimes refer to neither an extralinguistic reality (as we logocentrically presume language to do in our daily usage of it) nor to other signs in an ordered structure (as semiotic theory posits language does; and as post-structural theory holds is *all* it does). It instead resembles "the scream" (Lecercle 1985: 44) of the sense-devouring *délire*, the flipside of abstract, systematic, communication-enabling language, where language becomes material, instinctual—and very much individual.

2.2 Lynda Barry, "El Fagtastico," *The Freddie Stories* (Seattle: Sasquatch 1999), pp. 100–101.

In describing the genesis of his strange counter-language, Freddie explains how he "ran into the darkness to get free" (Barry 1999: 93), but this freedom is a double-edged sword. The constraints of language are eluded at the expense of communicability. Freddie's vivacious linguistic explosion enmeshes him in two parallel binaries: freedom versus constraint; and comprehensibility versus meaningless babble. The escape, here, is indeed into unfathomable darkness. As Freddie exempts himself from linguistic conventions, he exiles himself from the social discourse whose standardized practices enable communication. If communal language is the means through which human beings comprehend and exist in the world, Freddie's pseudo-language refers to neither extralinguistic reality nor a complex of inherited, meaningful signs, but to primal and disordered darkness.

The spirited chanting of *The Freddie Stories* is a radical example of convention-busting in Barry's work, but possesses a kind of non-referentiality that is a perennial if subtle theme. The view that language is a closed-off system, in which differential signs take their meaning only from their relative position to each other and not from a corresponding external reality, is central to post-structuralism. This notion is dramatized in Barry's strips in a variety of ways. It is playfully embodied by Freddie describing his mother reappearing after storming off in response to his linguistic rebellion with the dramatic and terrifically off-the-wall report: "Shhh! Shhh! The bathroom door opens and here come the flat feet of the queen of Spain" (Fig. 2.2). Next to his mother's amplified but banal rejoinder, "Why?!!," Freddie's is an arresting utterance, but there exists an exaggerated and obvious disconnect between the words used and the "real-world" referent implied. A subtler version of this disconnect recurs intermittently when characters "tr[y] mentioning some words about" (Barry 1990: 52) or "tr[y] to say some words about" (Barry 1990: 69) a particular topic. These phrases stack multiple layers of "standing in for" between the speaker and the thing they wish to convey. By "saying some words about" something, rather than merely "saying" it, the gap between the speaker's intention and what they manage to communicate is elongated. The "try" in each of the above utterances further undermines these multiple attempts at "saying" or "mentioning" something "about" a given subject, highlighting the difficulty of getting words to "do" things.

The difficulty inherent in words' representation of anything is peripherally evident in all the curious constructions examined so far, particularly those that betray an obvious parroting of phrases in slightly the wrong context. Putting the appropriate words in place of an idea is an ongoing struggle and though these kids frequently bump against the edges of the linguistic system in highly engaging ways, the extent to which they can contravene it and still convey anything at all meaningful is repeatedly shown to be curtailed. While functional meaning is not the only pertinent analytical feature of language, where it is surrendered to the point of absence, an utterance necessarily fails discursively. Sense in language depends on mutual agreement. The extent to which self-referential signs are closed off from any external reality creates a problem for conveying anything not already instituted, contractually approved, and accepted within discourse. Meanings not already communally recognized are effectively discursively prohibited.

Throughout Barry's work, the restrictions built into language's inherited contractual nature are most evident in attitudes toward gender and sexuality. Judith Butler's theory of performativity, exemplary of the poststructuralist stance that our perceptions of the world are produced by language, is particularly pertinent to the tussles with gender roles Barry's characters undergo. According to Butler, the categories into which we organize gender and sexuality exist not as natural distinctions, but as purely linguistic ones, through which we are discursively conditioned to recognize binary genders. Gender consists only in a "repeated stylisation [. . .] that congeal[s] over time to produce the appearance of substance" (Butler 1990: 3). Social subjects, "from the inception of existence," are "hailed or addressed by social interpellation" (Butler 1999: 120), and it is entirely through these ongoing acts of naming that our idea of categorical gender and sexuality distinctions is actually produced. As speaking subjects, we operate from a position "always already inside" (Butler 1999: 189) the ready-made and socially pervasive system of restricted interpellations, "fundamental[ly] dependen[t] on a discourse we can never choose" (Butler 1997: 2). We have only a limited number of ways of describing gender and it is these categorical descriptions, rather than any natural divisions, which institute the recognized groupings. To put it *very* simplistically, a girl is only a "girl" inasmuch as *she* is constantly referred to as such.

A prime explication of this thesis can be found in the strip "Mood Ring Cycle," in which Arna explains that "Girls have never wanted me. No part of me matches what they need to have to match. They have called me a boy. Maybe I am" (Barry 2005a). Gender here consists in certain normative traits and a failure to match these creates a kind of terminological problem for the ungirlish girl. Given the limited terms that are available according to Butler, if this "girl" is so manifestly un-"girl"-ish, then what on earth is she? Of her cousin, Arna says, "Marlys is a girl, but she isn't very good at it." One's sex, then, is something that one *does*, a set of rules that one must submit to in order to participate socially. Marlys's failure to enact her gender sufficiently well leads to periodic ostracism, whereas Arna's more consistent inability to "do" her gender right leads to a more entrenched social disconnection.

Butler's warning that punishment threatens "those who fail to do their gender right" (1990: 185) is further borne out by Freddie, whose linguistic revolt is a questionable success and whose gender confusion creates immense difficulties. His bizarre linguistic secession from the hegemony of normative categories is bound up with the self-created, binary-smashing guise of "El Fagtastico, dude-dude, lady-dude, lady-lady, dude-lady, I am all of these things!" (Barry 1999: 100). To say, as his sister Marlys does, that Freddie "is often called a fag" (Barry 1999: 3) is a colossal understatement. Everyone—children, adults, and Freddie himself—habitually term him as such, but this labeling of the preteen character is not related to actual sexual practices or preferences. Instead, "fag" seems to be the best-fit term to describe Freddie's failure to do any kind of gender right: wearing his sister's swimsuit (Barry 2007b: np) and his mother's bra (Barry 2007c: np), only able to sleep if wearing girls' pajamas, and occasionally declaring himself to be a girl (Barry 2003b: np), the clash between Freddie's self and the normative sexual categories available in language is more complex than an easily definable, if discursively underprivileged, homosexuality. No terms can adequately define him, and where Arna is socially isolated, Freddie becomes "culturally unintelligible and impossible" (Butler 1990: 189). Though his own weird language allows him to step outside the confines of conventionalized social discourse, it cannot render him any more "intelligible" to those around him, who operate according to shared rules that do not afford Freddie an appropriate position within the differential linguistic system. Whatever respite El Fagtastico's linguistic camp[2] provides, it does not protect Freddie against being victimized and rejected.

Barry's work betrays a peripheral awareness of the mundane and everyday ways in which gender is performatively instituted through a set of props: girlishness is noted to manifest itself through quantities of "clothes, hair and toys" (Barry 2002a: 185); young girls' ideal of grown-up perfection hinges on being "fully-developed" (Barry 2000: np); and a teenager bewails that a slew of high school-arbitrated defects could be counterbalanced through "stackedness" (Barry 1990: 14). These nods towards the performative nature of gender and language's limiting categorizations feed into the palpable suggestion of inauguration into constraining social discourse, insofar as it is so often children who creatively misuse language while adults aim to enforce conventional norms. Through a kind of linguistic initiation, these children are seen gradually being introduced into social discourse, and their ability to resist its conventions is frequently challenged. Through this, it becomes clear how identity might be produced linguistically, though in acknowledging that strategies for resisting these conventions *do* exist, it is necessary to temper the assertion that language absolutely produces the differentiated meanings through which we understand experience—for if this were the case, we could hardly identify and discuss these manifestations of language influencing and constraining meaning. Through the unconventionality of their uses of language, Barry's characters aptly demonstrate that, though language is indeed constraining and strongly *influences* the way we conceptualize the world around us, there is some scope for manipulating its conventions in order to draw attention to and even challenge discursive norms.

With regard to performativity, Butler allows that it is possible to resist the norms that are enforced through discourse. Though the system offers only limited terms, whose conventional iteration reinforces discursive norms, those norms can be challenged through a "variation on that repetition" (Butler 1990: 185). By repeating against type, and using normative terms in unusual ways, speakers can resist the constraints of the system from within. Marlys enacts a kind of naive reclamation of the word "queer" in her crudely self-crafted guide to this "great subject" (Barry 2000). Her use of the term is so matter-of-fact as to become banal. The sexual implications of the word are effectively neutralized through the mundane and innocent nature of Marlys's appraisal: pondering her readers' potential questions about queers, she preemptively offers, "What does a queer do when he sees a dog. Answer it depends on the dog. Maybe pets it." Marlys *is* conscious of the sexual meaning of the term, carefully explaining that some people "don't like queers" because "one thing they're thinking is the queers [*sic*] going to kiss them." This assumption of indiscriminate enthusiasm for anyone of the same sex is effectively deflated through the following dramatization: "You do so want to!"; "As if"; "Why not?"; "You get on my nerves." This exchange is so blandly artless as to make the fear it addresses seem positively hysterical in comparison. This strip is rife with the sorts of "improper use of the performative" (Butler 1999: 124) that Butler claims undermine, rather than reinforce, conventional connotations.

Butler's concern for the way language is used to impose a normative order on the world leads her to a different slant on misuse than that of Lecercle, though both agree that linguistic rebellion always takes place from inside the system of language. For Lecercle, the sense that a rule has been broken attests to the dominance of that rule, while for Butler, utilizing constraining terms in non-normative ways exposes the performative nature of those terms, and highlights the non-referentiality of the linguistic categories that impose order on the world rather than respond to it. The destabilizing power of linguistic resistance, in relation to the norms encoded in the system if not the hegemony of the system itself, is displayed when Marlys overhears her aunt and mother arguing that their respective sinning will turn each of their offspring into either a whore or a homosexual. Her ready response, "I dibs faggot!" (Barry 2005b: np), exemplifies the type of usage that "rework[s]" (Butler 1999: 124) conventionalized terms, invoking them in ways that work against the grain of privileged norms.

Butler makes clear that the constraints of the linguistic system can only be resisted from within. There is no position outside language from which speakers might resist the limitations it imposes, but, even from within it, we can identify and discuss these discursive restrictions. As such, though it is undeniable that "once human beings became language-using creatures this [had] a profound effect on their conceptions of everything" (Kitching 2008: 193), the view being advanced by this chapter stops short of positing meaning as *wholly* created by language. If this were the case, the alternative "improper" uses of the performative Marlys indulges in would not be possible. We would not be able to perceive, let alone discuss or challenge, the dominant norms language fosters. The system *is* restrictive, offering a finite set of terms, but the *use* individuals make of particular terms, in various combinations and in particular contexts, can challenge the norms and conventions engrained in discourse.

Barry's work, like Herriman's, shows that it is possible to play with the conventions of language, but her cartoons further emphasize the impossibility of shaking off these rules entirely. Misuse of language always carries its unconventionality along with it. However, the fact that the sorts of resistance discussed above are possible precludes the absolutist assertion that language bequeaths us a perception of reality that is entirely circumscribed within a wholly closed system. Therefore, though it demonstrates how language constrains speakers and *influences* our understanding of the world, this chapter also acknowledges the possibility of subversive, "improper" usage of its terms and rules, and thus adopts a kind of "middle course between the implausible idea that language 'passively' reflects reality and the equally implausible idea that reality is produced by language; between the naive view that discourse merely replicates the form and content of pre-linguistic reality and the equally simplistic view that reality is differentiated only post- or intra-linguistically" (Tallis 1995: 102).

Barry's work shows how language influences and stabilizes our understanding of the world (for example, providing binary, oppositional categories of gender), but does not absolutely control and create meaning (for example, also enabling us to identify and discuss those binary categories, and explicitly question them as these child characters do, if only through unconventional use of its limited terms). Despite tempering the extremes of post-structuralism, I have sought, here, to underline the centrality of language to human social life. While it is undeniable that the thriving visual culture emphasized by comics critics does away with any assumption that "language is paradigmatic of meaning" (Mitchell 1994: 12), the fact that language is our primary means of communication, on which our social existence hinges, *does* differentiate it from visual signification, and has crucial implications for how we use and process it.

The aim here has been in part to provide an anticipatory counterpoint to the issues explored in Chapter Seven, which shows that visual signification does not operate in the ways examined here. Images are not constrained by a *langue* but instead afford scope for "pure creation" (Barthes 1967: 15). The preceding analyses of quirky coinage, parroting, and the unintelligibility that comes with over-creativity all attest to the constraints of the *langue* and evidence the fact that linguistic signs are always signs *used* rather than created in the moment of their invocation. This is not to suggest that images are not conventionalized to a degree, but these conventions operate very differently within a motivated system, as we shall come to see. Visual images are simply not subject to the same communally ratified rules that are continually reinforced through mundane, everyday discursive habits, nor are they implicated in stabilizing and organizing our perceptions of the world.

A secondary goal has been to reinforce the claim put forward in the first chapter that language is, in many cases, a crucial element in comics, and the common insistence that words are always of secondary importance in every hybrid text is a mistaken move. None of the cartoons discussed here could convey much of a narrative without their outlandish and engaging textual content. The dexterity with which Barry crafts her child characters' idiosyncratic stabs at language further confirms that attending only to the information value of comics' language rather drains it of its richness and aesthetic value. Of course, Barry's childlike drawing style, the narrative punctuation of panels and speech bubbles, and framing of pictorial content are all integral to the overall impact of each strip, but frequently in

Barry's work words are primary. The literary value of her strips lies in their canny use of language and not the narrative content that this language is instrumental in conveying. The specific features of language addressed here are instrumental in enabling the specific literary effects her works exploit. Comics critics are of course quite right to insist that neither verbal nor visual signification should be privileged as better at communicating. However, this refusal of *hierarchy* makes an erroneous logical leap when it rejects the idea that any pertinent distinctions exist at all between these two very different signifying systems.

Chapter Three

Language in Context
The Spatiality of Text in Comics

Thus far, the focus has been on comics' incorporation of literary writing, and how those literary qualities depend on mechanisms specific to the linguistic system. This approach has been used to show what is lost by the habitual sidelining of comics' language. However, while it has been demonstrated how comics can achieve the same verbal prowess as prose texts, the specificity of the comics form and peculiar ways it can deploy language have so far been ignored. Critics' "search for comics exceptionalism" (Beaty 1999: 67) has led to many a dubious claim about features "unique" to the comics form,[1] and though it is important to avoid claims like these that do not stand up, it is nonetheless necessary to consider the medium's particularities. The preceding analyses have been deliberately skewed toward the sort of textually focused literary criticism that could be applied to traditional literature, examining features and devices definitely not unique to comics, but which they are capable of utilizing. Anglophone comics criticism would certainly benefit from a more attentive and thorough importation of these "scholarly traditions with which it might best intersect" (Groensteen 2006: viii), particularly where the neglected textual aspect of the form is concerned. My aim here has been to demonstrate that, far from being a secondary incidental consideration as the likes of McCloud would have it, comics can and should be viewed in terms of their use of literary language. I have also insisted, however, that such an approach is necessarily (obviously) incomplete, and as a closing statement to this first section will consider how literary language is put to work *specifically* within the comics form.

As we have paid an unusual level of attention to language in the preceding chapters, it should now be clear exactly what is lost through the critical vagueness that avers that "'[w]riting' for comics can be defined as the conception of an idea, the arrangement of image elements and the construction of the sequence of the narration and the composing of dialogue"

(Eisner 1985: 122). Such an expansive view of "writing" provides little scope for appreciating the genuine literary value that comics' linguistic element can possess. That said, due caution must be taken when applying neighboring analytical paradigms, such as literary close reading, to the comics form. Such applications can only ever be a starting point for a fully developed theory of comics; we cannot simply build comics theory from pieces of existing theory without attuning these to the art form's particularities. Though comics' separable elements are ill-served by approaches that fail to treat them as such, the form is certainly not reducible to its visual and verbal elements, and an adjustment of the existing critical frameworks is, perhaps always, necessary in order to effectively apply them to comics' interwoven components.

The problems surrounding notions of language and literariness that have become cemented within critical discourse on comics seem the result of a detachment from established critical traditions, which a more attentive augmentation of those traditions might guard against. However, it would be a counterpart error to attempt too rigidly to apply the standards, expectations, and practices of literary analysis to comics, without acknowledging their divergences from prose literature. Comics *can* be highly literary and, as demonstrated above, attending to their linguistic content enables us to validate this claim. However, not all comics—complex, rich, and thematically sophisticated as they may or may not be— employ literary language, or indeed any language at all. In promoting an approach to comics that considers linguistic content, I do not suggest that all comics can summarily be judged as if they were "a kind of literature," certainly not without expanding what that term implies to the point of losing sight of its specificity.

The expansive characterization of "writing" that equates it to broader narrative and artistic practices effectively undermines comics' claims to the linguistic dexterity that truly distinguishes literary from non-literary writing. The association between comics and literature has been increasingly open to question in recent debate (Beaty 2007: 7, Wolk 2005: 13), though it seems as if truly *literary* readings of comics texts have rarely been carried out in the first place. Such readings potentially offer a rich seam for criticism, but the caveat regarding automatically classifying all comics as literary works remains. Not all comics can be usefully critiqued according to literary standards, and while neglecting the verbal element results in a failure to appreciate language in comics, insisting that all comics are "a kind of literature" risks taking their linguistic component out of context. A flipside danger to conflating "literature" and "writing" with "narrative" and "art" is failing to acknowledge that comics' writing operates according to a mode different from prose or poetry. Though I would insist that literary comics are those that use language well, that is not to say that a text with mediocre or even poor language fails in any way: language-in-comics can only be evaluated within media-specific parameters.

Cases in point are Will Eisner and Alan Moore, both widely vaunted as great comics writers. Given the heights to which comics' deployment of literary language can aspire, the assessments of these two comics industry giants illuminate how literariness has been engulfed by a desire to applaud comics' achievements to the hilt, without always making a nuanced distinction between what can rightly be thought of as "good comics" and those which are much more specifically *literary* comics. Eisner, something of a sacred cow with an annual award named after him, remains an astonishing draftsman, whose cartooning style and innovative layouts were "years ahead of their time" (Wolk 2007: 168). Eisner is sometimes credited with inventing the full length "graphic novel," which term was hijacked in order to pitch comics into the literary ring, for his 1978 work, *Contract with God*. This work is in reality a series of vignettes (the term was actually first coined in 1964 [de Liddo 2009: 15]), visually stunning but lacking in the profundity to which it aspires, and which the ever-irreverent Douglas Wolk describes as "club-footed and mawkish" (2007: 172). Eisner's theoretical work makes evident that he considers verbal content secondary to visuals, explicitly emphasizing cartooning over words (Eisner 1985: 103). It may thus seem unfair to judge his writing in isolation from its context, but doing so serves to illustrate what is obscured by equating broad ideals of creativity or narrative with more specific *literary* value.

Generally speaking, Eisner's dialogue sounds reasonably colloquial and, along with most of his caption text, might merely be described as functionalist, deployed in service of helping the story along, rather than for aesthetic purposes of its own. It is, however, given to occasional clunkiness, as when a letter-writer confuses the tenses appropriate to his own vantage point and his reader's, instructing "I bought you a ticket – look in this envelope I put it in" (Eisner 2006b: 269). It can also be jarringly non-idiomatic, as when a wife dismisses her husband's rehashing of his baseball-playing glory days with the wholly unnatural phrase "it is fifteen years later Charlie" (Eisner 2006a: 40). When Eisner really lets rip, however, the awkward grandiloquence of his extended bursts of prose veer towards the embarrassing with such sentences as: "Gradually, unreasoned terrible fear mingled with grandiose dreams in the turgid, boiling plasma of his mind" (Eisner 2006b: 239). There are obvious, though rather questionable, semantic links between the bubbling overflow suggested by "boiling" and the swollen saturation suggested by "turgid," but it is dubious whether something actually can be both boiling and turgid at once. These verbal constructions are played entirely straight, with none of the deliberate mangling that characterizes Barry's and Herriman's dexterous composition of mishandled language. Eisner's alliteration is a far cry from the intentionally hammy games of *Krazy Kat*, sounding somewhat forced and unwieldy in his hands, as when he writes of subways: "it [the city] burrows into the earth for commutation catacombing itself with capillaries" (Eisner 2006a: 23). This mix of metaphors is bewildering, notwithstanding Eisner's apparent attempt to use the word "commute" as a root for the word from which it is itself derived.[2]

It is perhaps unfair to judge Eisner on the quality of his prose. His work is firmly rooted in the American mainstream industry, and transcends genre standards on almost every level, genuinely pushing the boundaries of the comics form. To subject his sentences to linguistic analysis takes them out of context, for adroit prose is really not the point of Eisner's work. Eisner was always chiefly a comics *artist* who privileged the visual as the driving force of any work, and who is generally praised as an all-round comics creator. Critical accolades characteristically subsume actual writing skills into general storytelling and creative capabilities. It can be galling, however, to find his work continually and uncritically held up as exemplary of great comics authorship, with no distinction made between his impressive artistic ability and visual inventiveness—and truly great *writing*, which other comics authors pull off with much greater skill.

There is an analogous objection to be made regarding the critical plaudits heaped on Alan Moore's comics, though the linguistic weak spots in his work are far fewer and subtler than Eisner's. Unlike Eisner, Moore undertakes the writing role in collaboration with various artists, and is thus more specifically held up as "an excellent writer" (Sabin 1996: 137), as well as an all-round creator. An undeniable creative colossus, Moore's ideas are magnificent, his narratives constructed with dramatic flair, and, as far as the comics form goes, he is indeed a "wizard at formalist exercises" (Gravett 2008: 31). But to cite Moore as one of the comics form's best writers reveals the disinclination, within comics criticism, to tease out the difference between great comics and great language-in-comics. Moore is capable of a sharp line, as the likes of the fascist cabaret tune in

V for Vendetta show, but the timbre of his prose is not so consistently polished as that of numerous other comics' writers—and ones to whom the "great writer" tag is not always so readily applied.

A self-confessed fan of Moore's, Wolk makes a concerted and explicit effort to counterbalance this bias by acknowledging Moore's lesser talents, which he interestingly identifies as chiefly residing in a handful of verbal "tics," not least Moore's fondness for rendering all speeches of import in an exaggerated "iambic gallop" (Wolk 2007: 235). The London tour undertaken by Sir William Gull in *From Hell* is narrated with an unrelenting rhythmic chant, presumably intended to lend the impression of terrible resonance. It is perhaps appropriate that the sweeping elucidation of his unhinged plan in this Gothic melodrama is turned into the grave, yet singsong dirge it is, but the unremitting regularity of the rhythm, maintained through a mildly inconsistent use of contractions like "'twas" and "'twould," risks becoming contrived. The theatrical V's similarly cadenced recitals, which Wolk also references, are saved from awkward artificiality by being framed as songs, and tempered by the character's frequent quotation of lyrics and verse. While readers will hardly expect naturalism from this outpouring of megalomaniac lunacy, the delivery veers towards a rather plodding *over*-regulation, as in such lines as "now *all* that's *left's* this *dis*mal *patch* of *grass*, grazed *bare* by *sheep*; a *yell*owed *waste* in *sum*mer's *heat*, a *quag*mire *if* it *rains*" (Moore & Campbell 2000: 4.10; my emphasis), and "'twas *thus* for *several mil*lion *years* – Then *men* re*belled*, per*haps* a *few* at *first*, a *small* cons*pir*acy – who *by* some *act* of *social magic, politics* or *force* cast *woman down* that *man* might *rule*" (Moore & Campbell 2000: 4.8; my emphasis).

This lumbering march may well play to Gull's madness, to the intricate orderliness of his plan, and the overblown nature of the story itself, but it risks exhausting the reader who has to negotiate its forced rhythms for several pages.

Moore's use of expository dialogue can also, on occasion, stray into clunkiness. Clarifying explanations are sometimes inserted into the mouths of characters who effectively *tell* the reader what they need to know, rather than the story *showing* them. When V asks Evey if she remembers the war that has plunged the country into totalitarianism, instead of relating her personal memories of the conflict, she gamely launches into a convenient explanatory summary of the war's events and consequences. Telling V, who has lived through the very same events, that "nobody knew if Britain would get bombed or not" later revealing "but Britain didn't get bombed," and carefully explaining to him that bombs affected the weather and caused famine as "the weather had destroyed all the crops, see?" (Moore & Lloyd 1990: 27), does not feel like an account of a mutual experience. The inclusion of details that both characters must necessarily already be aware of, which are already implicit in V's original question, are obviously reviewed here for the benefit of someone who was *not* there when all this happened—the reader. Such moments are not over-frequent, but neither are they rare. Exemplary is Evey's comment, "Oh it's raining. It must be cold" (Moore & Lloyd 1990: 172), which sets up the revelation that she has been so transformed by her experience she no longer even perceives the cold. In order for Moore to unveil this fact as a dramatic bombshell, however, he requires Evey to *notice* something she supposedly cannot feel, but wait for V's prompt, "Do you feel it?", before starkly and powerfully confirming, "No" (Moore & Lloyd 1990: 172). The close of this conversation is aptly emphatic and climatic: V has transformed Evey into a fearless agent of his resistance movement, effectively dehumanizing her in service of his own anarchic ends. The effectiveness of this dramatic final "no," however, is somewhat compromised by the jarringly artificial opening gambit, which leaves the entire conversation feeling too palpably manufactured and constructed.

Allowances must be made for a certain degree of explication through dialogue, as a work that showed everything, rather than reporting via occasional asides, would be tedious and overlong. However, as with any other narrative art form, conversations structured round a central revelation can be off-putting if not tempered with a sufficient degree of believability. The question is one of degree, as well as medium. Moore is by absolutely no means a bad writer and, as with Eisner, the above critique potentially risks taking his writing out of context, engaged as it is with a range of literary genres and traditions not necessarily concerned with realism or naturalism. But though Moore wholly deserves his accolades as a comics genius, and though mixed-media forms such as comics cannot be straightforwardly evaluated according to their use of one particular element taken in isolation, the persistent labeling of Moore as an "excellent writer" exposes how little critics attend to actual language in comics and how far "writing" is bound up with broader ideas of storytelling and creativity.

Comics are not, of course, reducible to literature. They are a visual-verbal form, and layouts, pictures, other visual devices, and plotting might justifiably take precedence over a well-crafted sentence. Language is just one of the form's elements, and may not be at the core of a particular text's aesthetic. As the examples above, particularly Moore's work, serve to show, writing in comics that may not stand up to scrutiny when removed from its context is not necessarily bad writing-in-comics. But this does not render writing negligible. It is not, for example, inappropriate to consider the dialogue in film (another mixed form). Rather, we approach this verbal component as we variously would the text of a novel, poem, or play, with a different set of standards and expectations in mind against which to measure the work. Comics' use of language therefore needs to be considered according to the specifics of the form, within which parameters the relative naturalism and expository serviceability seen in the examples above are judged differently to prose literature. The preceding chapters have dealt with consummately written cartoon strips, and have shown just how flawed is that strain of logophobia that blindsides critics to the potential of comics' linguistic component. The remainder of this chapter will counterbalance the linguistic analyses of Eisner and Moore with consideration of the work of Posy Simmonds, demonstrating in more detail what it might mean to look at language-in-comics. Simmonds is another literary virtuoso, but the focus here is how her works utilize the fragmentary nature of the comics page as an integral tool in constructing linguistic effects. Though still linguistically focused, this reading aims to showcase some form-specific ways of approaching comics' literary language, modifying the usual practices of literary close reading to account for the distinctive properties of this art form.

Posy Simmonds uses large chunks of text: it could never be said that "the words become secondary" (Varnum & Gibbons 2001: ix) to understanding her works. Passages of prolonged prose allow Simmonds to create a sustained tone and give her characters recognizable voices that sharply contrast with each other, something both Herriman and Barry also manage in their smaller bursts of text, but which Simmonds pulls off with a more prolonged grace and polish. In being unafraid to rely on text, Simmonds avoids the sort of clunky expository dialogue that can creep in when artists attempt to dress up telling as showing, using characters as a sort of chorus. Where telling is more appropriate, narration is allowed to hold sway, with depicted scenes used to show what is more fittingly shown. In addition to being aptly used and well-written, Simmonds's text is arranged so as to make full use of comics' fragmentation into speech bubbles, captions, and images. The arrangement of utterances within the two-dimensional space of the page is made integral to the way that text reads. Her arrangement of verbal content utilizes the sort of effects created by a poem's lineation or through the sort of spatial layout seen in pattern poems. This spatial arrangement informs the way text reads, assisting in creating literary effects.

Simmonds's layouts, with their prose passages, unbordered images, and traditional strip segments, are collage-like, and challenge the traditional conceptions of page layout that underpin definitions of the form such as that of the oft-cited McCloud. For McCloud, the interframe space or "gutter" and process of "closure" (McCloud 1993: 66–67) by which readers mentally bridge the two moments in time depicted in adjacent panels to infer a continuous narrative, are both central to comics and their exclusive preserve: "a kind of magic only comics can create" (McCloud 1993: 93). Horrocks outlines how McCloud constructs this definition of comics in order to foreground the particular feature he most values (Horrocks 2001: 2). McCloud's definition hones in on this one feature without ever attempting "to justify why 'Sequential Art' should be seen as the one definitive element in comics to the exclusion of all others" (Horrocks 2001: 2), even going so far as to reduce his central tenet to the epithet "space equals time" (McCloud 1995: 59), which has developed into something of an accepted standard within discourse on comics' formal makeup. Simmonds's work cannot be so simplified, as it resists reduction to chains of consecutive panels, instead drawing multifarious spatially distinct (but not necessarily sequential) elements into a network of interrelation. The kinds of "gaps" that inform her work are not merely spaces between momentary panels in sequential strips. In a direct challenge to McCloud, Robert C. Harvey examines a very different kind of "gap" in comics, between picture and caption, which the reader similarly "fills in" so that each illuminates the other, revealing their full import only through their mutual relationship (Harvey 2001). Though Harvey's analysis provides a valuable counterpoint to McCloud's emphasis on the "gutter" as the most—even only—pertinent gap within the comics form, by examining Simmonds's compartmentalization of text in particular, we can see how the spaces in comics over which readers must make imaginative links are far more diverse than either of these conceptions admits.

This "filling in," especially as described by McCloud, is no more than the comics version of the "intentional sentences correlatives" that Wolfgang Iser describes in prose fiction, which "disclose subtle connections" between the "component parts" of the text that together create "the world of the work" (Iser 1980: 52). McCloud attempts to claim that comics' "demand for active interpretation" and "participation" (McCloud 1993:

136) is somehow unique to the form, an assertion symptomatic of the widespread urge to find some aspect of the medium entirely specific to it. Many critics are apt to follow his lead. Thierry Groensteen and Charles Hatfield, on the other hand, both acknowledge the similarity between the operations that McCloud and Iser describe, though Hatfield does so with characteristic hyperbole, stating that comics are intrinsically *more* fractured and thus inherently *more* demanding of active participation than prose (Hatfield 2005: xiv), while admitting the two share in the general narrative principle that "no author worth his salt will ever attempt to set the *whole* picture before his reader's eyes" (Iser 1980: 57). The pertinent difference between comics and prose literature is that in the former these narrative gaps are *visible*, physical spaces on the page over which a *range* of elements—segments of text, whether brief caption, extended narration, or speech bubble; individual pictures; and whole panels—are all drawn into the reader's imaginative construction of the world of the work. Simmonds's loosely structured pages show just how reductive is the prescriptive "space equals time" definition and how Harvey's counterclaim still only accounts for a small part of comics' prolific fragments. Her canny spacing out of portions of text, or lexias, in particular shows how comics' spatial configuration is relevant to more components than just the panel, and that a *web*, rather than a sequence, best describes the range of relationships that resonate through these fragmentary texts.

I do not wish to suggest that the features McCloud and Harvey identify are not important to comics' operations, but rather to demonstrate that comics weave a connective tissue that enmeshes a multitude of textual fragments that can never be summarized by a single (or even taxonomic set of) "core" feature(s) that will comprehensively account for how we read them. The aim of this particular section is to challenge narrow conceptions of comics' narrative gaps, as well as further the challenge presented to critical logophobia, by showing how comics *specifically* put verbal text to use within their fragmentary, gap-riddled, multi-component form. I would argue that this spatialization of constituent elements is part of comics' *visual* arsenal, though crucially not a *pictorial* one. Common attempts to flatten word-image distinctions and impose a linguistic model on visual signification can blindside critics to the radical heterogeneity of the latter, a feature Simmonds's use of non-pictorial visual apparatus helps illuminate. Her work exploits spatial and typographical aspects of visuality to set up interplay between *textual* correlatives. Just as we link up panels, or pull together pictures with their captions, so too our comprehension of a text

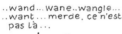

3.1 Posy Simmonds, *Gemma Bovery* (London: Jonathan Cape, 2001), p. 4.

"sparks across" (Kunzle 2001: 15) these other gaps, directing us to connect the web of relations between comics' multifarious fragments, including visually spaced textual lexias.

Simmonds adroitly spaces out fragments of text to maximize the comical gap between the inner monologue of the prose passages and her acutely realistic, humdrum dialogue, effectively creating setups and punch lines from spatially distinct lexias. In *Gemma Bovery*, for example, the pompous narrator Joubert[3] describes in authorial typescript finding a magazine clipping in Gemma's diary with the word "WANKERS" scrawled across the picture (Fig. 3.1). There is a palpable pause as the reader moves from the depiction of the clipping to the strip beneath, where the Frenchman Joubert sits, English dictionary in hand, mentally cogitating (in neat freehand) "wand . . . . wane . . . . wangle . . . . want . . . . *merde, ce n'est pa là.*"

The picture is necessary for contextualizing these thoughts: we need to know Joubert is searching for a translation of this word. But though the picture lends pause, emphasizing the gap that our comprehension "sparks across" as we reconfigure our gaze from text to strip, the joke's impact lies in the connection between the two verbal utterances. There is some humor in the juxtaposition of Joubert's visually and tonally authoritative report and the depiction of his bemused expression, but there is greater comedy in the credulous and fruitless search for comprehension through a chain of alphabetically proximate words shown in the textual fragment. It is the *visual gap* between these divergent *textual* strands, between the native's wielding of slang and foreigner's recourse to only dictionary-approved vocabulary, which gives the joke its impact.

Simmonds's work contains numerous examples in which the reader's comprehension "sparks across" a gap between text and image. In counterpoint to the above, when we read Joubert's assertion that his wife in no way suspects his obsessive preoccupation with their neighbor, the reader is inclined to flit backwards to the preceding strip and reassess his wife's pursued lips and raised eyebrows (Fig. 3.1). Comics criticism often contrasts the spatiality of the visual with language's linear, temporal progression (Varnum & Gibbons 2001: xi), and Simmonds's collage-like annotated layout utilizes this spatiality alongside the traditional sequentiality of strip cartoons. Her reading protocol is particularly loose, allowing the reader to move around the page and interpret the dispersed pictures, text, and strips, rather than following a regimented grid of panels. Here, Simmonds creates another pause, as we finish the paragraph before beginning to wonder if our self-important narrator is himself missing something in the preceding strip. This wry gag is funnier, almost arch, in the way it sends the trusting reader back from our narrator's pronouncement to look again at the close-up of his wife's shrewd, savvy expression, which is not seen from his point of view (she stands behind him), and which subtly undercuts his assertion. In contrast to the textual correlative of the first example, this operation relies on a gap between text and picture of the sort Harvey privileges, but performs a more complex correlation than picture with *caption*, and one that overrides the reader's progression through a sequential reading pathway.

In a similar example, Joubert pours his Gallic superiority onto Gemma's recently acquired makeover, laconically lamenting her high heels, miniskirt, and makeup, with an affected worldliness: "Don't young women realise how utterly bankrupt that image is? It's the currency of 40 years ago, of their mother's youth" (Simmonds 2005: 59). Three proximate pictures zoom in on Joubert's face and his widened eyes goggling over the top of his glasses. His evident fluster exposes his cool assertion of indifference as a self-deluding protest: "Really one had to yawn. I found her quite without allure" (Simmonds 2005: 59). In line with the previous example, and conversely to the one preceding that in which the reader was invited to quite literally read between the lines of dispersed text fragments, here we read between the series of images and the segregated passage of text, finding wry correlatives in between Joubert's protestation of indifference and his titillated gaze.

Joubert is vividly characterized. Simmonds excels at creating a tonal gulf between the prose passages voiced by the self-consciously literary Frenchman and the linguistic excerpts of the other characters, which are spatially juxtaposed for maximum emphasis. The most arresting turns of phrase are reserved for Joubert, who relishes his own overdramatic eloquence. He deftly mimics the Boverys' romanticization of their French country retreat, stating: "Nestling in its green embrace, their little house, with its smoke curling from the chimney, resembled the last scene of a fairy tale, the page where the protagonists will live happily ever after" (Fig. 3.2). This clashes with the casual cynicism he and his wife voice in the adjacent unbordered image: "Won't last long . . . two bad winters, they'll be off." This subverts the preceding vision, attributed to the Boverys but patently voiced by the effusive Joubert, who conjures a rose-tinted idyll of which the prosaic Boverys do not seem capable. Joubert slips as easily into undercutting his own projection, with the portentous, overtly narratorial declaration, "We'd seen it all before, this bourgeois fantasy. Foreigners – they move to France, bury themselves in their hectare of mud and wonder why they go mad." Joubert's tendency toward dramatization allows for some unreservedly poetic writing, as well as subtly mocking this proudly well-read, self-important figure. Contrasting tones are spatially offset so that they undercut, mock, or otherwise alter each other, requiring the reader to mentally draw these "units" of text into meaningful synthesis. Lexias thus come like a "'surprise' that is sprung upon the reader" (Harvey 1996: 81), their full import only revealed through their relationship to one another, just as Harvey describes picture and caption functioning in tandem. The physical gaps of the comics page delay this comprehension, heightening the feeling of revelation and giving each punch line teeth.

Simmonds's considerable "ear for the spoken word" (Garland 1999: np) is all the more impressive given the seismic shifts between fractured,

But I digress. It seemed that Gemma found everything about her new life in Normandy entrancing. One saw her in the market exclaiming over the vegetables, one heard her singing in the garden.

It was early summer.
Nestling in its green embrace, their little house,
with smoke curling from the chimney,
resembled the last scene of a fairy tale,
the page where the protagonists
will live happily
ever after.

I remember that
both Martine and I
had the same thought:
They won't last long...two
bad winters, they'll
be off...
Ah,
oui

We'd seen it all before,
this bourgeois fantasy.
Foreigners – they move to
France, bury themselves in
their hectare of mud and
wonder why they go mad.

3.2 Posy Simmonds, *Gemma Bovery* (London: Jonathan Cape, 2001), p. 33.

truncated bursts of speech (and Gemma's unpolished diary) and the carefully constructed, pseudo-intellectual, and vaguely foreign-sounding narration of Joubert. The measured report, "it's apparent that Charlie is ready to unburden himself" (Simmonds 2005: 9), contrasts with the sigh-punctuated, ellipsis-riddled stream that comprises this "unburdening": "-*Hunh*-I'll never get over her, Raymond . . . Never . . -*Hunhh*- . . it's the bad stuff . . . there's really bad stuff . . . -*Huuhh*- . . . can't handle it . . ." (Simmonds 2005: 9). Simmonds's dialogue is authentically repetitive, with bold format, underlining, capitals, and shifts in text size visualizing the modulations of tone that are natural to speech. Tonal emphasis is perceptible in Joubert's mellifluously flowing sentences, characterized by the formal qualification "I, Joubert" (Simmonds 2005: 20), but the contraction-heavy, semi-articulate speech benefits from these visual pointers, which actively assist in creating both the patina of realism and the gaping tonal gulfs between Joubert's narration and the other speakers. Of an early encounter with the fledgling expat in ecstasies in his bread shop, Joubert comments, "It pleased me that Madame stood for some moments in rapture, in reverence, transported by . . . *une pure volupté*, as she breathed the rich, warm aromas of my bread" (Fig. 3.3). In her own words, positioned so that they are the next words read, Gemma's raptures are less elegantly, more colloquially phrased: "Bloody hell, Charlie . . . I mean **25 different** kinds of bread! God, the French are incredible! I mean, they just know how to **live**!" Once again,

It wasn't until they came into my shop in Bailleville
that I saw Gemma and Charles Bovery
at close quarters.

It pleased me that Madame
stood for some moments in
rapture, in reverence,
transported by... *une pure
volupté*, as she breathed the rich,
warm aromas of my bread.

3.3 Posy Simmonds, *Gemma Bovery* (London: Jonathan Cape, 2001), p. 33.

the proximity of these two differently cast utterances, disjointed through their material presentation, creates a comic, rather bathetic effect.

Joubert recreates Gemma's tale from her stolen diaries, his dreamy, Frenchified lyricism thrown into relief by her own lack of polish, which exposes his tendency to manufacture details. Describing Gemma's growing hatred of her gloomy house, he reports, "Wherever Charlie is, he blocks the light. The rain falls, the muslin droops around the windows. All her possessions seem to retire into the shadows to die. The beams are gibbets of lynched, dangling things. And the deathly quiet. It ennerves her" (Fig. 3.4).

Gemma's source testimony appears beneath these last two sentences: "God this bloody place! It's like a morgue NOTHING happens! God I hate my life!" Joubert fabricates poeticisms, writing his own flowery tale around the pedestrian description in the diary.[4] The pertinent visual gap in examples such as this exists between lexias, which are drawn into collaboration so as to create setup and punch line from visually distinguished verbal utterances. The visual apparatus categorizes typescript as narration

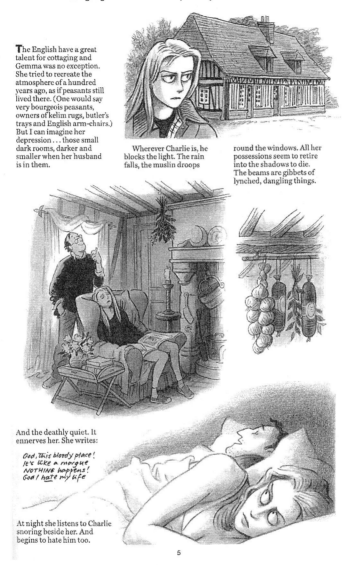

The English have a great talent for cottaging and Gemma was no exception. She tried to recreate the atmosphere of a hundred years ago, as if peasants still lived there. (One would say very bourgeois peasants, owners of kelim rugs, butler's trays and English arm-chairs.) But I can imagine her depression... those small dark rooms, darker and smaller when her husband is in them.

Wherever Charlie is, he blocks the light. The rain falls, the muslin droops

round the windows. All her possessions seem to retire into the shadows to die. The beams are gibbets of lynched, dangling things.

And the deathly quiet. It ennerves her. She writes:

God, this bloody place!
It's like a morgue
NOTHING happens!
God I hate my life

At night she listens to Charlie snoring beside her. And begins to hate him too.

5

3.4 Posy Simmonds, *Gemma Bovery* (London: Jonathan Cape, 2001), p. 5.

and freehand as diary, and the correlative relationship (in the form of significant dissonance) between the two verbal components is blackly amusing. The visual element ensures clarity, but functions like the "who's there?" of a knock-knock joke: it structures and contextualizes setup and denouement, but does not directly contribute to the humor. The gap that

Outside was equally disturbing: Gemma claims that when she went out sketching the landscape somehow immobilised her. After a while she couldn't draw. Anything. This doesn't surprise me. Normandy was, after all, the great outdoor *atelier* of the nineteenth century. How could one not be reminded of those giants of painting– Millet, Monet, etc? How could one not feel inhibited, one's efforts absolutely pigmy?

So on the day when she described herself sitting hunched at the edge of a harvest field, it was perhaps the thought of Monet's *Haystacks* that froze her drawing hand.

No reason at all I get totally freaked. Today it started with seeing a tick in the bracken – remembered reading tick bites are bad news . . also bracken spores give you cancer. Then couldn't stop hearing every rustle & twig snap behind me . . started thinking : Rabid animals . . . rapists . . . . . . French murders, like in the papers – killer is always local half-wit garagiste or else bloke in coat who asks the time . . . .

3.5 Posy Simmonds, *Gemma Bovery* (London: Jonathan Cape, 2001), p. 38.

the reader's understanding "sparks across" is a physical, *visual* gap, but one whose function is to segregate *text*.

Even Gemma's lengthier passages fall short of the elegance Joubert weaves around them. After an unproductive day's sketching, she writes, semi-grammatically, "No reason at all I get totally freaked. Today it started with seeing a tick in the bracken – remembered reading tick bites are bad news . . also bracken spores give you cancer. Then couldn't stop hearing every rustle and twig snap behind me . . started thinking: Rabid animals . . . rapists . . . French murderers like in the papers" (Fig. 3.5).

This unreconstructed musing follows on from Joubert's overtly culti-vated version of her reaction to the landscape. He declares it "somehow immobilised her" adding, unsurprised: "Normandy was, after all, the great outdoor *atelier* of the nineteenth century. How could one not be reminded of those giants of painting – Millet, Monet, etc? How could one not feel inhibited, one's efforts absolutely pigmy? So on the day when she described herself sitting hunched at the edge of a harvest field, it was per-haps the thought of Monet's *Haystacks* that froze her drawing hand."

This refined erudition belongs entirely to the high-minded, would-be aesthete Joubert. Graphically, Joubert's typed paragraph, imitating pub-lished (literary) texts, and Gemma's loose cursive sit in opposition, but the adjacent pictures also participate in this playoff, though not quite in line with the sorts of mental linking that either Harvey or McCloud describe.

Beside Joubert's tidy paragraph sits a small, neat representation of the Monet to which he refers, bordered with the likeness of a heavy gallery frame. Below this, above Gemma's own account, sprawls the vast rustic scene she contemplates, with its repetitive forms of hay bales receding into the unbordered distance, sky bleeding out into the white background of the page. According to Eisner, this device "speaks to unlimited space [. . .] encompassing unseen but acknowledged background" (1985: 45), and here it signifies an ungraspable vastness, representing an expanse that cannot be captured through replication, only alluded to. The unnerving landscape exceeds the tiny, framed picture, with its single shape dominat-ing a penned-in space, and the disparity between the two pictorial versions mimics the gulf between the two textual fragments. The real landscape is manifestly unframeable, overwhelming attempts to capture it within the page space. Beside it, not only Gemma's efforts but the artwork to which the cultured Joubert refers, are both rendered "pigmy." For Joubert, art is awe-inspiring, but for Gemma it is the diminution of *any* representation, including the thumbnail Monet, in the face of the boundless real that truly paralyzes her.

Through this multiway interaction, the conflicting, visually segregated lexias, and discordant pictorial representations draw out each other's significance, underlining the disparity between Joubert's and Gemma's accounts. The differences between the pictures' scope furthers the con-trast between the outlooks expressed. This effect depends on neither sequential movements nor a mere two-way trade between a picture and a caption. Instead, the four components connect in non-consecutive ways, drawing meaning from the *web* of relations that exist between them. The reader does not suture adjacent moments in time, but links proximate correlatives to make, not a temporal sequence, but a conceptual jigsaw. The significance of the two pictorial representations is brought to light by the two accounts, the one focused on the landscape and the other con-cerned with elevated artworks. The contrast between these visually com-partmentalized versions is crucial. The small artwork to which Joubert attributes sublimity is dwarfed by the representation of the real landscape and unacknowledged in Gemma's account. In retracing our way from Gemma's account through the diminishing versions of the landscape back to Joubert's, much is revealed about our narrator's desire to aggrandize art, and to recast reality in an artful manner. He exhibits this tendency in his continual recoloring of Gemma's sordid social life as a doom-laden tale of passion and despair, fretting constantly over the intertwining of her fate with Flaubert's fictional near-namesake. In the tableau above, he triumphantly holds up an artistic representation as the towering distillation of a reality that, in fact, is truly overpowering in itself. This maneuver is highly characteristic of Joubert and manifestly *unlike* his pragmatic foil, though he purports to be telling her story. This set piece depends upon each of its constituent elements acting in concert, and while the general relevance of sequential progression remains undeniable, the privileging of this linear narrative movement over more dispersed spatial relations here proves to be erroneous.

One final example from Simmonds's work emphasizes how comics' *visual* arrangements create *literary* effects. In *Tamara Drewe*, Beth Hardiman, long-suffering wife of the philandering Nicholas, begins to suspect he is "Lulling The Spouse" (Simmonds 2007: np): deliberately arousing her suspicions in order to consistently prove his alibi, flaunting his trustworthiness so that, Beth admits in her typescript voiceover, "After a bit you stop checking – It's humiliating. He's always where he says he will be, all innocent and plausible" (Fig. 3.6). This potentially conciliatory tone is wickedly undercut by the thought bubble below: "Devious bugger . . . " Once again, the comical correlative lies between the dissonant verbal statements. The mounting testimony to Nick's truthfulness, innocence, and plausibility seems to acquiesce that he is demonstrably above suspicion, but the rankling thought that follows upends this. The physical space between the two utterances forces a greater pause upon the reader, who must reorient themselves within the picture, adjust to drawn text after typescript, and pull together the apparent contradiction: he's always telling the truth/devious bugger. A prose-only version, "He's always where he says he will be, all innocent and plausible, devious bugger," retains the sense and humor, but has more clout when written: "He's always where he says he will be, all innocent and plausible. Devious bugger." The stronger break lends the punch line force, and when this swerving train of thought is disrupted by, not comma or full stop, but actual physical space, by different graphic forms, and by the embedding of one lexia in a picture, the

Nicholas has been doing this a lot recently. Telling the truth, lulling me.
After a bit you stop checking – It's too humiliating. He's always where he says he
will be, all innocent and plausible.

3.6 Posy Simmonds, *Tamara Drewe* (London: Jonathan Cape, 2007), np.

interruption is exponentially greater and the joke hammered home. In this
fashion, comics can fragment lexias in ways that rhythmically control the
reading pace, effectively inscribing comic timing on the page.

It has nowhere here been suggested that the deliberate sidelining of
pictures carried out in this section yields a comprehensive framework
for approaching the comics form. Instead, the intention is to gain some
semblance of critical balance and challenge the prevailing critical view
that underplays the potential importance of words in comics. The textual
component has been considered for its prose qualities alone, in service
of demonstrating how arresting and deeply literary that linguistic content can be in itself. It has also been shown that these linguistic effects
depend on the utilization of language's special features, which demonstrably differentiate it from (but do not therefore somehow make it superior
to) visual signification. In the final examination carried out here, language
has been considered through the lens of the comics form. In Simmonds's
work, we see how words may be deployed in ways that exploit comics'
spatial, visual nature. The goal here, beyond further exposing the errors
of logophobia, has been to show how comics' use of words has recourse
to *particular* visual-verbal effects. These effects, which engage with the
graphic side of text, are not special to the comics form. In everything from
pattern poems to advertisements, we can see how the visual potential of
text, the impact of its material form and compositional arrangement, is
ripe for creative employment. The material surface of the sign, and the
way that sign is incorporated into the two-dimensional layout of the page,

can both be brought into play and inform the way we read the text. Thus, the reader makes links over a multitude of narrative gaps in constructing the world of the work, significantly in excess of the oft-emphasized panel-to-panel and picture-to-text gaps—though these are important.

Like Herriman and Barry, Simmonds is a gifted *writer*. She skillfully evokes different voices and utilizes comics' fragmentary nature to empha-size the divergence of these textual strands. The literary quality of the writ-ing of all three authors should not be ignored because it is integrated with the pictures and other visual devices. That said, it must be recognized that the impact of the verbal text is manipulated by meaningful spatial arrange-ment and juxtaposition with pictorial content. Simmonds's untraditional page layouts segment text in ways that create pauses, turns, subversions, and punch lines. She directs the reading of her text through its spatial arrangement, controlling its rhythms visually, and carefully timing the unfolding of narrative elements and syntactic turns. Transitions between adjacent panels that represent brief chunks of diegetic time, by which crit-ics tend to characterize comics' narrative development, are perhaps the least interesting thing happening in her work. The productive correlation between text and images is central, but these collage-like layouts engage in a more complicated exchange than that of picture with caption, with multiple dispersed fragments drawn into a web of resonance. Linguistic content is vitally important to understanding this web, and plays its part in concert with its own visual materialization on the page. Graphic style, position, and relationships to other components within the reading pro-tocol all shape the way these words are read. This reading affects and in turn is affected by the pictorial content, and it is the evolving relationship between these within the web of the entire work that produces the text's full effect.

In examining the effects of spatial arrangements on text, an implicit challenge has been presented to that side effect of the conflation of signi-fying systems, which equates visual signification with iconic signs, reduc-ing "the visual" to "pictures." Spacing and typography, chiefly looked at here in terms of how they mold the reception of *text*, are vital elements in comics' visual arsenal, but do not operate as signs standing in for an iden-tifiable signified. These devices cannot be considered in isolation from the signifiers they materialize. They constitute the *material* contextual effects that distinguish *parole* from the repeatable conceptual signifiers that con-stitute the *langue*. Barthes says that "it is because signs recur that language is possible" (1967a: 70). The visual sign is always materially specific, and so is different from language whose mental sign-forms are repeatable, always partially subject to the context of their usage, yet with a prior, abstract existence of their own. Comics maximize the impact of language's graphic side, and thus signal language's particular *langue/parole* distinction by bringing the latter so forcefully into play. Comics' visual aspect cannot be reduced to its use of representational icons, nor is the form's linguistic content always reducible to mere supplement. Spatialization of text (and pictures, and panels) exerts *visual* influence on that text, and contributes to a text's effect as much as do pictures. Critics agree that the visual is vital to comics, but in acknowledging this we must not overlook the potential centrality of text—of material, graphic, spaced-out *words*—in shaping these visual works as much and potentially more than do iconic *pictures*.

PART TWO
Comics as Language

Chapter Four

The Hybrid Question
Interaction or Fusion?

By way of introduction to the widely accepted epithet that "comics are a language," this chapter tackles the issue of "hybridity" and explores the various ways critics characterize the conjunction of words and images in comics. The French critic Aarnoud Rommens, reviewing the essays collected in *The Language of Comics*, complains that the hybridity debate is crowded with ill-defined terms such as "partnership" and "integral language," which "fuzzy terminology [. . .] suggests its own conceptual inadequacy" (Rommens 2001: np). Much of the discourse around the issue of verbal-visual interaction does seem to justify this charge.

It is indisputable that words and images interact in producing comics' narratives; however, problems frequently arise when critics attempt to pin down the precise nature of this interaction. Critics often seize upon particular ways of combining image and text as being definitive of the form, though these definitions tend to account for a limited range of possible conjunctions, as we shall see. Furthermore, many critics routinely extrapolate from the notion of an *interaction between* word and image and posit a total fusion of word and image, suggesting that the two are subsumed into the comics form in a way that "transcends" (Whitlock 2006: 968) or "collapse[s]" (Hatfield 2005: 36) the very distinctions between them. However, a survey into the extensive range of ways comics actually combine words and images presents a challenge to these limiting definitions, exposing the failure of the common critical circumscriptions to account fully for the diverse practices that exist. Furthermore, the idea that words and images fuse into a kind of comics language can be seen to be pervaded by the same defensiveness that motivated the problematic logophobia examined in Part One. Many critics attempt to neutralize the perceived word-image hierarchy by positing comics' two semiotic modes as being subsumed into a new fusion-form, cast as a unified language in order to further the denial of any boundary lines between them. But though it is true that many word-image combinations rely on a generative trade-off between visual and verbal, this incontestable *interaction* must necessarily be predicated on there being two *distinct* components—the prerequisite for any *inter*-action to be possible.

The hybridity issue, at first glance, seems to split the field. Many critics expressly endorse the term, for example, claiming that comics are "a hybrid form of two separate media" (Cohn 2005: 237).[1] However, a robust counter strain of critics insist it is "a mistake to see comics as a mere hybrid of the graphic arts and prose fiction" (McCloud 1993: 92).[2] Yet any exploration of this apparent opposition soon meets with overlapping terminology. McCloud maintains that comics are not mere hybrids (we will come back to this word "mere" shortly), characterizing them as comprising an "interdependent combination" of words and pictures (1993: 17). This sounds remarkably similar to the "mutual dependence" Harvey describes in sanctioning the term (1996: 4). Harvey, along with Rocco Versaci, further characterizes this "mutual dependence" of words and images as a "blend" (Harvey 1996: 4, Versaci 2008: 13), while Hillary Chute and Marianne DeKoven, who also approve of the term "hybrid," support it by stating that "verbal and visual narratives do not simply blend together" (2006: 769). Further explication of these opposing stances is offered through distinctly similar descriptive terms like "weave" (Sabin 1996: 8) and "interplay" (Harvey 1996: 9), suggesting that, in part, the disagreement over "hybridity" is a semantic one. Though critics may disagree on the nature of comics' visual-verbal admixture, the debate is confused by a parallel disagreement over what sort of admixture the term "hybridity" actually connotes—which terminological muddle supports Rommens's complaints.

In part, the contention over terminology can be traced to a widespread desire to distinguish comics from illustrated texts. Most critics are keen to isolate *interactions* of words and images from other verbal-visual forms, particularly those considered juvenile such as illustrated picture books. This distinction can be demonstrated via two cartoons by Addams Family creator Charles Addams. There is some disagreement over whether single-panel cartoons should be considered as comics along with cartoons strips, serialized comic books, and graphic novels: generally, they are accepted as belonging to the same tradition, but are excluded by the likes of McCloud in order to privilege the sequential aspect of strips (Cohn 2005: 237). However, these single-panel cartoons enable a clearer explanation of the different ways text and image might be conjoined than is sometimes possible

"Just back up a little, dear, so you won't cut my head off."

4.1 Charles Addams, *Happily Ever After: A Collection of Cartoons to Chill the Heart of Your Loved One* (London: Simon and Schuster, 2006), p. 88.

within chains of panels whose multiple lexias and pictures connect in a complex web. Indeed, it is precisely this type of single-panel picture-caption pairing that is central to Harvey's conception of the form as being predicated on visual-verbal sutures, as discussed in the previous chapter.

In the cartoon above, the gag absolutely depends on both picture and caption being seen together (Fig. 4.1). The two contextualize each other, to the extent that each actually alters the way we interpret the other. We only see what is really happening in the picture—and what is about to happen next—in light of what the caption reveals. Similarly, the innocuous instruction only takes on its comically sinister meaning through a suturing with the picture, which reveals the circumstances under which that instruction is issued. The visual and verbal elements add to each other and the cartoon itself is greater than the sum of its parts, as the conjunction of visual and verbal produces new meaning not present in either element in isolation. It is this *productive* interaction that critics are keen to emphasize

"Is there someone else, Narcissus?"

4.2 Charles Addams, *Happily Ever After: A Collection of Cartoons to Chill the Heart of Your Loved One* (London: Simon and Schuster, 2006), p. 59.

in their discussions of blends, weaves, and fusions. The trade-off between caption and picture generates the joke. In contrast, the second example above comprises a co-presence of a caption, which tells the joke in its entirety, and a picture that illustrates that text (Fig. 4.2).

This cartoon would not pass Harvey's "litmus of good comics art" that seeks to "ascertain to what extent the sense of the words depends on the pictures and vice versa" (1996: 4). The text makes sense on its own, sufficiently implying the framing situation that the picture makes explicit. Neither picture nor caption radically alters its counterpart, as happens in the first example. The caption's joke may receive a certain *embellishment* from the picture—by the disgruntlement evident in the cleft-chinned, pouty-lipped, long-lashed face of Narcissus, or his exaggerated classical curls—but essentially the picture *illustrates* the caption without altering or adding to it. Critical accounts are routinely dismissive of this sort of illustration, foregrounding instead the sort of imaginative linking of text and image that is demanded by the first cartoon. The defensive impetus for favoring particular kinds of conjunction seeps through in the oft-repeated assertion that comics are not "mere" hybrids (McCloud 1993: 92, Sabin 1993: 9, Whitlock 2006: 969), as well as in parallel avowals that hybrid texts are distinct from "mere illustrations" (Meskin 2007: 370, Bartual 2010: 84) or "mere amalgamation" (Pratt 2009: 108), and that word and image do not "merely synthesize" (Chute & DeKoven 2006: 769) within them.

There seems to be a twofold aim in separating comics' use of words and images from illustration, both of which endeavor to glorify the form. The desire to differentiate comics from kids' picture books is frequently made explicit, although I have never heard that form referred to as "hybrid" outside of the comics scholarship that holds this illustrative "hybridity" apart. This non-interactive co-presence might better be described as "juxtaposition"—if indeed another term than "illustration" is needed to designate its operation—and it is useful to any analysis of comics to distinguish this from other kinds of visual-verbal conjunction. However, it is surely untenable to insist comics never undertake this kind of illustrative word-image coupling: the cartoon above is no less a cartoon because it does not exploit the interactive possibilities of the form as much as the first does, and though it is helpful to be able to account for their differences, it is a mistaken and apparently defensive critical inclination that "posits the blurring of words and pictures as a value in and of itself" (Chute 2006: 1024). The second goal seems to be to downplay the form's replication of the operations of literature and art (as shown in Part One, the fondness for the "literature" tag does not amount to a consideration of comics as texts incorporating literary practices). It is notable that the pro-hybrid camp usually avers the form hybridizes words and images, while the opposition protests it is not a mere hybrid of graphic art and prose literature.[3] Some critics acknowledge the form "employs narrative strategies closely connected to literature, on the one hand, and other pictorial narrative media, on the other" (Pratt 2009: 107). But even they are quick to point out that comics do not *only* replicate the effects of these two art forms, but also utilize their own, form-specific devices, such as panel sequences, page layouts, and speech balloons.

Aaron Meskin (2009) approaches the hybridity debate via Jerrold Levinson's genealogical definition of hybrid art forms: "An art form is a hybrid one in virtue of its development and origin, in virtue of its emergence out of a field of previously existing artistic activities and concerns, two or more of which it in some sense combines" (Levinson 1990: 27). This historical question is certainly an interesting one, but the specific mechanics of visual-verbal integration in particular works seems to be a separate issue to the question of whether comics also incorporate the practices of the recognized traditions of art and literature and can be shown to have descended from them. Much as literature is used as the default point of comparison for comics, critics are nevertheless keen to section off the form and present it as something other than the practices of literary writing lumped together with the practices of fine art. Comics demonstrably do utilize these practices (and, as I argue here, can and should be analyzed in those terms), but they certainly do *more* than replicate them, and the hybridity debate is often imbued with an eagerness to stress aspects of the form that are not inherited from these artistic ancestors. Difficulties with this only arise when critics extrapolate from the truism that comics are a medium "in their own right" (Sabin 1993: 9), with their own form-specific codes and conventions, to the point of claiming that this comics "language" actually elides the differences between the visual and verbal elements that make it up. Comics' own signifying devices will be examined in subsequent chapters, which will question how far these devices can be considered a system or language, but the present concern is not with comics' redeployment of the traditions of art and literature, but rather the ways they utilize visual and verbal signs in conjunction, and the dubiousness of the idea that the form's mixed nature[4] actually collapses the distinction between the visual and verbal sign systems it draws on.

Descriptions of comics' crossbreeding of words and images that are apposite do exist. The least problematic are those that include careful caveats, and avoid claiming to define the way the form itself weaves the two. Those that do purport to pin down an essential nature of the mixture risk failure unless they are so broad and general as to cease to be enlightening: beyond saying the form uses words and images (usually), it is not possible to declare in advance the role each element must take, for, as we shall see, the practices of comics texts themselves are extremely diverse. Common categorizations considered here include Harvey's suggestion that in the best comics words and pictures are joined "in such a way that the one 'explained' the other" (2001: 81). This is a useful description and one that

Harvey fleshes out convincingly, but even in the first *Addams* cartoon, which links up largely in the way Harvey describes, the operation is better termed as a mutual *alteration* or *subversion*, rather than *explanation*. Harvey is among those who imply that in this sort of conjunction neither word nor image makes sense without its counterpart, which is not exactly true: as the first example shows, caption and picture make perfect sense alone, but take on a very different meaning when read in light of the other.

Harvey is cautious enough to acknowledge that the sort of conjunction he privileges is not the last word in comics' hybridity (Harvey 1996: 9), but many critics are not so wary. David Carrier's suggestion that "the picture and the text work together to tell *one* story" (2000: 74), in which visual and verbal are "unified" (2000: 71) and "seamless" (2000: 4), risks being misleading. Like Harvey's assertion that the two serve "complementary narrative purposes" (1996: 7), these descriptions seem to elide the "gap" (Kunzle 2001: 15) between text and image. They suggest an easy cohesion that does not fit with the disjunction that generated new meaning in the first *Addams* cartoon. Some critics acknowledge this potential "tension" (Hatfield 2005: 37) between word and image: Chute (2006: 1,025), David Kunzle (2009: 23), Frank Cioffi (2001: 99), and Daniel Raeburn (2004: 7) all address particular works that are predicated on a "disjunctive" (Cioffi 2001: 99) relationship between text and image, and refrain from claiming that these particular operations are essential. Their respective characterizations of visual-verbal divergence aptly describe the particular texts on which they focus, but offer only a partial inventory of the broad spectrum of possible divergent combinations, which tidy taxonomies such as McCloud's seven types (1993: 53–54) risk simplifying into neat, rather limiting categories.

The following examples illustrate the limits of these different descriptions, demonstrating the mistake inherent in attempting to prescribe how comics *in general* deploy words and images. In most of the texts examined here, word and image diverge, and this deliberate focus aims at rebuffing the suggestion that word and image might collapse seamlessly into each other. The overriding point made by this chapter is that, though the mutual exchange between visual and verbal is pertinent to any examination of comics, the nature of that exchange cannot be defined for the form as a whole. There is no essential nature of comics' use of words and images, and attempts to construct one betray a certain critical defensiveness insofar as they so often tend to foreground the more attractive of the available practices, while sidelining those (such as illustration) that do not bolster

'. . . of course indoor games are an extra.'

4.3 Ronald Searle, *The Terror of St. Trinian's and Other Drawings* (London: Penguin Classics, 2000), p. 57.

the form. In the St. Trinian's cartoon above (Fig. 4.3) the product of the mutual exchange between caption and picture is a sense of incongruence (which amplifies the already somewhat incongruous depiction of hard-drinking, snooker-playing public schoolgirls). The picture undercuts the prim proviso offered by the caption and it is the jarring inappropriateness of the pairing, which is anything but "seamless" or "complementary," that generates the humor. Springing that "surprise" on the reader that Harvey describes, caption and picture can only be conceived of as "unified" insofar as the comical sense of incompatibility is the objective of the strip.

In the following excerpt from the graphic novel adaptation of Paul Auster's *City of Glass* by Paul Karasik and David Mazzucchelli, we see an elegant visual-verbal divergence that cannot be aptly designated a "duel" (Kunzle 2009: 23) or "contradict[ion]" (Raeburn 2004: 7), though the two do not exactly tell "*one* story." The sequence describes the metaphorical

4.4 Paul Auster, Paul Karasik and David Mazzucchelli, *City of Glass* (London: Faber and Faber, 2004), p. 8.

relationships between author Daniel Quinn, his pseudonym William Wilson, and main character, the detective Max Work. Wilson is described as a ventriloquist, Quinn himself the dummy, and Work "the voice that gave purpose to the enterprise" (Fig. 4.4). The text states Work has "increasingly come to life" for Quinn, and the visual-verbal layering of what this might mean adds real poignancy to this sequence. Bereaved of his wife and son, Quinn has grown increasingly reclusive, and this sequence fleshes out the potential pun on Max Work's name to show that this living presence is no more than inanimate sheaves of typed pages. There is something strangely touching about the depiction of the character, an archetypal hard-boiled detective, as a sort of companion-cum-helpmeet, seen in the center-right panel tucking the sleeping author into bed. But this oddly tender representation is undercut by the panel that sprawls beneath it, extending from the central area so that the pages of which Work actually consists rain down and flood Quinn's apartment. His "comrade in solitude" is no more than the solitary pursuit of a writing career, and it is only his work—the lonely industry of writing—that gives him any purpose. Clearly, it is this composite message, with all its double-edged pathos, that is intended by phrases like "unified," "*one* story," and "complementary narrative purposes." But the literal depictions of textual metaphors and layering of representations that first amplify then undercut the suggestion that Work offers Quinn comfort—work by a kind of dissonance not best described as "seamless." The effect of the sequence depends on the palpable and resonant gap between what is said and what is seen, with word and image necessarily remaining distinct in order for this reciprocal offsetting and countering to occur.

This dramatization of a metaphor is a recurring feature in *City of Glass*. In one sequence, the pictures effectively stage the suggestion that the perambulations of the elder Peter Stillman (hereafter "Stillman"), which form letters if traced on a map, are "like drawing a picture in the air with your finger . . . . . . the image vanishes as you are making it." The pictures show city streets disintegrating as footsteps pass over them, and the metaphor is extended to show brick fragments vanishing into notebook pages, dramatizing the fact that Stillman's coded message exists only because Quinn chanced to map these steps in his notebook. These pictures do not alter the text or add information, and the verbal element (though possibly less so the pictures) makes sense on its own. However, the pictures contribute much more than a tautological illustration: picture and text are drawn into a rhetorical transaction, gaining in aesthetic impact rather than hard content. The artistic value of this segment and its combined elements is rather depleted if couched only in terms of information value. As mentioned, the habit of stressing that pictures, just as much as words, are "an effective way to communicate information" (Versaci 2008: 7) mistakenly sets the functional dispensing of information above aesthetic impact. The atmospheric contribution these pictures make is not negligible because they contribute little additional narrative information: they are metaphorical, engaging, and imaginatively arousing.

Chapters One and Two both dealt with the much-vaunted necessity of pictures, not text, "carrying the burden of the narrative" (Meskin 2007: 369), and this insistence emerges throughout the hybridity debate. As already mentioned, and as seen again in the example above, demanding that pictures partake in dispensing plot information neglects consideration of the aesthetic impact they lend a work. Daniel Arasse, cited by Thierry Groensteen, distinguishes between "'iconic' detail and 'picture' detail," pointing out that any account of a painting must consider both "the drawn elements" and "the manner in which they are drawn" (Groensteen 2006: 125). To risk simplifying this to the point of flippancy: the Mona Lisa is not "about" a woman sitting in front of some rocks. The downplaying

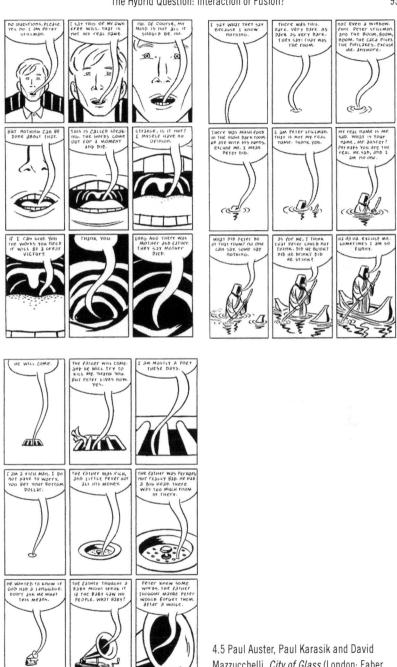

4.5 Paul Auster, Paul Karasik and David
Mazzucchelli, *City of Glass* (London: Faber
and Faber, 2004), pp. 15–17.

4.6 Paul Auster, Paul Karasik and David Mazzucchelli, *City of Glass* (London: Faber and Faber, 2004), pp. 27–28.

of illustration, and concomitant insistence that pictures must undertake active narrative duties, both stem from the logophobia discussed throughout Part One. The overstatement of the essential importance of pictures arises from the habitual and defensive comparison with literature: the logical implication is that if the pictures are not involved in conveying the story, then comics are "merely" prose narratives with some embellishing visual decoration, which leads critics into overstating or circumscribing their informational value as a way of carving out an appealing identity for the form. It is in order to differentiate comics from prose narratives and art, whose properties they might otherwise be charged with simply duplicating, that it becomes imperative for pictures to be involved in narrating.

The mistake inherent in this becomes clear when we look at the two recitals of the backstory of Peter Stillman junior (hereafter "Peter"), locked in a darkened room by his father for nine years during his childhood. This tale is first narrated by Peter himself in a cryptic and sprawling manner. Words issue from the depths, the tails of speech balloons reaching ever-downwards: down Peter's throat, and the throat of the boatman of the Styx who rises from the waters, from the mouth of the figure in a cave painting, from a drain, down a plughole, and more (Fig. 4.5). Caveman, boatman, drains, and the descents into the recesses of the speaking body all suggest penetrating interiority and depth, connoting Stillman's unhinged plan to isolate Peter so he would learn "God's language" (Auster, Karasik & Mazzucchelli 2004: 20), a pre-Fall Ur-language which connects words and things. But most of all, this unfathomable sequence of images is weird. Emerging from it, the reader shares in Quinn's three-panel shocked silence, mesmerized but mystified.

The account of Virginia, Peter's wife and guardian, is told with pragmatic clarity, elucidating everything that might not be deducible from the rambling, elliptical account delivered from the depths of Peter's damaged mind. Less consuming than Peter's account, Virginia's version entails some depictions of the conversation that might be classed as illustrative— a tedious prospect if these respectively sixty-five- and twenty-panel conversations were entirely visualized in this way. Her account is additionally emblematically represented by bluntly schematic icons, which duplicate her plainly informative tone and purpose (Fig. 4.6). Indeed, it is only when emotion starts to creep in, with the phrases "monstrous experiment" and "I'll be damned if I'll let anyone hurt him again," that these businesslike pictograms briefly give way to a drawing of the suddenly impassioned speaker. The shift itself is telling. Peter's story is comprehensively narrated by the text, as is expedient. Neither adding, altering, nor explaining what the words tell, the pictures run parallel to the text, redolently evoking the tone, manner, and feeling (rather than literal meaning) of these accounts in a highly suggestive and arresting way.

This dramatizing operation reaches its peak in *City of Glass* in the highly metafictional visit Quinn pays to author Paul Auster and his family, where he is taunted by reminders of the wife and son he lost. The reader *sees* Quinn's real reaction to this confrontation in the third panel below (Fig. 4.7), while a polite conversation carries on around the violent image of his literally piercing agony. There is no direct referential crossover between text and picture, but this refusal to tell "*one* story" is highly eloquent. In a way, the picture illustrates Quinn's feelings, but it is the divergence of text and picture that really illustrates—or rather *performs*—Quinn's repression of his emotions, dramatizing the failure of human connection that sees him retreat when those feelings threaten to resurface. This conjunction of text and picture is anything but "seamless" or "unified," yet is no

4.7 Paul Auster, Paul Karasik and David Mazzucchelli, *City of Glass* (London: Faber and Faber, 2004), p. 96.

better characterized as a "contradiction" or "duel." Instead, text and picture threaten to peel away from each other, though this divergence carries its own very powerful message.

No discussion of comics' supposed "indissoluble" (de Liddo 2009: 20) hybridization of text and image can fail to address Chris Ware's "I Guess." Comprehensive analyses of this piece already exist, but lean toward the dubious suggestion that its stunningly unconventional interplay of text and pictures somehow amounts to a blurring of the distinction between the two. Hatfield's insightful close reading is somewhat compromised by his admission that the form works via a tension between codes, and concurrent claim that the form therefore "destabilize[s] this very distinction" (Hatfield 2005: 37) between visual and verbal. It is hard to see how a tension between two codes can amount to a blurring of their very separateness, though Hatfield is far from alone in making this logical leap. Ware's technique in this strip is to essentially graffiti a childhood memoir *across*

4.8 Chris Ware, "I Guess," *Quimby the Mouse* (London: Jonathan Cape, 2003), pp. 39–41, p. 40.

a generic superhero tale, enacting the ultimate antagonism of visual and verbal. Words and images do not so much contradict each other as refuse to acknowledge each other's existence. The work is "radically disorienting" (Hatfield 2005: 38) and taunts the reader to try and connect the two narrative strands. The sequence shows how the comics form spatially intertwines word and image, yet also asserts their independence from each other. Woven together on the page, they resist the suggestion that their distinctness might thus be eroded by willfully telling two utterly separate stories across the one space (Fig. 4.8).

The overriding point made so far is that the vast majority of the "rules" suggested for characterizing comics' co-deployment of text and image are untenable, describing only a limited range on the spectrum of existing possibilities. It is a mistake to elevate characterizations that aptly describe particular examples to the status of a definition: having made much of the distinction between illustration and mutual exchange, for example, I have referred to works in which pictures *do* illustrate, and while these indeed may not be "using to the fullest the resources of the medium" (Harvey 1996: 4) (or at any rate, not utilizing that *particular* resource), they are comics nonetheless. The fact that visual and verbal so often diverge, that they take part in an *inter*-action, raises questions about how far their mutual exchange can be characterized as a "single unified language" (McCloud 1993: 47) whose multimodal resources collapse indissolubly into one another. Whether applied to comics' visual-verbal consistency or the form's conventionalized signifying practices, the notion that they are "a language with their own grammar, syntax and punctuation" (Sabin 1993: 9) remains a highly questionable one, oft-cited, rarely elucidated, and, where it is, widely inconsistent and not entirely credible.[5] The core problem is that the analogy between comics and language is often used rhetorically: the conventional devices that critics refer to in no way correspond to the "grammar, syntax and punctuation" that structure language, and these terms are seemingly invoked for their associated cachet. Unfortunately, this metaphorical use of the term "language" becomes tricky when applied to a form that actually draws on language proper. Critics cannot hope to properly account for the various linguistic, pictorial, and hybrid operations of the form by conflating these different modes, or by "rewrit[ing] the definition of 'language' to reflect this broader sense of multimodalism" (Cohn 2005: 239). The different systems comics utilize need to be addressed on their own terms, just as much as the form itself needs to be considered "in its own right," and conflating these very different operations in order to rhetorically lionize the form only undermines the theory that purports to take the form seriously.

Calling the comics form a language bolsters the medium, and additionally shelters it from the suggestion that it replicates graphic art and literary devices simultaneously, with no unique selling point of its own. The art form's genealogical history does not preclude its having developed practices and techniques not inherited from its forebears, but critics' keenness to highlight these becomes distorted into a notion that its twin modes collapse into a unique, fused language of its own. In truth, "comics rarely mobilize truly specific processes and techniques" (Groensteen 2006: 23), and this applies to the interplay of visual and verbal, despite critics' best efforts to claim that "[a]mong the popular traditions, none mix text and image more persistently, or diversely than comics" (Hatfield 2005: xiii). Examples abound of diverse mixtures of visual and verbal. Typography aims at creating various evocative visualizations of language's graphic form. The paintings of Dexter Dalwood make haunting appeals to the "collective conscious" (Saatchi Gallery nd: np) via their contextualizing titles, for example evoking foreboding and horror through labeling a swank, sunlit Sixties interior *Sharon Tate's House*. Film and television, in many ways more fitting comparisons than literature given their multimodalism, inclusion of iconic representation, and suturing of elliptically joined shot sequences (Christiansen 2000, Cwiklik 1999: 62), are also capable of conjoining visual and verbal so that our understanding "sparks across" the gap between the two. An exemplary sequence from the series *Arrested Development* sees the young son of a wealthy family, who has already been noted to believe their Mexican maid actually lives in their kitchen, seek revenge for an accidental misdemeanor: as the voiceover recalls "what Buster did to what he thought was Rosa's car with what he thought was Rosa's favorite toy," the viewer sees the boy running down the front lawn to throw a hand-vacuum at a bus.

These visual-verbal interactions show that the generative hybridization often used in comics has counterparts in diverse other forms, and is certainly not unique to it. It will already be obvious that I think the word "hybrid" is an appropriate one for describing these visual-verbal conjunctions: the term does not readily suggest illustration or juxtaposition as some critics seem to fear. On the contrary, it implies an interwoven totality that could not exist—or signify—without both its constituent forebears. But the word acknowledges that this new whole is formed from two constituent elements, totalities in *their* own right that are ontologically separate entities, and so avoids the problems inherent in positing the form as a "language," whose interacting elements somehow override their dual consistency. The above examples point to the range of visual-verbal media—including advertising, magazines, websites—that hybridize words and images in ways comparable to many of the comics examples discussed so far, all working according to an interaction between textual and pictorial content. I wish now to consider a more specific submission in support of comics' unique duality: the speech balloon.

The speech balloon is the special preserve of the comics form in a way that little else is. Though its antecedents date back to medieval times, the device recognizable as the modern speech balloon was born with the form, invented when comics proper emerged from its precursors.[6] It is the sort of conventionalized sign that goes some way towards justifying attempts to call the form a "language." We read the balloon's shape as an indicator of how something is said: dotted outlines, for example, usually denote whispering; serrated edges may indicate a voice relayed electronically or with volume, which we deduce according to other picture elements and textual context. We know to read these balloons "neither purely as holes in the picture nor as things depicted" (Carrier 2000: 29), recognizing by learned convention their relationship to the diegesis: not visible in the world-of-the-work as they are to the reader, these forms represent diegetic material nonetheless, visualizing for the reader what is audible for characters. Speech balloons make the notion of comics as a semiotic system tenable in a way the form's integration of other semiotic systems does not, and the ways cartooning institutes its own codes and conventions will be fully apprised in Chapter Seven. For the present, I want to consider the position forwarded by some critics that it is in the speech balloon that the distinction between word and image breaks down.

Carrier espouses a common idea that through speech balloons comics "bridge the word/image gap" (2000: 28). However, he explains this bridging as owing to the speech balloon's placement within the picture space, an issue of proximity he seems to conflate with the separate issue of whether text alone, or text and picture together, carry the narrative. Carrier draws heavily on Kunzle's examination of pre-nineteenth-century proto-comics (Kunzle 1973) and, along with Harvey (1996: 107–9), argues that these forerunners lack their modern counterparts' interactive hybridity because they are chiefly narrated by text accompanied by pictures that do not contribute to the story. (As noted above, it is generally assumed that for pictures to be "integrated" they must "carry the narrative.") Both Harvey and Carrier align this non-interactive juxtaposition firmly with captions, conflating the visual-verbal interactions that characterized the new comic strips that emerged around the fin-de-siècle, with the simultaneous emergence of speech balloons, by which these earliest examples of modern comics are recognizable. Oddly, Harvey's own work elsewhere examines productive mutual exchanges between pictures and their captions (Harvey 2001), and it is never explained why captions might be less likely to participate in a mutual exchange than dialogue in speech balloons.

4.9 Paul Auster, Paul Karasik and David Mazzucchelli, *City of Glass* (London: Faber and Faber, 2004), p. 6.

Both Carrier and Harvey appear to confuse *position* with *function*, overemphasizing the relevance of a lexia's placement and failing to distinguish this issue from the question of its role. They respectively suggest that "the speech balloon [. . .] establishes word-image unity that distinguishes comics from pictures illustrating text" (Carrier 2000: 4) and "the inclusion of speech balloons within the pictures gives the words and pictures concurrence" (Harvey 1996: 108). However, the second example used in this chapter should indicate that spatial concurrence does not necessarily preclude illustrative co-presence and guarantee productive interaction: the picture would be no more implicated in the conveyance of the joke if this direct quote of a caption were placed in a speech bubble within the picture space. The role words play is not determined by their position, and the undue importance placed on it rather weakens Harvey's and Carrier's arguments. However, the speech balloon remains a convincing proponent of comics-as-language (or, at any rate, as symbol system) insofar as it reads as a conventionalized sign, recognized as a visual signifier of sound whose border and script affect how we interpret particular instances of its use. This visualization of words precludes the easy dissection of visual and verbal that is possible where captions and pictures are concerned, and thus appears to challenge more robustly the idea that words and images might "maintain their differences" (Chute 2006: 1,025) in comics. It is this graphic rendering of language, more than interactive function, and certainly more than the preoccupations with position and diegesis examined above, that presents the most efficacious challenge to the distinction between visual and verbal.

Carrier does dwell on the issue of language's graphic form. Although he conflates this with the balloon itself, equating the visual form that frames the text with the verbal content within, he acknowledges that the reader is additionally "aware of the visual qualities of the chosen type, which we read in the ways we read handwriting for signs of someone's character" (2000: 30). Akin to typographers, comics artists visualize verbal signs, creating graphic forms that have implications for how we receive the text itself. In *City of Glass*, Quinn's first encounter with Peter, via telephone, visualizes the source novella's description of his voice as being "unlike any [Quinn] had ever heard" (Auster 1988b: 6–7), "machine-like, fitful [. . .] rigid and yet expressive" (Auster 1988b: 15). The undulating lines, unevenly textured letters, and childlike mix of capitals with lowercase that realize this voice (Fig. 4.9) all suggest the strange intonation of a man raised in a darkened room and not taught to speak until he was rescued in adolescence.

It is the layering of these visual connotations over verbal signs that Eisner refers to when he says that "text reads as an image" (1985: 10) in comics. This epithet is embraced by numerous critics because it once again blurs the distinction between visual and verbal by suggesting the latter *becomes* the former when its graphic form is utilized in this way. Raeburn goes so far as to assert that this layering of visual and verbal renders comics "both of these things at once and therefore neither" (2004: 17), a baffling statement that again posits comics' interactive duality as somehow undoing that very dual constitution. It is undeniable that this use of drawn words "establishes continuity between image and word" (Kunzle 2009: 22) and layers the effects of each over the other. But to cite this graphic rendering of words (shared with typography, advertising, and graphic design) as evidence that the distinction between visual and verbal might be "specious" (Chute 2006: 1,025) is an oversimplification. The fear that word and image are seen to be "dethroned and debased as soon as they are side by side in a mixed media" (Groensteen 2009a: 9) evidently prompts many critics to seek to claim the form collapses these distinctions, not only interacting but actually fusing the two media. But the significance of these words' graphic form is only evident in relation to other words. These drawn letters only suggest what they do because they differ from other instances of the same letters across the text, and it is in this ability to distinguish between repeated verbal signifiers and their varying specific graphic forms in which the distinction between verbal and visual persists.

Roy Lichtenstein's *Sweet Dreams, Baby!* (1965) presents a central verbal signifier that is absolutely archetypal of comics' style. The visual form of the classic comics-speak "pow" is complicit in signifying along with the text: the word's size, its central position, the dynamic angle it is tilted off the horizontal, its vibrant color, bold outline, and overlapping letters all connote the same violent impact denoted by the linguistic signifier. But word and image are not indissolubly lost in this double-signification. Both elements "retain their traditional denotive functions while affecting each other in complex, form-determined ways" (Kannenberg 2001: 176). That is to say, this powerful "pow" is both visual and verbal at once, but does not then somehow become neither. We lose nothing of either of the separable visual and verbal elements, though each adds something to the other.

If we were to consider Lichtenstein's bold, dynamic, colorful central word alongside its traditional rendering in standardized typescript, we would recognize two varying instances of the same signifier. These signs would be vocalized in the same way, although on the page the reader *additionally* decodes the visual form each word takes. Saussure tells us that the linguistic signifier is abstract—a mental picture of a sound pattern that exists as part of that differential, conceptual system of language that constitutes the *langue*; the sign, on the other hand, used in a particular instance of *parole*, is always concrete (Saussure 1983: 120–21). It is in this *langue/parole* distinction between concrete signs used in particular contexts and abstract signifiers that are repetitively re-invoked across multiple contexts that the distinction between verbal and visual persists. In the instance of the drawn versus typescript "pow," it is clear the distinct visual contexts affect how the same linguistic signifier is interpreted.

W. J. T. Mitchell notes that all texts "incorporate visuality quite literally the moment they are written or printed in visible form" and suggests that therefore "the medium of writing deconstructs the possibility of a pure image or a pure text" (Mitchell 2009: 118). While the former notion is indisputable, the latter only tells part of the story about how language and images are received and processed (and it is far from clear how language's graphic form deconstructs the possibility of a pure image). Any sign, used in a particular instance of *parole*, will depend *in part* on its context for meaning. That context may be the tone of voice used in verbalizing the sign, it will include where the sign is uttered and in relation to what, and may involve the material, visual form the sign takes on a page (or whatever surface it is written, drawn, or carved upon). But this sign—a particular, concrete instance of a repeatable signifier—still signifies according to the *langue*, although its specific meaning in a particular context emerges from a collaboration between those prior denotations, connotations, and associations that make up the signified and the material specifics of the context in which the sign is made concrete. It is that preexistent abstraction, separable from the various material contexts that realize it in a physical form, that distinguishes verbal from visual: language's conceptual signifiers are only subsumed into graphic visualization or "imagetext" (Mitchell 2009: 118) when deployed in specific utterances. In short, text actually reads as *part of* an image, both visual and verbal "retain[ing] their traditional denotive functions," but *gaining* something in their mutual trade-off. As stated, it is the repeatability of verbal signs that Barthes says is the very thing that makes language possible, and the use to which comics critics have tended to put Mitchell's notion of "imagetext" ignores the *langue/parole* distinction in suggesting that the influence of particular material contexts on a words' meaning presents "an inseparable suturing of the visual and the verbal" (Mitchell 2009: 118). Thinking back to the twin instances of "pow" described above, we can distinguish between the two material contexts and the single verbal signifier that recurs in both. The verbal signifier is that which the two different images share, and their visual forms on the page are as distinct from that verbal signifier as the two material signs are from each other. It is through this *langue/parole* distinction that "imagetext" can be sundered and the visual and verbal elements of these material signs still distinguished from one another.

We decode visual signification only in part through learned associations. Lichtenstein's painting mobilizes fairly loose conventions, his suggestively bright colors and heavy outlines being read largely intuitively. More established is the association of standardized typescript with the authoritative, professionally published texts that comply with this regulated presentation, such as newspapers and books. It is by learned convention that we recognize the typewriter script that opens and closes *City of Glass*, and through intuitive interpretation of content that we understand this to indicate an authorial presence investigating and recording Quinn's story, resonant with the text's metafictional overtones (Fig. 4.10). We are accustomed to responding to the contexts in which verbal utterances are encountered, and comics critics overstate the uniqueness

4.10 Paul Auster, Paul Karasik and David Mazzucchelli, *City of Glass* (London: Faber and Faber, 2004), p. 137.

of comics' visualization of language, perhaps because literature, with which it is so often compared, suppresses this graphic aspect by adhering to uniform standards that mask its materiality. Sabine Gross notes that "learning to read means learning to stop considering letters and words as images" (1997: 31), and this operation is assisted by the self-effacement carried out by standardized typeface. In comics, as in pattern poems, the graphic form of language is engaged with and exploited—we encounter visualized verbal signs too in the likes of advertisements, magazines, and corporate logos, though it is notably rare for comics critics to pursue this obvious similarity when the comparison with literature is at once more attractive and fosters the suggestion that such graphic words are comics' own peculiar attribute. The fact remains that the exploitation of language's visual form is not unique to comics, nor is it true that this materialization of verbal signs destroys the distinction between word and image, though admittedly the meaning of a sign as used in a specific instance cannot be extracted from its particular material context. This works to jarring effect in "I Guess," where an explosion dramatic enough to warrant a sound effect in the visual strand coincides with the banal linking word "when" in the textual thread. The two different meanings, "superimposed on themselves" (Foucault 1983: 23) by the materialization of the sign in an unexpected context, exemplifies in an isolated material sign the visual-verbal dissonance that the entire piece trades off.

The perceptual distinction between the *particular* material instance of a visually arresting verbal sign and the abstract, repeatable signifier it realizes produces a kind of "back-and-forth movement between iconic and symbolic signification" (Gross 1997: 24), which is very similar to the "back-and-forth of *reading* and *looking*" (Chute 2008: 452) that occurs between picture and caption or dialogue. In this chapter's opening example, that picture-caption gap was abundantly evident. The cartoon's "unified" narrative end depended on a disjunction: caption and picture contextualized each other, each subverting what the other initially (independently) appeared to signify, and springing a "surprise" on the reader who imaginatively leapt across the gap between them. Speech balloons further the sense of unity, not by placing words within the picture space, but by materializing words in very imagistic ways. In these drawn words, whether they appear as dialogue, sound effects, or other text, the perceptual gap between visual and verbal persists in the distinction between *langue* and *parole*. There remains a "qualitative difference" (Gross 1997: 22) between those arbitrary linguistic signifiers, drawn from the *langue* and recognizable purely through convention, and intuitive, more loosely conventionalized, motivated visual forms.

Numerous examples have shown there is no definitively "comicsy" combination of words and images. Distinguishing between the different kinds of interaction proves useful, illuminating exactly how the form achieves its vastly varied effects. None of these operations are exclusive to the form, however—with the possible exception of the speech balloon, which we have already said does not constitute a special kind of hybridization, though the use of the device might be said to "belong" to comics. Neither can particular types of combination exclude a text that uses sequences of panels from being counted a comic, much as critics might like to fence off the likes of "mere" illustration. In consistently maintaining the distinction between visual and verbal, I do not deny the extent to which visual and verbal are integrated in comics, affecting each other and generating the meaning of the whole text by way of their effect on each other. Visual and verbal forms take part in a mutual exchange in comics, but this interaction does not override their distinct nature, and attempts to claim this interweaving constitutes a new "language" frequently expose themselves as rhetorical assertions intended to deflate the perceived word-image hierarchy. These assertions are problematic precisely because they gloss over the specifics of how language, visual signification, and this particular hybrid art form are actually structured. It can surely only be through a more scrupulous application of theoretical terminology that critics can hope to further the legitimization project with which so much recent criticism remains preoccupied.

Chapter Five

Comics as Network

Sequentiality features nearly universally in critical attempts to nail down a definition of the comics form, as alluded to in relation to Simmonds's networked compositions. This emphasis stems from Eisner's *Comics and Sequential Art* (1985), for though Eisner posited comics as *one particular kind* of sequential art, subsequent expansions of his definition, such as McCloud's (1993), have accentuated this aspect of comics still further. Indeed, it has come to so dominate theoretical conceptualizations that the form itself is sometimes rebranded as Sequential Art (*Thought Bubble* 2011: np). It is through reducing the form to this one feature that critics are sometimes led into dubiously categorizing diverse, historically distant artifacts as comics for reason of their sequentiality. Though some critics query the fruitfulness of constructing a definition of the form in the first place (Meskin 2010: 4, Witek 2009: 149, Lefèvre 2010: 38–40), the practice and its focus on sequencing remains an entrenched part of the critical discourse. The collaborative "filling in gaps" between sequential panels, previously discussed primarily in relation to Iser's notion of sentence correlatives, is in fact "an experientially rooted way of making sense of the world" (Christiansen 2000: 117). Ernst Gombrich explains that "there is no representation [that] leaves nothing to the imagination" (1952: 181): we fill in odd unheard words in conversation, overlook misprints and deduce the correct word when reading, and infer familiar images from loose or abstracted representations. The readiness with which we do so is testimony to the "importance of guided projection" (Gombrich 1952: 171) in interpreting *all* representational material. The process McCloud terms "closure," then, has sundry counterparts beyond Iser's theory (indeed, McCloud himself acknowledges this sort of guided projection informs all acts of perception, though critics citing his work tend to promote the simultaneous claim that the comics medium rests on this process "like no other" [1993: 65]). The process compares, for example, with the way we mentally group broken lines and proximate forms into continuous gestalts, and, as some critics acknowledge, with the way we suture cinematic cuts, understanding fractured film scenes as whole narratives (Pratt 2009: 111–14, Beaty 1999: 68). Critics bent on proving comics' worth alongside literature commonly dismiss this latter analogy (Hatfield 2005: 52, Køhlert 2010: 685), and the issue of film's formal similarity to comics will surface throughout the ensuing discussion.

Sequentiality lies at the heart of many attempts to describe comics as a language. Gaps between sequential panels are supposed to constitute the form's "grammar" (McCloud 1993: 67, Whitlock 2006: 968, Chute 2008: 455), while the creation of larger narratives from successive panels is frequently likened to the cumulative meanings of words and sentences in language (Raeburn 2004: 7, Saraceni 2000: 96). The linguistic nature of sequential panels is explicated with unusual precision by Cohn (2005, 2007, 2010), who is more careful than most critics in distinguishing visual language, which he characterizes as "sequential panel-to-panel relations (syntax)" (2005: 238) from "other forms of visual communication" (2005: 236). Cohn notes that critics tend to invoke disparate ideas like "visual communication," "pictorial icons," and "the comics form" as interchangeable synonyms that can all be likened to verbal language (Cohn 2005: 237–38), conflating diverse representational practices into a highly generic version of the linguistic semiotic model. Conversely, Cohn specifies that visual images might be "deemed a 'language' only when systematic features of sequence arise – that is, a grammar" (Cohn 2005: 238). Thus, his conception of comics' grammar is more rigorously linguistic than many critics', for whom any kind of encoded representation is enough to warrant comparison. For Cohn, systematic sequence, or syntax, distinguishes visual *language* from other kinds of visual signification, and his method of diagramming the syntactical structures through which we read panel sequences (2010) proves to be an enlightening methodology.

The other critical concept utilized here is French critic Thierry Groensteen's notion of arthrology. European (particularly Francophone) comics criticism is broadly acknowledged to be more sophisticated than its Anglophone counterpart (Christiansen & Magnussen 2000: 9, Rommens 2002: np, Baetens 2001: 147), but though the two traditions scarcely overlap, the translation of Groensteen's major work *The System of Comics* (2006) into English makes him a relevant figure in both arenas—though his assiduously academic text was tellingly labeled "gibberish" (Rifas 2007: 100) by a reviewer in the *Comics Journal*. Groensteen's notion of arthrology describes the relationships, both linear and translinear, between panels. It is through attending to not only the sequential progression of the narrative, but to "a dechronologized mode, that of the collection, of the panoptical spread and of coexistence, considering the possibility of translinear relations and plurivectoral courses," that Groensteen is led to espouse the network rather than sequence as the appropriate structural model of the form (2006: 146–47). The process of braiding more specifically describes a forging of links between panels "founded on the remarkable resurgence of an iconic motif (or of a plastic quality)" (Groensteen 2006: 151). Iconic resonances, which bridge dispersed panels and draw them into correspondence, can override linear narrative progression, and close readings of these operations prove to be instrumental in challenging Anglophone critics' preoccupation with sequentiality.

Both Cohn's proposed grammar and Groensteen's arthrology assert the importance of non-linear relationships. This chapter looks at two texts— the famous *Watchmen* (1995) and the avant-garde *Metronome* (2008)—that utilize non-linear plotting and resurgent motifs to complicate the basic sequential progression that characterizes *all* narrative forms. Film criticism provides useful terminology for describing many of the devices involved, and indeed even critics resistant to this comparison frequently invoke shot depth, *mise-en-scene*, and editorial cutting to describe the operations of panel composition and transitions. The limits of the cinema analogy (for it is only a comparator, not outright counterpart to the comics form) are often drawn in such a way as to favor the literary association or champion the form "in its own right," which can lead to some rather questionable assertions. It is, for example, stated that the comics form "differs from the only proximate medium of film – also a visual, sequential art form – because it is created from start to finish by a single author" (Chute & DeKoven 2006: 770)—far from a universal identificatory qualifier.

A more common error is to equate comics' panels with film frames, foregrounding the resemblance between a row of panels and a reel of frames or storyboard layout (McCloud 1993: 8, Harvey 1996: 178), which rather undermines the comparison from the outset given that these objects are manifestly not *cinema*. The more appropriate comparison, as some acknowledge (Cwiklik 1999: 62, Versaci 2008: 14), is between panels and *shots*, with transitions functioning like cuts that the reader/ viewer mentally links to infer a continuous narrative. This chapter highlights the greater structural similarities between comics and film, as compared to prose literature, though with the caveat that crucial differences do exist. It is recognized, for example, that film's moving images control the pace at which a work is consumed absolutely, while comics' static

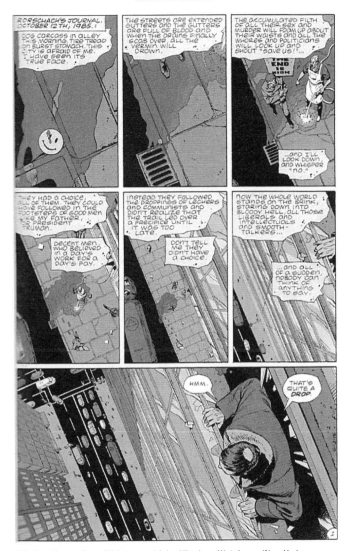

5.1 Alan Moore, Dave Gibbons, and John Higgins, *Watchmen* (New York: DC Comics, 1995), book 1, p. 1.

printed images must use other means to guide and influence a "self-paced reading" (Hatfield 2005: 74). Furthermore, in comics "simultaneity replaces linear narrative hierarchy" (Bennett 2010: np). That is to say, unlike film, whose shots are viewed one at a time, comics panels are co- present on the two-dimensional page. As we shall see, within the page, simultaneous panels can participate in webs of interrelationship that violate narrative sequence, and it is these non-linear relations that truly distinguish comics from other forms of narrative sequence.

Both texts considered here have notably cinematic openings. *Watchmen* begins with a dramatic zoom that pulls up from an enigmatic smiley badge lying in a blood-soaked street, ascending to a high-rise window to peer down on the street below (Fig. 5.1). The incremental rise over six panels emphasizes the plunging drop, as the street diminishes to a distant miniature and the building's facade soars up from the ground, consuming more and more panel space. The final panel sprawls out across the page's full width, encompassing both the distant street and the sheer plane of the building's vertical front falling away, its height underscored by sharply converging perspective lines. The sudden shift from regular, three-panel rows to this dramatically splayed panel cannot be replicated on cinema's fixed screen space. Comics thus have recourse to dimensional flourishes that cannot be replicated in film, but, in the dizzying zoom that apes the movement of a camera, this text constructs an undeniably cinematic overture.

There is something similarly cinematic in the opening of *Metronome*, which reads as a kind of "semantic locative" (Cohn 2010: 136), an extended pan round a slickly modern apartment that functions as a lengthy, moody establishing shot. Conducted over discrete, static panels, rather than through the actual tracking of a camera, this panning-by-increments takes in objects with the regular, pulsing beat of the metronome that underscores the entire work. The text's reading protocol is only revealed gradually, as an initial scattered montage settles into perceptible zoom-outs and panning conducted across horizontal rows in the pages reproduced here. This opening gambit lasts several pages, and might well test the patience of a cinema viewer, but the comics form militates against this as the reader can scan compositions such as these extremely quickly. The gradual zooms and steady panning create a contemplative aura, and though the repeated forms and rhythmic movement mean this can be taken in at a glance, the slow, brooding movement suggested by the contents is not compromised. The relationship between reading pace and story duration will be discussed in due course, but these opening zooms and pans show how comics can evocatively mimic the techniques of cinema, even if the experience of reading them is somewhat different.

Cinematic devices are further emulated through cuts in scene and perspective. *Metronome* particularly, concerned as it is with interaction and conflict, often opts for the classic shot-reverse shot device (Fig. 5.2). As

5.2 Veronique Tanaka, *Metronome* (New York: NBM Publishing, 2008), p. 39.

these shifts between bickering characters are simultaneously visible in a continuous row, we see an additional suggestion of distance: the characters look at one another over their shoulders, so that the adjacent figures are always either turned away from one another, or, in the central two panels, looking away. This subtle hint of the friction between them is made possible through the simultaneity of these sequential panels, but the quick-cutting between characters isolated in their own frames is highly redolent of the familiar camera technique.

It is common to foreground the elliptical nature of comics and contrast the effort that goes into mentally linking discrete panels with the supposedly "passive" (Hatfield 2005: 33) and "effortless" (Harvey 1996: 175) viewing of motion picture frames that flow seamlessly and automatically from one to the next. However, the closely linked action of Fig. 5.1 and 5.2 here passes so smoothly that the act of mentally suturing their content becomes near-automatic, a "largely unconscious and mechanical operation" (Groensteen 2006: 10). Equally, the more jarring, imaginatively demanding cuts that can occur between comics' panels can also be emulated cinematically. Films such as *Memento* (2000) or *21 Grams* (2003) test the viewer with scrambled plotlines that unfold backwards (*Memento*) or through scattered snippets (*21 Grams*), forcing the reader to piece together the overarching story from fragments that reveal further information gradually, continually clarifying or modifying what has gone before. This operation works by the same principle as Iser's sentence correlatives, and the *visibility* of the gap the reader must bridge in comics does not set the form apart from other narrative media that have recourse to similar narrative elision. The specific demands placed on the reader and relative "difficulty" in mentally linking fragmented elements vary from text to text and are not the special preserve of any particular art form. The "fetishization" (Groensteen 2006: 112) of the interframe space is linked to the defensive touting of "the kinds of things only comics can do" (McCloud 2000: 7), which counters the perceived assumption that comics are a debased and lowly form with vociferous insistence that they are in fact uniquely complicated, sophisticated, and involving. Specific comics are precisely as sophisticated as their specific content, and the particular level of engagement involved in piecing together the story is entirely dictated by that content—as it is with any narrative art form.

In unfolding their convoluted, flashback-laden narratives, both *Watchmen* and *Metronome* rely on the reader to deduce the relationship between disparate narrative threads. Both texts use the image of a photograph to segue into flashback, but these cuts are easily interpreted, heavily signaled by the content. *Watchmen* splices a flashbulb image in between a depiction of the photograph and a panel that shows that photograph's figures "live," breaking their pose in the moment after the picture has been taken. It is thus obvious from the surrounding content (a photograph of the bygone Minutemen; the Minutemen themselves in conversation) that the text's time line has delved into the past, and further dispersed correlatives help anchor this transition: a sly Polish reference identifies the younger Sally Jupiter, whose adult daughter has already told the reader in another strand of the narrative that her mother assumed that surname "because she didn't want anyone to know she was Polish" (Moore, Gibbons, & Higgins 1995: 1.20). The silent *Metronome* indicates just as effectively that the narrative moves from viewing a photograph, framed atop a piano, to the moment of its taking, by zooming into the picture then zooming out to show the still image on the screen of a digital camera, while the photograph's subject is seen rubbing her flash-dazzled eyes in the background. This sequence seemingly moves into the past *through* the photograph. These photographs make the temporal shifts apparent, but the process of mental suturing is often intuitive: the location of a particular scene in a story's deep structure simply becomes apparent from correlatives that are progressively meted out. Just as when a film cuts to another scene, the unfolding content gradually allows us to infer, more or less explicitly, how far and in what direction we have moved within the world of the work. The sequential transition across panel gaps, then, is perhaps less important than a general engagement with the "dechronologized [. . .] . panoptical spread" of correlations threaded through a text's wider content.

In underlining the commonalities between comics and film, this chapter remains mindful of their differences, particularly those afforded by the *spatial* nature of comics and *simultaneity* of its multiple panels on a two-dimensional page. This feature, illustrated by the moving-in sequence in *Metronome* (Fig. 5.3), is a genuine point of distinction between comics

5.3 Veronique Tanaka, *Metronome* (New York: NBM Publishing, 2008), p. 28.

and other narrative media. The camera first zooms out from a smiling face (an identical image to the one captured in the photograph) and then pans down to take in the shoulder strap of a rucksack and suitcase, letting the reader know what is happening here. The arrangement of these motions across the two rows results in a split panel effect at the right-hand edge, with the woman's upper and lower body aligned so that we cannot help but see a full-length image, skipping over the gap that bisects this figure and mentally configuring the divided panels into a continuous form. The eye overrides the sequence here, perceiving a composite figure that breaches the reading protocol.

Watchmen also makes use of the split panel device. Concluding a peripheral subplot with the blowing up of a ship, a full-width panel unfurls to accommodate the explosion, with three panels underneath together mirroring this single-panel row (Fig. 5.4). In the full-width panel, the shading of the sky has ample room to fade into darkness as we move away from the violent glare of the explosion itself. The intensity of light in the upper panel is emphasized through its contrast with the row below: dramatic shadows are thrown over the nearside of the driftwood and across the sand, which is bleached a lighter shade than in the mutedly toned panels below. Reading this segment, the reader does not naturally move from each panel to the next, obediently following the ritualized reading pathway, but scans the entire composition, making comparisons between the upper panel and the three lower ones that together replicate its composition. The reader partly processes this bottom row as one image, even while perceiving it is divided into three. However, we also see the differences

5.4 Alan Moore, Dave Gibbons, and John Higgins, *Watchmen* (New York: DC Comics, 1995), book 10, p. 18.

that arise as we move across this subdivided scene, which signpost the time shift that takes place as we traverse the row. The moon sinks. Smoke disperses and drifts away. The choppy waters calm: the final panel shows shimmering shadows of pier posts on an undulating, glassy surface, broken in the preceding panels by a surging wash round these posts, while emphatic black surface ripples gradually diminish. Finally, a sketch seen on board the boat washes up on shore. This "tension between linear and tabular readings" (Hatfield 2005: 53) is sometimes recognized as a special preserve of comics, enabling groups of discrete, sequential panels to simultaneously act as whole units. This operation, however, is elided by the entrenched critical emphasis on sequence, and, furthermore, the ways in which comics can override a sequential reading protocol are far more diverse and dispersed than this one acknowledged device.

Watchmen additionally utilizes intercutting plots to override panel-to-panel sequentiality. For example, it arranges parallel plots into columns that violate the left-right, top-bottom nine-panel grid that is maintained throughout most of the book (Moore, Gibbons & Higgins 1995: 3.6–7) and elsewhere alternates between two disparate scenes within a standard grid (as in Fig. 5.17), creating in both cases a kind of continuous visual "meanwhile." The point being stressed here is that comics can and often do override their own narrative sequentiality. It is through the *spatial* nature of comics' sequences, co-present on the two-dimensional page, that the form truly differs from comparative narrative media, film in particular. Critics do frequently acknowledge the spatial nature of panel sequences, and many point to this feature as distinguishing comics from *temporally* sequential motion pictures (Meskin 2007: 371, Versaci 2008: 16, Pratt 2009: 114). However, following McCloud's emphasis on transitions, panels' spatial relations are all too often discussed in terms of sequential adjacency. As a result, two-dimensional spatiality tends to take a back seat to linear narrative progression, with critics overstating the importance of the visible interframe space and risking downplaying non-linear relationships. This approach is solidified by conceptual definitions that center on sequentiality, enabling at best limited and at worst distorted accounts of the form.

In an incisive article, Cohn identifies manifold problems with current conceptions of panel transitions. Cohn expands from the narrow focus on panel transition, so far problematized in relation to the easy replication of these narrative effects in other media, to consider the problems of the "more radical" idea of "temporal mapping" (2010: 130). This theory is apotheosized in the already-cited maxim "space equals time." The initial problem Cohn identifies is the implication that *all* transitions must therefore signal shifts in time (2010: 130), a suggestion he notes is rather undermined by McCloud's own taxonomy, which identifies "subject-to-subject" and "aspect-to-aspect" (McCloud 1993: 70–72) transitions that entail shifts in space or viewing position, but not necessarily time. McCloud's theory, according to Cohn, is symptomatic of a much more pernicious issue: "the belief that *panels* equal *moments*" (Cohn 2010: 131). The idea that panel sequences work as a kind of "map of time" (McCloud 2000: 206) is key to current conceptions of the form. The panel is seen *definitively* as "a narrative morpheme that uses space to represent time" (Round 2007: 316), and it is this specific use of the semiotic model to couch these narrative units in terms of the medium of language that is here contested.

Metronome's metrically marching sequences decompose actions, breaking movement down into snapshots (Fig. 5.3), and from this it is clear how McCloud's simplistic take on panel sequentiality arises. However, the semantic locatives Cohn identifies, exemplified in the extended establishing shot that opens the text, simply do not fit into the "space equals time" schema, *placing* a story's action but not representing a moment in its unfolding. The inclusion of text is often seen to lock time into a panel, according to how long it takes to read dialogue or narration (Screech 2005: 102, Abbott 1986: 162). However, Cohn points out that "the properties of space and time being compared [by McCloud's temporal mapping theory] exist on two entirely separate planes of analysis. While the space McCloud refers to is based on physical distance, the sense of time he refers to is entirely a mental construct garnered from the contents of the panels" (Cohn 2010: 131). That is, time in comics is *fictive* time: a panel *represents* a stretch of action, but does not necessarily contain the amount of time the words in the panel take to read. Cohn points to examples that *signify* a duration of time or whole event visually: the classic "smoke-veiled fight" encapsulates the multiple actions of many flying limbs within an obscuring dust cloud, while in "polymorphic" panels a single figure is shown several times over, suggesting an ongoing action mapped by the path of the figure's movements within a single image (Cohn 2010: 132–33; for an example see Fig. 6.4). We deduce the diegetic duration suggested by the pictorial content, rather than measure this according to the time it takes us to read verbal (or for that matter visual) content. Relating the physical space to narrative time proves erroneous on many fronts, but betrays a poor acquaintance with narrative theory that is suggestive of a limited interaction with established scholarly discourse. McCloud's equation of text space and story time obliterates the distinction between fictive time and its representation within a narrative, between story and plot. The relationship between narrative duration and fictional duration is pertinent to all narrative forms, and the direct equation of the two assumed by the theory of temporal mapping is highly questionable.

Cohn asserts that the layout of panels may affect "the physical *rhythmic* pace in which those panels are read" (Cohn 2010: 131), but this pacing remains distinct from the story-world time represented in a given sequence. The example below from *Metronome* does not indicate the woman stands looking out of the blinds for three "moments" before the

5.5 Veronique Tanaka, *Metronome* (New York: NBM Publishing, 2008), p. 34.

5.6 Alan Moore, Dave Gibbons, and John Higgins, *Watchmen* (New York: DC Comics, 1995), book 1, p. 14.

man approaches (Fig. 5.5). Instead, this sequence signals an indeterminate stretch of inactivity before the man's fist (which will reappear later) interrupts this stasis by materializing ominously in the foreground. At this stage in the story, cracks are showing in the couple's relationship and the woman's claustrophobic boredom has been made evident. Like the opening establishing shots, the repetition of these three panels indicates a lingering, moody hiatus that is invaded by the close-up fist, which disrupts the medium-depth perspective the preceding panels linger on. It is a climatic appearance, looming suddenly in the last panel, and it is the panel's terminal placement in the row, rather than the precise number of momentary panels preceding it, that creates the sense of a lull broken.

In *Watchmen*, similarly rhythmic sequencing occurs in Rorschach's three-panel approach to an oblivious quarry he will violently press into revealing information (Fig. 5.6). Rorschach's approach spaces out a small amount of action, building up tension by slowing the pace at which that action is delivered to the reader: where an instant materialization would

5.7 Alan Moore, Dave Gibbons, and John Higgins, *Watchmen* (New York: DC Comics, 1995), book 11, p. 28.

emphasize speed and dynamism, the gradual, purposeful steadiness with which Rorschach bears down on his victim is instead coldly menacing. Slowing down the pace at which this action is *delivered* is only partially significant of the speed of the action itself, additionally insinuating the tone the narrative aims to establish. By lengthening narrative time in relation to diegetic time, the detached, almost robotic calm in this predatory approach is drawn out. Cinema too is capable of playing with narrative duration, but in comics "the visibility of the interframe space makes rhythm more salient" (Miller 2007: 109). Precision is crucial here: the interframe space does not make fluctuations in narrative pace inherently "comicsy," but *metrical* effects—the sense of a beat—are genuinely more readily exploitable within strings of discrete panels.

My point here is that the sequential arrangement of panels pertains to narrative effect, particularly reading time, and not necessarily, or even predominantly, to elapsing story time. At the culmination of *Watchmen*'s countdown to doomsday, where an artificially created life-form is tele-ported into the heart of New York City, detonating a shockwave that kills half the population, the three-by-three grid established as the text's stan-dard layout becomes compressed (Fig. 5.7). These rows of six narrow pan-els depict frantic panic, but the top row does not imply any progression of story time, instead working as a tableau, a claustrophobic series of snap-shots depicting a terror-stricken crowd in a single moment. In the bottom row, two casually acquainted characters dive into each other's arms as the background turns to a blistering white and the figures are vaporized, dis-sipating into a blurred shape that echoes the five-to-midnight motif that runs throughout the text. The speed of the action—that is, the amount of story time elapsing—is deduced entirely from the *content*: this instinctive dive for comfort or protection is a momentary action, it can only be sud-den, and it is this content rather than the size or spacing of the panels that tells us this. The narrow spacing is suggestive of speed, because the reader takes in many closely linked slivers showing infinitesimal movements in a sort of zoetrope effect, and because the increased number of panels cre-ates a feeling of acceleration across this row. At the same time, however, breaking this action down into so many smaller movements prolongs it. The sense of desperation in this agonized, drawn-out striving toward each other lends this segment urgency and renders it deeply poignant. To reit-erate, the narrowness of the panels increases the pace of *reading*. The sense of *story* time passing is entirely dependent on the content that indicates it, while the way that content is broken down across these panels actually elongates our experience of the action depicted. Thus, these panels create a sort of hyperactive slow-motion effect, with reading pace accelerated and the story's action stretched out and slowed. Both rows here manipu-late the relationship between reading time and story time to great narra-tive effect, but there is a marked difference between them, despite their identical frames. The difference lies in the different ways content is meted out within these rows, and it precludes the oversimplistic prescriptions implicit in some critics' equation of narrowing frames with a consistent, particular shift in the pace of action (Raeburn 2004: 8, Kunzle 1990: 349).

It should be noted that the narrowness of the panels in Fig. 5.7 is entirely relative to the standard panel size the text establishes through basing itself on a regular grid of nine. This structure underpins each page. Deviating panels, such as those in Fig. 5.1, 5.4, and 5.7, tend to subdivide or combine clusters within that structure, maintaining the baseline arrangement. The interpretable *significance* of panels' size might thus be comparable with language, insofar as each panel is valuated according to its relative position within a system of panels. However, this system does not extend beyond the bounds of an individual text. Rather than an overarching symbol system that imposes standards on all texts from without, comics' panels are defined relative to other panels within their particular text, and each text is (relatively) free to institute its own standards. Spatial arrangements are made significant in *Watchmen* through the deliberate adoption of a benchmark structure, which flags up any deviations. The layout of *Metronome* too is foregrounded and significant: its rigidly maintained four-by-four grid of perfect squares gels well with the cleanly simplified drawing style and the regular beat of the metronome that runs throughout. But though these two texts both self-impose compositional regularities to great effect—the first via telling deviations, the second through scrupulous uniformity—there is no external, preexistent standard against which the significance of individual panels within particular works can be measured. The straightforward grid might provide a default layout (besides which artists like Chris Ware can be judged experimental), but a particular panel is only vested with significance according to its specific relational value within an individual text. Thus panels within layouts are signs *made*, not *used*, and are thus more readily comparable with the visual rather than linguistic system.

In the preceding examples, it has been reading pace that has been most clearly manipulated by the dimensions and frequency of panels, while story time is more specifically controlled by the way depicted action is broken down across a sequence. There is a further objection to the notion that the size and spacing of panels must directly organize the reader's understanding of fictive time, one highlighted by Harvey's numerous expert close readings (1996), which emphasize how composition actually responds to depicted contents, spatially framing action rather than indicating its duration. When Adrian Veidt fights off a would-be assassin in *Watchmen*, the customary grid is clustered into a number of outsize panels spread over a double-page, with two columns of three flanking a central spine-straddling panel that runs the full height of the page (Fig. 5.8). This pivotal panel is sized to frame the action within. The tall vertical emphasizes both the upswing of Adrian's weapon, and the trajectory of his attacker down into

5.8 Alan Moore, Dave Gibbons, and John Higgins, *Watchmen* (New York: DC Comics, 1995), book 5, p. 14; p. 15.

the water. Arranging these large panels across the double-spread styles this section as big, bold, and dramatic, with roomy panels more comfortably accommodating the dynamic dives, thrusts, and tussles. The pace of *reading*, here, is fast because we consume these pages far more quickly than we are accustomed to, glancing over a mere seven panels in a space normally reserved for eighteen. However, the sense of diegetic speed is a result of the way the action is broken down across these panels. While Fig. 5.6 breaks a smooth single movement into interim steps, the action here is not closely linked but proceeds by elliptical leaps: the weapon that deflects a bullet in the third panel has already been re-swung and struck its target in the fourth; diving after his attacker in the fifth panel, Adrian has already mastered and hauled him to his feet in the sixth. It is these gaps in *action* that create a frenetic pace, along with the cinematic shifts in shot depth and perspective that are themselves forcefully dynamic. The content plays a vital role in lending meaning to this dramatically enlarged layout, which could easily connote contemplative stasis if the contents so suggested it.

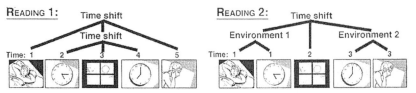

5.9 Neil Cohn, "The Limits of Time and Transitions: Challenges to Theories of Sequential Image Comprehension," *Studies in Comics*, 1.1 (2010): 127–47, Fig. 10.

Layout and content essentially take part in a similar mutual exchange to text and image, though as Chapter Nine will argue, the former more usually relies on the latter for its meaning. We can thus see that it is *content* that indicates story time elapsing, with the layout of panels lending narrative pace and showcasing action, rather than telling the reader how much diegetic time elapses.

In his own debunking of the pervasive principle that sequentiality represents the "essence" of the comics form, Cohn sets out a far more convincing model of comics-as-language than is traditionally offered. He identifies unconscious hierarchical groupings through which the mind understands sequences of panels. Setting himself in direct opposition to McCloud's temporal mapping, Cohn demonstrates how readers mentally group panels into subsets, or chunks, which are understood in relation to other parts of the sequentially arranged work. Crucially, he shows how this understanding is organized by hierarchical structures rather than linear ones. Though we read comics sequentially, and indeed progress linearly through any narrative text, Cohn shows that it is not these linear relationships that guide our understanding. The meaning garnered from these chunks emerges through the conceptual content: that is, it is deduced, and does not arise according to "some overarching default principle like 'space = time'" (Cohn 2010: 142). Using a custom-made, structurally ambiguous example (Fig. 5.9), Cohn demonstrates two distinct possible readings, which make sense of the sequence by imposing a hierarchy of subsets onto it: the first of these readings assumes that each panel represents a separate moment in time, but the second, equally plausible reading considers the first two panels and then the final two as occurring at the same time and in the same place, and these pairs as separated by a time shift, which hinges on the central panel and is denoted by the two clocks. Cohn points out that McCloud's theory of temporal mapping and taxonomy of transitions could not adequately account for the ambiguity of this sequence, offering no way to capture the

Acceptable grouping

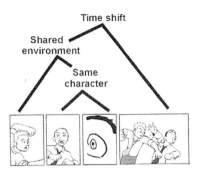

Non-acceptable grouping

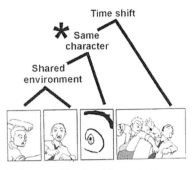

5.10 Neil Cohn, "The Limits of Time and Transitions: Challenges to Theories of Sequential Image Comprehension," *Studies in Comics*, 1.1 (2010): 127–47, Fig. 11.

differences between these two possible readings or the possibility of both existing for the same sequence.

Cohn further identifies rules and constraints governing how these groupings occur, and it is these hierarchical principles he likens, convincingly, to a "grammar" of comics. Cohn's structural hierarchy states that: "panels representing the same time and character should be grouped first, followed by panels at the same time but different characters, then finally with panels in other times" (Cohn 2010: 142). This is demonstrated by his diagramming of the groupings that order the sequence above (Fig. 5.10). From this, we see how the first three panels do not signal any temporal shift, but rather focus the reader's attention on different aspects of the same conceptual moment for narrative effect. By interpreting them according to a hierarchical structure, the reader is able to deduce that the widened eye groups with the character in the preceding panel, which larger unit (or clause, though Cohn does not use this word himself) is additively grouped with the first panel, showing a different character within a shared environment. This larger unit is then drawn together with the final panel to denote a shift in time. This example shows how readers mentally divide strips into logical perceptual units organized into hierarchies, and not governed by the linear reading order. Cohn finds in comics an organizing principle that genuinely bears comparison with language's grammar. Tellingly, this comics grammar overrides the sequentiality that superficially links panels with words in sentences. Cohn thus reaches the same conclusion this chapter aimed to establish through other examples:

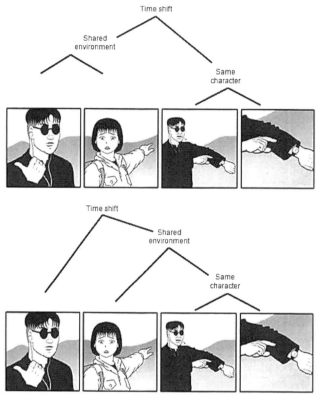

5.11 Veronique Tanaka, *Metronome* (New York: NBM Publishing, 2008), p. 37; with diagrams.

the sequential nature of narrative does not hold the key to understanding the comics form, and over-general comparisons with the linguistic structural model little illuminate the way texts are organized and read.

In looking at cinematic effects, and the difference between story pace and diegetic time, only limited attention has yet been given to the nonlinear relationships that are threaded through comics. The likes of split panels can be seen to utilize spatial, rather than sequential relationships on the comics page, and the emphasis placed on linear sequentiality through the "sequential art" tag risks sidelining such non-sequential connections. Cohn's theory avoids this, and his account of hierarchical groupings explains more persuasively how readers navigate strips through the comprehension of chunks that additively relate to other parts of the sequence—preceding as well as proceeding. Cohn wisely does not push the language comparison too far, never attempting to find comics' equivalents for language's phonemes, morphemes, clauses, and sentences, though his account of perceptual chunking corresponds to the accretive understanding of a sentence built from clauses that may refer backwards as well as forwards. Cohn further notes that McCloud's theory confuses text and story duration, and fails to account for the sorts of ambiguities his own grammar elucidates. An exemplar row from *Metronome* offers no basis for assuming temporal shifts occur between every panel: the fourth panel's zoom-in represents a change in viewing position, not time, emphasizing the intransigent pointing to the watch by extending its textual duration, but not necessarily its story time (Fig. 5.11). There is a definite time shift between this pair of panels and the first panel, but there is no indication that time elapses between either panel one and two, or two and three—or, potentially, one and two and three, though only the former two possibilities are diagrammed above.

These readings quantify the degree of ambiguity that exists within this segment, and both readings account for the possible simultaneity of certain represented actions: the first reading is particularly compelling, temporally uniting the first two panels linked by the horizon line that flows across them, so that the two figures pointing in opposite directions (away from each other) are read as a temporally simultaneous unit vested with obvious symbolism. Ultimately, both these readings shed more light on the ways readers interpret strips than McCloud's taxonomy offers.

Cohn's compelling rejection of temporal mapping has implications for the issue that began this chapter, namely the critical habit of grounding definitions of comics in sequentiality. However, Cohn also rejects what he sees as the alternative approach described by Groensteen's concept of arthrology. *Watchmen* proves to be a particularly instructive text in elaborating the semantic, iconic, and compositional links described by arthrology and braiding. The text revels in creating resonances intricately woven throughout its serialized issues (the "chapters" of the collected edition). The five-to-midnight motif, referred to earlier, recurs on clock faces that explicitly count down to the cataclysmic finale—and appears also as veiled allusion in manifold other forms (such as the last panel of Fig. 5.7). Groensteen's influence on the Anglophone field is far less pervasive than McCloud's, but his theory deserves closer attention here for two reasons. Firstly, the principle of arthrology is particularly relevant to the two texts considered here, which rely heavily on non-sequential iconic resonances. Secondly, having endorsed Cohn's repudiation of McCloud's conception of panel transitions, I want to question his concurrent rejection of arthrology. Arthrology avoids the principle mistake of much Anglophone criticism by conceiving of a *network* of connections rather than privileging linear sequential progression. The inclusion of recurrent motifs is, of course, not the special preserve of any narrative medium. However, Groensteen grounds his theory in comics-specific elements (panel frames, page layouts, speech bubbles, and visual forms) and in networks of relationships between these forms as arranged over two-dimensional pages and throughout entire printed texts.

Cohn is correct that arthrology, like the temporal mapping of panel transitions, does not systematically describe structural ambiguity in strips and cannot map the hierarchies by which strips are additively understood or the possible varying interpretations. But the examples against which Cohn measures arthrology's capabilities are custom-made to illustrate his point, and Groensteen's theory proves valuable for analyzing more dispersed connections, particularly compositional and figurative. Cohn further objects that arthrology is a "broad concept" (Cohn 2010: 137), comprising "loosely defined principles of connection" (Cohn 2010: 128), but there seems to be no error inherent in addressing a varied set of connective principles. Cohn further protests against the very expansiveness that would appear to give arthrology its advantage over McCloud's narrow focus on transition and adjacency. Specifically, he objects to the notion that "every panel exists, potentially if not actually, in relation with each of the others" (Groensteen 2006: 146, cited in Cohn 2010: 137). Cohn points out that this would entail a potentially incalculable complex of resonances that "without any explicit underlying structure to guide such connection [. . .] would be overwhelming for human memory to handle" (Cohn 2010: 138). However, there is no suggestion either that every connection *will* resonate with every other or that readers must pick up on every actual resonance on first reading in order to understand the text. Ultimately, the two methodologies do not set out to describe the same operations. Though it is true that Cohn's grammar provides a more systematic means of diagramming the perceptual connections necessary for understanding a strip's content, it utterly ignores the myriad subtle echoes and repetitions that reverberate through a complex artwork, which are not negligible if they are not discernible at first glance and that are included under the "broad concept" of arthrology.

Cohn in fact carefully brackets off the "artistic interpretation" (Cohn 2010: 129) that underpins McCloud's claims about reader involvement, and is essential to an awareness of the subtler and more dispersed iconic and compositional resonances that fall under the term braiding, separating it from the "unconscious processes" (Cohn 2010: 129) by which readers intuitively group and hierarchize sequences of panels. For Cohn, it is the very inaccessibility of this process that is "comparable to the creation of meaning by words in sentences" (Cohn 2010: 129). That is to say, we process speech without being consciously aware of the cognitive operations through which we reach the understandings we do. Though an emphasis on "basic comprehension" (Cohn 2010: 129) has hitherto been resisted, it must be conceded here that Cohn's theory provides a more precise and enlightening means of explicating how the mind processes panels-in-sequence by a process of accretion. It is additionally more scrupulously grammatical in nature than manifold other stabs at describing comics' grammar, and finally does at least explicitly differentiate between the basic comprehension of information, and active interpretation and analysis of rich, complexly woven threads of relation. Cohn claims that "panel transitions and arthrology are appealing as notions because the reader (or author) can directly experience them" (Cohn 2010: 140). It certainly seems that the emphasis on transitions fosters an attractive characterization of the comics reader as a uniquely imaginative and engaged participant, consciously interpreting the text in a manner far removed from the supposed "inert spectatorship" (Hatfield 2005: 33) of film-watching. However, I cannot concede the dismissal of arthrology, even if some of the correlations it describes indeed "would overload the working memory of the human mind" (Cohn 2010: 137). In admitting there is value in mapping the structures through which we cognitively process strips' basic informational content, which Cohn's hierarchical grammar enables, it remains true that this grammar pays no heed to comics as artworks. As an approach to comics' communicative efficacy, Cohn's scheme is a welcome advancement, but Groensteen's notions of arthrology and braiding facilitate an aesthetic appreciation of intricately networked figures and compositions that this functional grammar does not even attempt to address.

Metronome, in which incrementally progressing rows initially appear to work according to McCloud's moment-to-moment conception of panels, draws its hypnotically rhythmic effect in part from the iteration of iconic forms throughout the text. From its first pages, the work sets up a lexicon of objects (photograph, mask, picture, lava lamp, piano, fan, and of course the metronome itself) that recur with a pulsating frequency. The repetition of these objects plays up the claustrophobia of the apartment

5.12 Veronique Tanaka, *Metronome*
(New York: NBM Publishing, 2008),
p. 65, plus detail; p. 35.

in which the central relationship, once confined, starts to disintegrate. The sense of being hemmed in is an emerging theme of the text, neatly represented by the oft-revisited picture that includes a bird, whose form is duplicated in the scene showing a trek outdoors (which enlivens her and bores him). The circular picture contains within a frame a fragment of the expansive outdoors that sprawls across two rows of split panels,[1] the shapes of helicopters over the city providing a point of contrast to the soaring birds in the countryside (Fig. 5.12). This picture is further drawn into play with the text's erotic undertones by the placement of the already suggestive tree image beside a compositionally evocative panel depicting oral sex to create a veiled visual pun, a head coyly obscuring what the picture makes explicit symbolically (Fig. 5.13). In incorporating the freewheeling bird and resounding with bodily forms, this picture does not merely signal a "vague sense of 'connectedness'" (Cohn 2010: 142). It embodies the ties that bind the central couple together, making graphic their connection and shared history, while also alluding to the tensions that will eventually pull them apart.

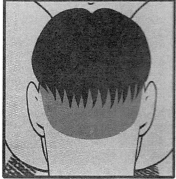

5.13 Veronique Tanaka, *Metronome* (New York: NBM Publishing, 2008), p. 20.

5.14 Veronique Tanaka, *Metronome* (New York: NBM Publishing, 2008), p. 59.

In combining its key attributes of visual echo and metrical cadence, *Metronome* frequently devises dramatic reveals, a steady panning or zoom that springs a final surprise on the reader. The steady dripping that regularly appears, formally similar to the fluid blobs of a lava lamp and metrically similar to the beating of the metronome, are shown at the text's end to be drops of coffee spilled during the story's climatic fight. This unveiling not only explains these recurrent drops, but assists in anchoring the segues in and out of flashback, signaling that the scene in which the male protagonist contemplates the disarray, which resurfaces throughout the text, takes place at the end of its *story*. Perhaps the most arresting use of the reveal is the repeated zoom in to and out from an eye, that regularly opens and closes scenes. On its final outing, this device exposes an eye blackened in the fight that finally destroys this faltering relationship (Fig. 5.14). This familiar movement is rendered shocking in its final evocation, the recognized form disfigured by the heavy black shape, starkly geometric in its emblematic representation of a bruise.

The clear line drawing style of *Metronome* effectively makes repeatable signs out of visual images. In stressing the importance of language's constitution in minimal units, I have implicitly alluded to the significance of visual signification's non-minimalism. While verbal signifiers can be

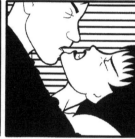
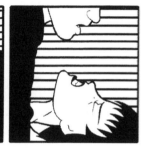

5.15 Veronique Tanaka, *Metronome* (New York: NBM Publishing, 2008), p. 31, p. 44.

decomposed into minimal morphemes, images' multiple gradated variables (eight, according to Jacques Bertin: two dimensions, size, value, texture, color, orientation, and shape [1983: 7]) collaborate to make a complex, multi-elemental sign—essentially, already a *text*. It has further been argued in the preceding chapter that where verbal signs must be drawn from a preexistent *langue*, visual signs are not limited in advance this way. Visual *parole* can create new signs, and while repetition is possible it is not inevitable as it is with inherited language. *Metronome*'s drawing style, which pares down physical forms to simplified, almost diagrammatic shapes, deliberately plays to the *possible* repeatability of visual forms: the repeated zooms mentioned above all resonate with each other, but some utilize absolutely identical forms. Some comics critics have suggested that as pictures become more abstracted and symbolic they become like words (Hatfield 2009: 133, Raeburn 2004: 18), but though these "reduced" visual representations here take on the repeatability of verbal signifiers, they continue to operate differently from words. When the pained expression of the woman struggling with a heavy houseplant recurs in an awkward, even mildly aggressive sex scene, the exact replication is noteworthy (Fig. 5.15). Any strained grimace here would have aptly conveyed the difference between this clumsily forceful act and the dreamy, grey-and-black depictions of the couple's "honeymoon period," but reusing the

5.16 Alan Moore, Dave Gibbons, and John Higgins,
Watchmen (New York: DC Comics, 1995), book 2, p. 11.

exact same few lines, which could be superimposed on each other, speaks volumes. Not simply allusive (like the echo between the different eyes) but embodied and total (like the repetition of the man's eye), these recurrent forms tie the two different contexts unfavorably—and tellingly—together. Repeatable words only become *significantly* repetitious if their iteration is flagged in some way, made obvious through proximity, or the repetition of clusters of words or by some other contrived emphasis. The exact repetition of pictorial forms, however, is never incidental. Using simplified—we might say abridged—images here fosters an exact repetition of iconic, representational images in different contexts, but the effect this arresting and unexpected replication creates is markedly different from that of inevitably iterated verbal signifiers. This replication is subtle, but, once noticed, arresting, and it is precisely this sort of braiding that Cohn's grammar does not address.

Watchmen's sometimes relentless inclusion of arthrological echoes borders on tricksiness, but though less sparely elegant than *Metronome*, its formal intricacies are impressive. The text tends strongly toward performing repetitious links over scene cuts, for example segueing into and out of flashbacks by using strikingly similar panel layouts to suture adjacent panels depicting the same characters at distant times (Fig. 5.16). The repetition of expressions, stances, and viewing angles smoothes over these cuts, though often rather overdetermines scene shifts. Some of the verbal links in particular begin to feel like a display of cleverness for its own sake: the voiceover technique, for example, where a conversation from one story thread is narrated over an intercutting story thread is wryly used when a elevator-attendant's line "ground floor coming up" (Moore, Gibbons & Higgins 1995: 1.3) is inscribed over the flashback depiction of a character being flung out of a high-rise window to his death. This waggish signaling soon starts to feel contrived, however, as when a reference to a character who "doesn't care *how* people dress" (Moore, Gibbons & Higgins 1995: 3.9; emphasis in original) captions a panel showing another character putting on a suit—by telekinetically animating it. The text's *visual* echoes, however, can be highly effective: in the example below, the lines etched onto the forehead and cheek of the character in the first panel, and tired droop of his features, are suggestive of the time that has passed between these two representations. Along with the likes of Fig. 5.4, these devices exemplify the operations described by braiding and arthrology.

Visual echoes are not, of course, out of reach of other narrative media, namely film. However, the ways a text like *Watchmen* puts these echoes to work is sufficiently specific to the form to warrant special attention. It is, for example, hard to conceive of another form that could contrive the pivotal symmetry of the fifth chapter/issue. Hinging on the double-spread fight scene (Fig. 5.8), each page is formally a mirror image of its counterpart, with thematic content, composition, and even color to varying extents taking their place in a palindromic structure. Cohn is quite correct in noting that, on first perusal, the reader's mind is unlikely to take in and process such minutely arranged complexities, but they are nevertheless present and pertinent to the tightly laced intercutting narrative threads and self-referentiality the text so relishes. The tightly braided webs of interrelation these recurring visual formats create certainly transcend the "non-stop continuous linear transitions" (Cohn 2010: 138) that are foregrounded through the emphasis on sequence. In one sense, Cohn and Groensteen both advocate non-linear readings as the basis for understanding comics, but Cohn does so only on the small scale in the service of mapping our basic cognitive comprehension, while Groensteen aims at the large scale at an engaged and attentive interpretation of the complex threading of allusions and motifs throughout the text. To reject the latter, as Cohn does, because its full significance is unlikely to be grasped in one reading is a dubious proposition. To risk flippancy again, no one pretends they "get" every allusion in *Ulysses* on first reading, or even ever; conscious artistic interpretation may indeed be needed to reveal such devices.

The utilization of page space will be revisited in Chapters Six and Nine, but is pertinent to the issue of sequentiality, particularly in the case of the

5.17 Alan Moore, Dave Gibbons, and John Higgins, *Watchmen* (New York: DC Comics, 1995), book 5, p. 12.

aforementioned intercutting plot strands that periodically alternate across *Watchmen*'s nine-panel pages. These interlocking strands effectively leap-frog consecutive panels, disrupting a linear reading as they weave together separate scenes (Fig. 5.17). Comprehending which panels relate directly to which is largely a matter of deduction based on content, but the text also utilizes color, subtly off-setting a unifying set of tones in one strand with a contrasting set of dominant colors in the other. This visual patterning remains peripherally visible even as we focus on one panel at a time, helping to distinguish these narrative threads and drawing the whole page space to the attention of the reader. The text thus overrides transitional relations, accentuating what Wolk describes as the "'tick-tock' effect" (2007: 239) of these interlocking strands, foregrounding the page as an integrated unit and drawing each sequential panel into its complex whole.

The text's famed *Black Freighter* device, which intercuts the main narrative with scenes from a comic book being read by a character, furthermore differentiates the pulp comic book pictures with a grainy texture distinct from the "real" story world (Fig. 5.17). The narrative shifts between these strands are of course signaled by the content as well, but the shifts are eased through the additional use of visual cues. The grainy texture of the *Black Freighter* panels is exemplary of the kind of visual signal whose meaning is established within a text, their significance reasserted for the reader each time they recur. This comic-within-a-comic makes further use of non-pictorial visual cues: the scroll-like caption boxes, looking like torn and off-color parchment, clearly differentiate captions that belong to *The Black Freighter* comic book from the text frames used for *Watchmen*'s main narrative. Most caption boxes are unobtrusive white oblongs, and tend to contain text in speech marks, denoting a conversation continuing from an intercut storyline, as described above. The *Black Freighter* segments further develop this technique, with scrolls from *The Black Freighter* comic appearing in panels concerned with the main narrative and speech bubbles from that narrative also appearing in panels depicting images from *The Black Freighter*—their tails tellingly pointing out of the panel and merging with the interframe space, indicating speakers external to the depicted scene.

The competing verbal strands that accompany each other throughout these alternating panels perform the same waggish interplay noted above: a reference to arms dealers making a killing from wars is juxtaposed with a scroll describing gulls as "scavengers"; the caption "This sudden confrontation with morality induced an odd clarity within me" is coupled with a newsstand vendor's homespun insight: "I mean, all this, it could be gone: people, cars, T.V. shows, magazines . . . even the word 'gone' would be gone" (Fig. 5.17). These referential lexias tend to justify Wolk's observation that "occasionally Moore threatens to sprain an eyelid from winking so hard" (2007: 249), but the way they are materialized illustrates an important point. As cues indicating the diegetic level of pictures and text, the scroll-captions and grainy texture might be termed visual symbols, rather than pictorial icons. That is, they represent by way of a convention that which the text establishes. The use of scrolls for the pirate narrative is, of course, a motivated choice, but the reader comes to interpret these forms automatically, learning to recognize these scrolls and the grainy texture as indicating the comic-within-a-comic. This texture cue in particular is an arbitrary sign; a learned association "read" like words. However, crucially the association of this visual signifier with a signified is established within the text itself. This conventional sign is created on the page through continual reinforcement and is not inherited from a preexistent, constraining system. Though these sorts of visual symbol are largely arbitrary and conventional, as is language, they do not become entirely like language. The distinction drawn here between visual symbols and pictorial icons—a distinction that attests to the heterogeneity of visual signification as distinct from language—will be fully explored in Chapter Seven. Suffice it to say here that these non-pictorial visual symbols—the colors, textures, and frames that distinguish Rorschach's diary, his rough-edged speech balloons, Dr. Manhattan's inhumanly blue ones—are all signs that are *made* within the individual text. They are deliberately devised, and thus remain distinct from words, for all their significance is learned and read rather than iconic and deduced via resemblance.

The distinctions between types of visual sign and their variable levels of motivation have deep implications for the comparison of images and comics to language. Such distinctions are particularly pertinent to the issue of sequentiality as it is the recurrence of these signs, drawn into resonant networks that permeate the text, which allows them to be read. Recurrent visual devices such as these come to make sense gradually, with close attention and sometimes even repeated readings eventually teasing out the nuanced arthrological connections that braid every panel "potentially if not actually" to every other, and that iteratively vest non-iconic visual forms with new significance. Frequently in *Watchmen* entire panels (or their pictorial content, at least) are repeated, creating bridges between non-adjacent panels often separated by many pages. These correlations often only reveal themselves upon repeated readings. The death of the Comedian, which opens the text, is exemplary. It is revisited several times, always intercut with another narrative thread. Initially, detectives investigating his murder are alternated with depictions of his death. Later identical images appear interspersed with other panels (and different voiceover

5.18 Alan Moore, Dave Gibbons, and John Higgins, *Watchmen* (New York: DC Comics, 1995), book 2, p. 27.

text). These panels themselves are repetitions drawn from disparate scenes from the Comedian's backstory, forming a sort of life-flashing-before-your-eyes montage that encapsulates in a single page the threaded networks of flashbacks and multiple narrative threads that cumulatively make up the text's entire story (Fig. 5.18). These panels finally recur inter-cut with the confession of the Comedian's killer, a startling revelation that assaults the expectations the reader has built up, forcing a reassessment of everything previously read and exemplifying the interruptive process of "anticipation and retrospection" that Iser describes (1980: 54).

The replication of whole panels is immediately apparent, and though they recur separated by many pages (and appear in different places on the

5.19 Alan Moore, Dave Gibbons, and John
Higgins, *Watchmen* (New York: DC Comics,
1995), book 2, p. 7.

page, the significance of which will be touched on in Chapter Nine), their
correlation is graspable on first glance. It takes a much greater familiarity
with the text, however, to notice the similarity in composition between
one of these death scene panels (the fifth panel in Fig. 5.18) and a panel
from a fight that occurs in the Comedian's younger days (Fig. 5.19). This
panel surfaces before the first recurrence of the Comedian's death (that
is, between the first and second times it is shown), and its visual echo
only really reveals itself through a familiarity with the repeated images it
resembles. It is only when we are accustomed to the scenes of the murder, effectively carrying a memory of them that functions like the mental
picture of a signifier, that we are able to see the similarity of the panel
below to the one above, and recognize it as a slightly altered instance of
the recurrent composition. That this correlation is beyond the comprehension of the first-time reader does not make it irrelevant, as Cohn suggests in setting his highly specific grammar in opposition to Groensteen's
expansive conception. On close reading, this visual echo *is* perceptible,
and effectively ties the Comedian's wayward life to his eventual death. This

is a more nuanced braiding of life and death than occurs in the second recital of this death, spliced with scenes from throughout the Comedian's life, though both link dispersed panels together in ways that violate the text's sequence. Noticeable only for a reader who has already read the whole book, this panel invokes previous *and later* panels, drawing them into an evocative network of exactly the type that arthrology describes.

The issue of sequentially is a vexed one primarily because of the skewed emphasis placed on it by many critics. Though visually obviated by the interframe space, sequentiality itself does not distinguish comics from any other narrative media. This chapter has suggested that it is the spatiality of the sequence—the simultaneity of sequential panels on a two-dimensional page—that really separates comics from its nearest comparative medium, film. The sequential passage of panels need not have any direct relation to the passage of story time, though it can be used to dictate reading time and control narrative pace. Space can also be used for dramatic and aesthetic ends: emphasizing action, dramatizing a spectacle, or assisting in creating a certain mood. The network model proves a valuable one here, illuminating how comics can create bridges between non-consecutive panels that are visibly co-present on the page, and conceptually co-present with all other panels throughout the text. Some of these connections are glaringly evident, but they may be more subtle, only revealing themselves upon closer, active analysis. The extent to which these networks contribute to our understanding of the text, which examination of *Watchmen* and *Metronome* has shown can be considerable, suggests that it is the very ability of comics to violate the sequential nature of narrative that in fact distinguishes the form. The dispersed connections may mirror the sentence correlatives Iser describes, but differ in being embodied, physical repetitions. The braiding of panels simultaneously present on the same page has no comparison in other media, asserting a connection that bridges the sequence in the eye of the reader, even as they are following it. Through being spatially arranged on a two-dimensional surface, only comics can visibly override their own linear progression.

Of the theories that aim to describe the operation of reading sequential panels, McCloud's notion of temporal mapping, with panels equaling moments, is the most widely accepted and the most problematic. It aptly describes certain kinds of transition—and very common ones—but it certainly does not define the medium as a whole, as he purports. Cohn's explication of cognitive "chunking" of sequences into segments processed hierarchically is valuable in explaining how readers unconsciously comprehend strips. Cohn's theory also furnishes us with an unusually viable comparison with language in demonstrating a systematic organizing principle that governs how sequences of panels make meaning. It does not, however, provide any insight into approaching relationships between more dispersed panels throughout a narrative, which Groensteen's arthrology does. It is notable that both these theories hinge on a back-and-forth reading of panels, rather than attending only to the linear sequence, as McCloud and many subsequent critics have done. Sequentiality is a cornerstone of current conceptualizations of the form, and, as we shall see, the network model that has here been used to evaluate and contest that focus has further implications for how we theorize the makeup and operations of the comics medium.

Chapter Six

Sequentiality as Realism

Conceptualizing comics in terms of linear sequencing does not provide quite the scope it is often credited with for differentiating comics from other narrative media. Nor does this understanding of the form offer a sufficient basis for explicating how we read and process these texts. As *Watchmen* and *Metronome* have shown, any demarcation of the relationship between (text) space and (story) time will only ever be typical, not definitive, and the medium facilitates much greater narrative diversity than the "space equals time" rule suggests. As has been mentioned, and will be further demonstrated in Chapter Seven, the various facets of visual signification are not so constrained as the linguistic system. This is particularly true of comics' sequentiality, and though broad *trends* exist for arranging panels to suggest progressing moments in time, there are manifold other possibilities for constructing a narrative within the subdivided page space. It is in exploiting this two-dimensional aspect that comics themselves present a compelling challenge to conceptions of the form as essentially sequential. This challenge extends beyond the effects of simultaneity and of threaded networks of interrelation, for there exists a variety of possibilities for constructing reading pathways that create complex and very visible webs on the page. The work of Chris Ware exploits the deducible nature of visual signification to make complex, intricate, often explicit use of comics' structural web, and in doing so creates an alternative to what might best be thought of as the "naturalism" of the linear narrative sequence.

The emphasis on linear sequencing props up the comparison between comics and language by effectively pinning down the temporal basis of (spoken) language into a similarly linear, but spatial, sequence on the page. However, we have seen that text-space and story time cannot be so simplistically and directly mapped onto one another as this account suggests. Emphasizing the essentially one-dimensional linear sequence undersells the very facet of comics that in fact distinguishes it from other narrative forms: its two-dimensional basis on the page. The concept of "sequential art" downplays the *simultaneity* of the sequentially arranged units on the page, which critics regularly acknowledge but rarely foreground in sequence-centered definitions of the form. Unlike the shots and scenes of film and theater, which are two-dimensional in themselves but that are viewed in transit and strictly one at a time, comics' segments are visible simultaneously and, as the split panel device shows, can enter into correspondence to the extent they act like units, interrupting and diverting a sequential reading. Comics criticism underemphasizes this valid point of distinction by aligning the conception of comics' formal makeup with narrative linearity. All narrative forms progress sequentially, but while the likes of film and theater progress temporally, offering a single window onto the world of the work, comics panels participate in both a sequential narrative and the totality of the page layout. All narrative forms can, analeptically or proleptically, override their diegetic sequencing, but as we have seen, only comics can potentially override *textual* progression.

Ware's "Big Tex" strip turns an entire page into one big split panel, a technique traceable to Frank King's *Gasoline Alley* in the 1930s (Raeburn 2004: 4). A full-page depiction of a backyard is subdivided into panels representing segments of the scene at various points in time (Fig. 6.1). To say time is represented spatially here would be a lazy formulation: text space maps onto story space, the entire page acting as a "window" onto one scene, and each panel's temporal location is represented through its content. The larger narrative, over passing years, is indicated by the changing seasons, growing sapling, timeworn and recent graves, crumbling house, and conversational snippets—but not by space *per se*. Read according to the conventional z-pathway, the narrative unfolds backwards, adhering to the prototypical mapping of text space onto story time that many critics promote to a formal definition (Chute 2008: 452, 2009: 342).[1] However, this surface conventionality belies the actual experience of reading the strip: with its sparse cues and yawning indeterminate shifts in diegetic time, the reader is not disposed to read "Big Tex" from start to finish and then stop. Given its brevity, which places the whole piece before the reader's gaze on a single page, the strip encourages scanning, retracing, and hopping around (something the printed medium particularly facilitates [Eisner 1985: 80]). The piece is not grasped merely by "filling in" the gaps between adjacent panels, but by deducing the relevance of each fragment of content to all the others, no matter their proximity and order: the vertically contiguous third and sixth panels, for example, are best comprehended as a correlated pair, the instruction "now you take care of this place, y'hear?" jarring with the later dilapidation of the house, which occurs earlier in

6.1 Chris Ware, "Big Tex," *Acme Novelty Library Number 7* (Seattle: Fantagraphics, 1996), p. 28.

the reading pathway but needs to be interpreted in light of the (textually) later panel. The simultaneity of these fragments renders the house a unified form on the page, poignantly emphasizing the disparity between the segments. The reader must locate each segment within a diegetic time frame in order to understand the strip, but the sequential movement back through time, which obviates this diegetic placement, does not account for the strip's distinctive impact so much as the segmentivity and simultaneity, which are the special preserve of the form.

If anything, this full-page split panel technique plays to the potentially ambiguous connection between text space and story time, by representing a unified space that endures through various time shifts, while fracturing that space to suggest the passage of time over a given space. The whole image persists in the reader's peripheral vision, even as we move through its various segments, deducing time shifts from their content. It is comics' narrative breakdown, plausibly (but rarely) proposed as a defining feature of the form (Harvey 1996: 109, 2009: 38), which inscribes shifts in story time onto text space. Groensteen has suggested that the English term "breakdown" is insufficient for conveying the "cutting out" implied by the French *decoupage* (Groensteen 2008: 90), which describes not only the apportioning of story content into discrete panels, but the demarcation of a particular viewpoint by each panel (that is to say, whatever sliver of the story world is visible implies an "off-screen"; as with film, what we are shown and from what vantage point matters). "Big Tex" exploits both elements of narrative breakdown, cutting out segments that fit into a larger composition and showing potent snippets from an expansive fictive time frame. Crucially, it is narrative breakdown—segmentivity, rather than sequentiality—that carves out distinct temporal locations within the world of the work, and the simultaneity of these segments, which the form peculiarly affords, is here exploited to great effect. This use of narrative breakdown signals the potentially complex relationship between text and diegesis, as well as tying fragmentary panels into a networked totality. Thus, despite its apparently conventional gridding and straightforward progression backwards, the strip actually demonstrates that two-dimensional narrative breakdown distinguishes comics from other, strictly sequential narrative forms.

The simplicity, albeit deceptive, of "Big Tex" is atypical of Ware, whose compositional style tends toward the variously sized panels and uneven, yet scrupulously neat tessellation showcased below (Fig. 6.2). The differently sized panels disrupt the default z-pathway, and, particularly on the recto, the entire page is consumed as a kind of tableau. The reader naturally groups similarly composed panels into segments, but there is no fixed prescription for processing these segments in a particular order. The eye gathers the three panels straddling the spine that depict Jimmy's father, and only from here moves up to the upper left row that would be the usual starting point for the next page. The image of the hand on the shoulder, repeated down the right-hand column, leads the eye with it, so that the reader arches around the central panel. Despite this perceptible trajectory, the page must be pondered. It can only be comprehended upon careful consideration of all the segments as part of a symbolic whole, not a series of "moments" read through linearly. Within the rerouted reading

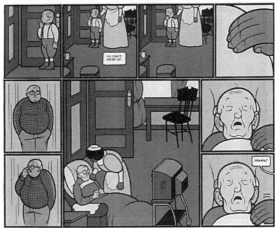

6.2 Chris Ware, *Jimmy Corrigan: The Smartest Kid on Earth* (London: Jonathan Cape, 2001), np. Images appear as double spread in original.

order, there is no sense in which the reader moves through fictive time while moving over space. In fact, we do not really progress through story time, but rather view it symbolically collapsed in on itself, past metaphorically resonating with present through a literal, physical simultaneity on the page: on the verso, Jimmy's grandfather as a child responds to a knock at the door and, in the adjacent panel behind a screen door, we see Jimmy's father in late middle-age.

The shifting between late-nineteenth century and contemporary narrative threads that takes place in these pages is not a jump cut of the kind that would broadly comply with the "space equals time" axiom, but works by a kind of staggered splicing that is sustained across the page, representing past infiltrating present in a highly symbolic way. This reaches its peak in the palimpsestic central panel on the recto. In the right-hand column, the hand of the black maid on the shoulder of Jimmy's grandfather as a child is echoed in the hand of his black adoptive sister, Amy, on the shoulder of the same man in old age. These "moments" are compressed in the central panel in which the maid in cap and apron places a hand on the shoulder of the old man slumped in front of the TV in an easy chair. That Amy turns out to be a biological descendent of this maid adds a dynastic echo to the visual repetition of the hand-on-shoulder image. The layering of narrative threads in the central panel is highly suggestive of the passage of time across (or within) static space. Time collapses, and through this abstracted and non-naturalist portrayal the key theme of resurgent family history is neatly encapsulated: the violation of the "space equals time" principle proves lucidly eloquent.

Layering temporal locations in a single panel complicates the diegesis. The assumption that panels house fictive moments, which pass by as we progress through them, suggests a certain critical credulity with regard to the illusion of realism comics can create. In collapsing the fictive temporal sequence, Ware casts off this illusory realism. The panel below (Fig. 6.3), in which a girl returns to her childhood bedroom at different stages in life, sleeping in a different spot each time, provides an illuminating analogy: the different positions in the room, pertaining to different times in her life, help "keep all the pieces in place." The segmentation of the room space imposes a sense of order, just as the segmentation of a narrative into panels creates a sense of order in comics. Crucially, though, this is a *conceptual* order. Intangible memories are kept in alignment through their organization into different points around the room, and fictive time lines are ordered through their arrangement on the page, but the potentially fluid relationship between page space and story time allows for revealing disruptions in the illusion of a consistent diegetic world organized spatially. The accumulation of time within one panel here represents a conceptual co-presence of past and present, complicating the diegesis through a palimpsestic overlaying that the form's two-dimensional constitution well affords. It is the "all at once" (Varnum & Gibbons 2001: xi, Raeburn 2004: 25, Versaci 2008: 16) aspect of this two-dimensional text space that distinguishes comics from other linear narrative forms and on which conceptualizations of this "unique" form would be most appropriately based.

6.3 Chris Ware, *Acme Novelty Library Number 18* (Chicago: Acme Novelty Library, 2007), np.

The tangling of fictive time lines does not, of course, genuinely break the diegesis. For that to happen, elements from outside the story world would need to be drawn into it, and the comics form has a number of ways of blurring the line between the intra- and the extra-diegetic. Panel frames, for example, are inscribed on the same surface as characters and settings, but tacitly understood as existing on a different plane. However, in a strip from Winsor McCay's *Little Sammy Sneeze*, the central character's violent sneeze shatters the panel borders that contain him (McCay 2007: 62). In McCay's dazzlingly virtuoso *Dream of the Rarebit Fiend*, one episode shows an enraged lover shredding the panel from the inside, tearing at its edges till the strip dissipates into a drawn heap of tattered fragments (McCay 2006: 79). Similar is the invasion of the interframe space by the eponymous hero of Marc-Antoine Mathieu's *Julius Corentin Acquesfacques* series, who traverses this space to get back to an earlier moment (Mathieu 1993: 28 cited in Miller 2007: 132). Such innovations truly disturb the presumed separation between page plane and story world. Of course, all forms can play with diegesis. But the simultaneous presence of extra-diegetic objects (such as caption and title subframes, and speech

6.4 Gianni De Luca, *Hamlet*, trans. by Barbara Graille (Paris: Les Humanoïdes Associés, 1980), pp. 18–19.

balloon and panel borders) and diegetic elements on the same page surface means comics can do this in fairly form-specific ways—which interesting area unfortunately falls outside the remit of the present study.
Though this diegetic play operates on a different level to the confusion
of times lines examined above, the two are analogous in that they both
disturb the illusion of realism. By compressing multiple fictive "moments"
into a single panel, the impression of a "window" onto a consistent world
is destabilized, and any assertion that time and space are related according
to hard and fast rules undermined. The trends toward which the medium
tends function like the "realism" or "naturalism" of prose and painting,
commonly used conventions read with ease, but by no means therefore a
neutral reflection of reality. *Defining* an art form according to such conventions is extremely limiting, and Ware's work demonstrates how far the
default practice of lining up panels to stand in for a sequence of moments
can be shelved in favor of less "realist," more interpretive strategies.

Paul Gravett asks of panels such as Fig. 6.3, comparable to Cohn's polymorphic panels in depicting the same figure multiple times, "If we are
able to suspend belief as far as perspective is concerned and accept the

illusion of a three-dimensional world represented on a two-dimensional plane, why not suspend belief on the level of time-based perspective and accept that a multiple-instant 'reality' can be portrayed in a single frame?" (Gravett 2008: 27). This question aptly compares the "time-based perspective" of comics that McCloud and others elevate to a structural absolute with the learned conventions by which we interpret perspective drawings. Gravett raises this issue in relation to Gianni de Luca's convention-defying adaptation of *Hamlet*, which all but does away with traditional panels (Fig. 6.4). Narrative breakdown remains key, but action is segmented not into discrete panels but through multiple representations of the same figures arranged in smooth visual trajectories that create a tangible sense of movement across a page. The roving figures seen above, choreographed like actors on a stage according to Gravett (2008: 29), form fluid reading pathways that the reader can hardly resist following. Though these layouts are unorthodox, the "eye streams" they form on the page guide the reader into interpreting broken down movements as a smooth flow of action, creating an impressive illusion of animation from static pictures.

This technique, superficially the same as Ware's multi-instant panels, has a very different effect in de Luca's hands. Where de Luca plots segments to embody a serpentine flow of movement creating an illusion of a multi-instant "reality," Ware's "'dead' [. . .] mechanical" (Wolk 2007: 123) style conjoins distant points in time in a way that actually foregrounds abstraction. Fig. 6.3 enmeshes four preceding, diegetically dispersed depictions of this girl in her bedroom by repeating them compressed into a single panel, thus creating an impossible image—or, rather, an overt symbol that defies the illusion of a consistent reality, but still makes perfect, *metaphorical* sense. Properly speaking, this panel functions not as a symbol in the Peircean sense, but as a *metaphor icon*. Charles S. Peirce's distinction between symbolic (arbitrary), iconic (motivated), and indexical (direct, causative) signs can sometimes get lost in colloquial, idiomatic usages of terms like "icon" and "symbol." (McCloud, for example, often uses "icon" as a catch-all, interchangeably used to describe words and images, while "symbol" is invoked as a type of "icon," referring to simplified images [1993: 28, 2000: 1–2]; it would be unfair to call this usage erroneous since McCloud simply does not intend these terms in their instituted, technical sense, but it is unfortunate that the precise distinctions they afford are thus often muddled.) Strictly speaking, as there is a logical relation between the composition of Fig. 6.3 and its significance, it is not an arbitrary symbol but a motivated icon. It is not an icon of the *image* type, the subdivision of iconicity that describes representation through straightforward material likeness, and which we tend to conflate with the entire category of motivated signs in defining it. Rather it is an icon of the *metaphor* type, depicting a representative character of a signified. That is, the depiction is suggestive of the abstract idea but does not (could not) embody physical likeness. These distinctions prove useful in checking critical tendencies to claim that schematic pictures, such as Ware's, become "like words" in their abstraction, and the issue will be further explicated in the next chapter, which deals with the breadth of types of sign that exist under the banner of "visual signification."

The point to be emphasized here is that in this shared technique of polymorphism there is scope for both an illusory representation of a consistent story world and a more conceptual visual representation the reader can nonetheless interpret though it represents an abstract idea more than a fictive "moment." This kind of conceptual representation pertains to the allusion already made that the "space equals time" principle is comics' equivalent of naturalism. In art theory "it has become an accepted fact that naturalism is a form of convention" (Gombrich 1952: 305), and I would suggest that the mapping of (text) space onto (representations of fictive) time functions in a comparable way. Easy to read, familiar, and so readily grasped as to seem "invisible," using serial panels to stand in for fictive moments works like the naturalism of prose or painting in encouraging us to read *through* the medium and share in the illusion of a fictive reality. But just as Western perspective drawing does not "define" the art of painting, nor the construct of realist prose constrain literature, so comics are not defined by the convention that so many critics elevate to a formal definition. Delving into Ware's work further will show exactly how far the form can deviate from this set of conventions, both in terms of representing concepts rather than fictive stretches of time, and in constructing convoluted, and even non-linear reading pathways from the arrangement of segments.

The composition below (Fig. 6.5), exemplary of the *Building Stories* series from which it is drawn, maps story segments onto a three-dimensional building plan, and it is through this network of related strands, rather than linear progression, that the narrative as a whole is elaborated. There are sections of this overtly representational diagram that work as sequential strips, progressing linearly and, if not "containing" moments, then standing in for an action or event in the diegetic world. But these strip sections form a complicated web, whose significance depends more

6.5 Chris Ware, *Acme Novelty Library Number 16* (Chicago: Acme Novelty
Library, 2005), np.

on their relationship to one another than on either reading sequence or
diegetic order. There is, for example, no easy way through the upper right
section that depicts a neighbor lusting after the story's protagonist. It is
useful to fit this segment into a general diegetic time frame, but it is not
necessary to pin these panels into an exact sequence (whether textual or
diegetic), leading as they do in multiple directions and merging into multiple nodes on this network. We naturally begin in the leftmost upper-
most panel, but from here may move rightwards to close in on the man

mooching in his room, or downwards (following an explicatory arrow, and moving through a fight scene, where we may or may not pause) to a "reverse" image of the first panel that shows this man staring out of the same window but from the outside. When we reach the section showing this man fantasizing over the neighbor he has just seen, it can be followed downwards (presuming we enter it after following the top row) before expanding slightly leftwards into increasingly lascivious musings, or, alternatively, the reader can reverse back on themselves and re-enter the network via the close-up of a smashed picture that plugs into the aforementioned fight scene in which that picture is smashed. Attempts to describe this intricate network soon make clear that verbal summary is less illuminating than the visual map itself (I cannot, for example, safely direct readers to the "seventh" panel and expect concurrence). It is less important to construct a linear sequence through this piece than it is to understand the relationships between its various parts. Though the basic information of the strip (man is in turbulent relationship, lusts after neighbor) can be regurgitated in prose, the non-linear strip, with its multiple intersections and bi-directional pathways, more aptly conjures up the tangle of mundane encounters, secret yearning, and social disconnection in which Ware specializes: even in the proximity of the building, lives lived literally on top of each other are sectioned into lonely pockets.

This narrative web can only be understood as a holistic composition, and the sequence in which we approach each section is not always important. Ware often leads the reader down dead ends, uses visual cues to guide them in unexpected directions, and asks them to cross and re-cross other narrative threads: the sequential reading protocol of prose is flouted in the extreme. Cohn has shown empirically that comics readers have recourse to hierarchized strategies for deciphering complex layouts (2008), which guide our reading. However, like the mutable conventions of pictorial realism, these can be flouted, forcing readers to guess and test potentialities until "a consistent interpretation has been found" (Gombrich 1952: 204). For example, Cohn found that, when faced with a multiplicity of possible directions, readers prefer to move rightward even if this also entails an upward movement, resorting to a downward reading direction only when no rightward option is available (2008: 6). This strip's start and end points are made clear by their traditional top-left and bottom-right locations, the words "and so" further indicating the conclusion of the strip in two wryly juxtaposed scenes: the lecherous boyfriend is huddled beside his girlfriend, while the subject of his fantasy, who gave that girlfriend her conciliatory flowers for free, is upstairs alone as usual. Everything between the obvious start point and this poignant, even bitter end is constructed like a multiply-looped Möbius strip. The girlfriend on the street corner in the bottom right is "amplified" in the inset strip across the bottom that follows her into the shop on the corner, while a thought bubble emanating from her head in this strip leads back to the fight that prompts the flower-buying. The fight is heard through the floor by the neighbor above, who is inserted into the building backdrop by an arrow. Another arrow ties the boyfriend post-fight into the middle-tier apartment where he watches his neighbor leave, and this arrow bisects the fight itself, thus drawing it into play. Though there is an implicit sequence to events and clear entry and exit points, it proves to be the connections between segments, not linear sequencing, that elucidates the story. The complex layering of simultaneous storylines relies upon the diagramming of interwoven relationships to make clear what traditional naturalism would struggle to so evocatively embody.

Building Stories, of course, recalls Georg Perec's architecturally structured *Life: A User's Manual*, but also resonates with the connection Art Spiegelman makes between the Latin root of "story"—*historia*—which refers to both "picture" and the horizontal division of a building. The conflation is derived from the placement of narrative stained glass windows in churches, which meant that each building story was literally a row of pictures (cited in Gatti 2008: np). The knock-on metaphor of comics-as-buildings could play to simplistic ideas about panels as windows onto the illusory world-of-the-work, but Ware's architectural plans, which weave a complex narrative web, do this metaphor more justice. His maps draw segments that are both spatially (textually) and temporally (diegetically) dispersed into dense networks whose relationships, rather than sequential reading order, explicate the story. These diagrammatical strips, so unlike iconic realism, are nonetheless motivated—and deducible—rather than symbolic, wholly conventional signs like words: we feel our way round these circuitous compositions, responding to visually embodied links such as arrows or "eye streams," which disclose conceptual connections rather than a diegetic, temporal order. The building-based strip above compares with the convoluted family tree that charts the aforementioned biological connection between Jimmy Corrigan and Amy (Fig. 6.6). The functional information of this spread (that Amy's grandfather's half-sister was also half-sister to James the Elder [Jimmy's grandfather]) is dramatized through double-ended arrows, a timeline of headshots that moves

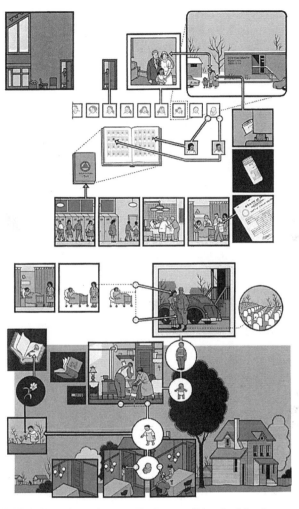

6.6 Chris Ware, *Jimmy Corrigan: The Smartest Kid on Earth* (London: Jonathan Cape, 2001), np.

backwards in time as the reader follows the usual reading direction, and a circuitous reading pathway. The first page alone links a wedding photo to an adoption scene, this scene via a birth certificate to Amy's birth, and her birth *back* through the history of her teenage parents; from their yearbook, we are led to the timeline, showing Amy at various ages, and from here we reconnect with the wedding photo where she is seen as a girl *and* with the page's natural entry point showing her in adulthood.

This intricate network not only elucidates this complex family tree, but aesthetically evokes the tangle of numerous lives, secretly (and silently) intertwined.

In examining the varied, distinctly non-realist ways text space can be used to articulate story time, I have alluded to the ways comics artists can create reading paths, guiding the reader through deducible or embodied connections that deviate from the conventionalized linear sequence of prose. Of course, comics can and do utilize the convention of the z-pathway, but as visual signification can *create* signs more readily than language (as has been mentioned, and will be fully argued in Chapter Seven), a range of strategies is available for enticing the reader into connecting segments in ways they have not necessarily been taught. As seen in the above compositions (this word seems more appropriate here than "strip"), Ware occasionally resorts to arrows, sometimes subverting the guidance they appear to offer by making them double-ended and thus multi-directional. Arrows have been termed "primal" (Foucault 1983: 33) signs in that their shape directly encodes their meaning, and Ware manages to invent other, similarly deducible ways of leading his readers in the desired direction, creating from elements in his texts "shape that formulates order" (Foucault 1983: 33).

In the strip below (Fig. 6.7), the speech bubble-like "tail" that anchors the shrilly large and vibrant "RING" to some off-camera source serves in part to direct the reader into the adjacent panel to which it points. (The "staggering" effect of the left-hand block, whose horizontal divide does not align with the lower frame of the third panel in the top row, disrupts the traditional grid here. Though the preference for moving rightward before downward, which Cohn identifies (2008: 6), also alleviates the potential confusion, Ware's additional visual guidance assists the transition.) The "K-KLK" sound effect of the answerphone sutures these two panels with a visible stitch across the interframe space, while the huddle of blue and white thought bubbles, one of which also strays into the interframe space, creates a visual cluster that guides the eye smoothly into the adjacent panel, mitigating against the possible temptation to travel downwards into the lower left panel that sits in neat alignment with the first two. The reverse direction of the center-right segment, with its black background, is easily indicated through discrete arrows that bulge across the panel frames, but the steady repetition of this composition and the disorientating backwards motion of this cluster aptly convey the pulsing flurry of Jimmy's confused and panicky thoughts here. Deceptively conventional

6.7 Chris Ware, *Jimmy Corrigan: The Smartest Kid on Earth* (London: Jonathan Cape, 2001), np.

looking at first glance, this strip has a definite reading order lacking in the warren-like network above, but still manages to encode an unexpected reading pathway, not through learned conventions but through the intuitive, deducible guidance offered by physical shapes on the page.

A further exemplar of embodied trajectories is the *Building Stories* composition below (Fig. 6.8), which incorporates a literal march back through time in a winding blue "caterpillar" that paints a dotted line for the reader to follow. For all its meandering reading pathway, this strip is a very smooth ride (which is not always the case; Ware's layouts can take some fathoming). Starting with the title text and following the obvious route through the strip below and the content beneath that, the reader is led by long, snaking arrows through a column of lexias and visual symbols, and to a characteristic "timeline" following the building's landlady from girlhood to her current situation as a "lonely old woman." Another wavery white line positions her within the building, and then guides the reader to the foot of this winding "string of renters" on whom she relies for financial support. Following this bold, blue eye stream guides us through a series of lexias that actually read backwards *up* the page, ascending through a fragmented description of "a fifty-year long caterpillar" that has "clattered and wormed its way through her doorways and hallways . . . stepping . . . stomping . . . slamming . . . ." At this point, another thin guiding line takes over from the "stepping . . . stomping" chain of legs to take us back up to a

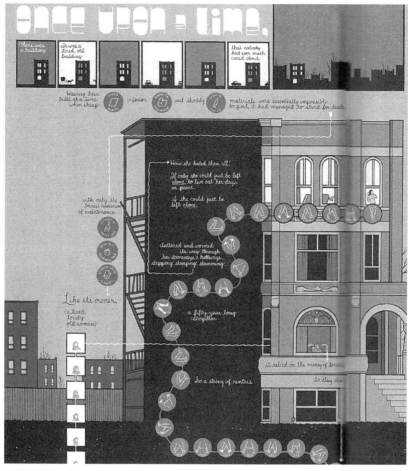

6.8 Chris Ware, *Acme Novelty Library Number 18* (Chicago: Acme Novelty Library, 2007), np.

conventionally arranged expanse of text. This reads: "How she hated them all. If only she could just be left <u>alone</u>, to live out her days in peace . . . if she could just be left <u>alone</u> . . . ," and the trailing off of this final lexia, which leaves the reader momentarily dangling in search of direction, effectively hands the gaze back over to the marching caterpillar of renters, who continue along the traditional left-right path until they reach—indeed, align with—the current tenant, a young woman fearful of the old lady's fate, who feels "entirely, 100%, horrifyingly, alone" (Ware 2007: np). The underlining of that one word "alone" in the landlady's thoughts is hardly necessary to emphasize the powerful conjunction of the longed-for and dreaded isolation. The heterogeneous system of visual signification (if, indeed, it can be thought of as one single system, rather than a complex of intersecting systems) has recourse to a multiplicity of devices to guide the reader round the page. Though comics may appeal to our tendency to follow prose's conventionalized z-path, they equally may flout this convention, using the likes of encoded, primal arrows or embodied, deducible eye streams. Ultimately, the arrangement of segments is the choice of the artist, not the rule of the system. Through a canny exploitation of comics' segmentivity and the simultaneity of those elements, the artist can guide the reader through reading pathways that are anything but conventional or linear, and elicit great aesthetic effect from the arrangement and apportioning of story information.

The snaking blue discs in this strip recall de Luca's snaking procession of Hamlets in that each simply carries the reader's eye automatically, relying little on prior tutoring to prompt movement in a particular direction. Ware concretizes reading pathways in ways that make lexias do an awful lot of work, both visually and because they themselves only make sense when assimilated with proximate lexias in a linked series. The circuitous, board game-like composition below (Fig. 6.9) is typical: the natural entry point is the large, clear center, and from here lexias lead the eye round the design, sequences of words tying together the scattered parts of this web. An arrow leads outwards from the end of the sentence in this initial circle to a text box, whose own final two words are repeated adjacently, carrying us further along the page. The rotated G (that almost, in its curving shape, asks us by itself to swivel the book round and proceed with our viewpoint once again revolved) is repeated, thus carrying us down into the expostulation "God!" from whence we move through a mini-strip to the imagined crossroads of "my life." Though multiple arrows point to three different places this life "could go," only one way out of this really makes full sense, and that is to opt for the leftmost box (looking now at the page on its side), which sits in a three-quarter circle with the other two, connected via the curving text that semantically continues from the thought bubbles leading up from the miniature strip to make the full statement: "Every possible direction my life could go seems utterly unbearable and repulsive to me . . . ." We are prompted to follow the page this way as much because it yields a full sentence as because the forms on the page guide us this way. Just as Gombrich describes us doing in interpreting unfamiliar painting styles through guided guesswork (1952: 204), here we test the various possibilities and are led to follow the path that yields consistent semantic

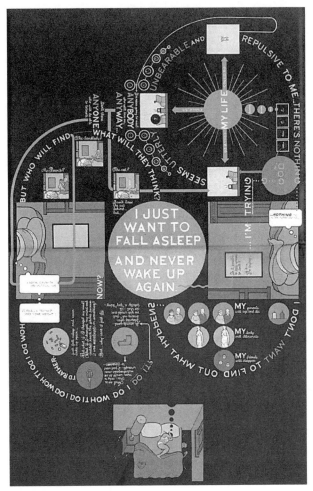

6.9 Chris Ware, *Acme Novelty Library Number 18* (Chicago: Acme Novelty Library, 2007), np.

sense: the text itself *embodies* the pathway, and the direction it is written in dictates where the reader goes next. In this way, Ware's strips are not open to the contents-free schema that Cohn uses to explore readers' approaches to complex layouts (2008). Groensteen too, following Henri van Lier, proposes the "multiframe," the sum total of the frames and borders that subdivide a text's page space and organize content, as the basis for understanding the form (2006: 24). Ware's strips resist reduction to a multiframe "cleansed" (Groensteen 2006: 24) of iconic and verbal content.

Graphic textual content *is* form, with writing, necessarily sequential, creating on the page visual forms that guide our reading.

Words structure this network. The circular lexia just discussed concludes with the beginning of the next clause in these (visually) churning thoughts, "There's nothing." Another rotated G and ellipsis leading to a proximate thought bubble prompts us to turn the page again and continue "nothing to look forward to." From here, still under the influence of the preceding circular formation, we push on through the reflected arc below: "I don't want to find out what happens," which is, once again, a semantically logical follow-on.[2] This particular section of the composition is read according to a negotiation between what reading conventions prompt us to try, how visual forms elicit our gaze, and what semantic sense confirms as correct. The route we take is interrupted by revolutions of icons and text on the page, asides, dead ends, and nodes leading in alternative directions. We nevertheless deduce a pathway, not by following a conventionalized sequence, but by feeling our way along possible paths, resorting to a process of trial and error when convention and intuitive cues are lacking, until led to a satisfying conclusion that allows us to draw the fragments we are presented with into a larger meaningful whole. Representation is once again highly diagrammatic and metaphorical, and does not deal in a straightforward mapping of diegetic time, whose passage is *conceptually*, rather than iconically represented here. It is fear of time passing, and not fictive time itself, that we read in this complex and interlinked web of revolving, circuitous anxieties, an abstracted, intangible signified, but one that is adroitly mapped in Ware's multi-directional, multi-layered composition.

Text is also integral to the *Quimby the Mouse* composition below (Fig. 6.10). Gene Kannenberg provides an insightful close reading of how lexias both guide the gaze and are in themselves significant here: the reversed reading direction leads us backwards after the initial "title" line; the self-consciousness of the disingenuous backwards statement in the center is betrayed by the red left-right keyword; the superimposition of "anymore" and "make me," along with the alignment and coloring that pull the single sign "you" into two contrary statements, dramatizes conflicting emotions; the slaloming reading direction and Expressionist lilting of the architectural design similarly indicate oscillating sentiments (Kannenberg 2001). But having already considered words' role in creating reading pathways, and elsewhere dealt with the pretext this radically physical "imagetext" offers for denying verbal-visual distinctions (in which Kannenberg

6.10 Chris Ware, "I'm A Very Generous Person," *Quimby the Mouse* (London: Jonathan Cape, 2003), p. 56.

participates), I want to look at two other aspects of this strip that challenge the notion of comics as Sequential Art. The word "being" that at first glance appears to float unanchored is, we later notice, aligned in a neat vector with the words "can't stand" and the less obtrusive, overlaid "alone." There is no fixed point in the reading protocol where this hovering, symbolically unarticulated phrase, "can't stand being alone," is intended to be read. It is detached, yet omnipresent, read in relation to the rest of the strip rather than at a particular point, and offers the whole piece an additional flavor. The scattering of extra-diegetic Quimbies (sprinkling money; hammering, propping up, and dangling from letters; fuming off-stage below left) are also pertinent to the issues discussed in this chapter. These avatars are not incidental. They add to the intricacy and multi-layering of the strip, foregrounding, through their non-natural style and extra-diegetic positioning, the highly conceptual nature of Ware's representational technique. They too have no prescribed position in the reading protocol, reading as part of a composition but not a sequence, and rupturing rather than partaking in the illusion of a diegetic story world. Here again, then, it is clear that the relationship of fragments within a total composition, rather than the sequence in which those fragments are read, is crucial, for many of these fragments stand in for more abstract concepts rather than representing fictive moments.

The sheer variety of different sorts of networked relationships seen here casts considerable doubt on the "space equals time" epithet that commonly distills the critical focus on and elevation of sequentiality within comics theory. These include breakdowns that ensnare disparate (fictive) time frames into the same space, whether a unitary composition (Fig. 6.1) or single panel (Fig. 6.3), so past and present jostle and collide on the page. Other compositions abandon traditional panels for an intricate map of relationships in which the connections between elements, rather than a rigidly prescriptive reading order, elaborate the larger narrative. I have placed greater emphasis here on narrative breakdown—segmentivity, and the simultaneity of those segments on the page—as the feature that truly differentiates the comics form from other narrative media. It is that facet of this particular printed form that allows comics to complicate, even override the inevitable sequential progression of their narratives.

It is this ability to disrupt textual sequence that makes the question of reading pathways a pertinent one. Within comics, both encoded and intuitive or embodied connectives can be used to *create* reading pathways that differ from the conventional z-grid. This creation of signs on the fly, as opposed to *use* of preexisting signs, distinguishes the motivated (and therefore deducible) visual system from the arbitrary (and wholly learned) linguistic system. In demonstrating that relationships between segments are often more pertinent than linear progression through those segments, particularly in Ware's work with its unusual level of abstraction, it becomes clear that readers frequently do not move through story time as they take in different parts of the strip, but instead respond to the whole composition. Textual, pictorial, and abstracted visual elements are all riddled with

- Shelley

6.11 George Herriman, *Krazy & Ignatz: 1919–1921*, ed. by Bill Blackbeard (Seattle: Fantagraphics, 2010), p. 95 (original publication date 10 October 1920).

significance, but do not necessarily "naturalistically" represent elements of the story world. As well as advocating the web analogy, I have proposed that McCloud's pithy definition of comics might better be conceived of as a kind of realism principle, at least loosely comparable with the rules of perspective that inform—but do not constrain—Western art. But this "convention of the real" (Barthes 1967b): 73), as fabricated as the perception of depth on a two-dimensional canvas or the "degree zero" of self-effacing realist prose, in no way defines or constrains the form, though it may function as a kind of default mode.

It may appear rather self-serving to use the work of Chris Ware to disprove the sequential basis for understanding comics, given that his work is so manifestly boundary-breaking—the virtuoso exception that might prove the rule. For this reason I want to conclude with a comparative example from *Krazy Kat*, also a non-naturalist and convention-defying body of work, though not so radically structurally extraordinary. To some extent, sequentiality is key to the reading of this strip (Fig. 6.11), but it is not a linear, panel-to-panel reading. In addition to the breakdown into eight panels, three visual trajectories cut *across* the sequence: Ignatz's machinations run across the top of the strip, the appearance of Krazy runs along the bottom, and numerous ancillary characters offer comment on the ascent of the brick, creating an eye stream that reads rightwards and *upwards* across the sequence. The reader's gaze is guided into following each of these trajectories in turn, and though we understand that each towering panel stands in for a fictive instant, with the triple-level action in each one to be interpreted as simultaneous, we do not move through the eight panels in linear fashion. Instead, we scan and rescan the various relationships between the various segments (panels and actions) in this composition. We connect the consecutive actions of each trajectory, the tiered actions within each panel, *and* the unfolding fictive moments that each whole panel represents. This composition does not complicate narrative time as Ware often does, and is extremely simple in its representation of a coherent story world, but it nonetheless functions as a network, rather than a sequence: exploiting the possibilities specifically offered by the comics form, it gains its aesthetic impact by partially overriding sequential narrative progression.

PART THREE
Images as Language

Chapter Seven

Asterios Polyp and the Structure of Visual Images

Much reference has been made to the broad analogies critics often make between linguistic and visual signification. There exists a marked critical drift towards framing the distinctions between visual and verbal as somehow specious. Both the simplified, abstracted pictorial style of cartoon drawing and the comics medium's disparate non-pictorial elements (such as speech bubbles, panel borders, and the like) are suggested to function like language. These elements are often seen as being "as abstract and symbolic as words" (Hatfield 2009: 133). For many critics, when an image's iconic resemblance is pared down and schematized, and/or where a high degree of convention underpins a visual sign-form, then the distinction between images and language diminishes, with the cartoon visual sign being recognized and read like a word (McCloud 2000: 2, Raeburn 2004: 7, Cates 2010: 96). (There is an interesting logical leap, noted by Cohn [2005: 239–41], between this proposition that certain kinds of conventionalized abstracted images are comparable with words, and the follow-on claim that the comics form *itself* is therefore a language, somewhat akin to treating the system of the English language and the literary form of the novel as synonymous.) But, as we shall see, important distinctions persist between the sorts of conventionalized, abstracted shorthand used within comics and the system of verbal language. There can be identified, within discussions around convention, abstraction, and arbitrariness in these signifying systems, a certain lack of precision that facilitates suggestions that abstract or conventional visual signs operate in a manner akin to words. A closer focus on the facets of the visual system alluded to throughout— namely its continuously gradated, rather than discrete, nature, and relative lack of constraint by a preexisting *langue*—thus enables a convincing challenge to be brought against such claims.

 I have already argued that language's constitution in arbitrary minimal units and its constraining *langue* are both crucial to explaining how

certain literary operations work, but such assertions necessitate a coun-
ter-demonstration that visual signification is constituted differently, and
that this formal makeup is equally pertinent to its workings. The aim in
undertaking this is to show how the conventions of cartooning, and the
ways we read and interpret texts that utilize it, are misrepresented by critical accounts that equate the structural models of the verbal and visual
modes. As already mentioned, attempts have been made by some critics to delimit "units" consisting of individual marks or groups of marks,
which have an identifiable signified within the complex of a whole picture, such as the eyes or mouth of a character, and which can be likened
to the phonemes, morphemes, or sentences of verbal language.[1] These
attempts to decompose continuous visual forms into discrete units are, at
least, precise in their invocation of the original semiotic model—perhaps
in keeping with the structuralist focus of 1970s-era European approaches
to the comics form. Such exercises are rarer within Anglophone scholarship, although Harrison (1981) creates categories of "picts," "pictoforms,"
and "pictophrases" that map onto language's double-articulated building
blocks and larger semantic units—but without ever actually explicating
what items, forms, and figures within a picture he sees as corresponding
to these hypothetical levels. Attempts to find discrete, minimally meaningful units within the continuous gradations of visual signification have
obvious problems, though the lack of such attempts within Anglophone
scholarship might be argued to relate to a muted interest in the minutia
of semiotics, which Francophone criticism was already moving past when
Anglophone comics criticism began to emerge. Thus, the already-estab-
lished fact of comics' semiotic similarity to language is much vaunted, but
little explored within the latter field, which demonstrably tends toward
broad interpretations, positing codes, conventions, and representation as
adequate qualifiers of language; the precise semiotic specifics might well
seem to be a done deal. But significant objections can be raised against
this widely embraced tenet, against both the nebulous understanding of
linguistic structure that facilitates such broad comparisons and the more
detailed attempts to descriptively force images—and comics' cartoon
images in particular—into the semiotic model of language.

Drawing on Mort Walker's tongue-in-cheek "dictionary" of cartoon
shorthand, *The Lexicon of Comicana*, it can be shown how far these partially motivated, partially conventionalized signs can be likened to the arbitrary signs of language. The distinction between motivated and arbitrary
signs raises the issue, mentioned previously, of the potential for *making*

visual signs: visual signifiers can be invented on the page, their context and, more especially, their form imbuing them with significance, in contrast to the inherited system of language. Critics seeking visual equivalents to language's constitutive features seem to shore up the "linguistic imperialism" (Mitchell 1986: 63) of semiotics, which offers the language model as the basis for all systems. Broadly, there exist two key strategies for extending the semiotic model to images: the first, outlined above, sees some critics try and describe visual signification in the terms afforded by the original semiotic model; secondly, there are those who attempt reconfigure the model of language so that it better suits visual signification. Mitchell, Kress, and van Leeuwen all seek to shift emphasis onto material, contextual language as a way of dismissing the *langue*, thereby subtly adjusting the model of language so that it better accommodates visual images (Mitchell 1994: 97, Kress and van Leeuwen 1996: 9). Groensteen is rather more convincing in simply querying the assumption that all semiotic systems must have a *langue* (Groensteen 2006: 7), allowing that the initial model of language may not be applicable to all other systems without adjustment. In examining comics' visual elements, I would advocate just such an adjusted model for approaching visual signs, using the linguistic structure as a point of comparison for outlining a more precise and specific conception of the semiotic structure of images, whose continuity and motivation are as pertinent to their operations as language's discreteness and arbitrariness have been shown to be.

As ever, the intention here is not to posit either system as inherently superior or more apt for particular subjects or types of representation. Instead, I am taking aim at the perceptible defensiveness that has bequeathed to comics studies a critical framework constructed in order to promote the visual to the (perceived) higher status of language. The overstatement of sameness between visual and verbal springs from a critical history that at once has often sought to align the comics medium with literature and also to elevate its position within a supposed hierarchy of word and image. This attitude to the relationship of comics and images to language is implicitly challenged through a critique of the accepted commonalities between visual and verbal semiotic systems, and through a more rigorous application of the established source theory to a particular text—David Mazzucchelli's *Asterios Polyp*. In doing so, I hope to show that this more precise, semiotically driven dissection of comics' images better accounts for cartoon devices and the ways we interpret them, which demonstrably depend on properties specific to visual signification.

7.1 David Mazzucchelli, *Asterios Polyp* (New York: Pantheon, 2009), np.

It must be acknowledged that conventionalized visual signs do exist, and these do not strictly resemble the things they represent, but are instead read on the basis of prior knowledge. Though no one seriously invokes the terminology he creates, Walker's suggestion that the likes of speed lines ("hites" [1980: 30]) and sweat drops ("plewds" [1980: 28]) are readable signs whose significance depends on accepted, standardized practices is convincing. The bubbles floating round a character's head that indicate "drunk," for example, or the stars that signify a concussed daze, are not really interpreted deductively, but have become standardized, and are decoded through familiarity with the convention. Like language, such signs are culture-specific: the string of radiating zeds that signify "sleep" in Anglophone and European comics are replaced in Japanese manga by a bubble emanating from a character's nose (Sabin 1996: 228). However, conventionalized though these signs may be, there is a degree of motivation at work in many. Speed lines and the jagged, splayed shapes that represent impact (Fig. 7.1) are both, if not exactly deducible through resemblance, at least highly suggestive of their signifieds. Kunzle charts the development of these types of devices through the work of Wilhelm Busch, prior to whose work naturalized forms of speed lines, such as blown-back clothing or trails of water, had been the norm (Kunzle 1990: 351–55). Certain of these now-ubiquitous abstract forms are in a sense diagrammatic: speed lines plot a figure's trajectory from its origin, but in an allegorical way. The visual trace of the figure's passage is suggestive of the tangible swiftness of its movement. There is, therefore, a certain rationale behind the relation of signifier and signified here, that simply does not exist for words.

Speed lines here are labeled "diagrammatic" in the Peircean sense, and the technicality of this term is crucial. Unlike Saussure, who hypothetically posited all signs as arbitrary (and in fact queried the fitness of semiotics for describing "natural" signs, such as mime [Saussure 1983: 68]), Peirce differentiated between symbolic signs (arbitrary, purely conventional), iconic signs (motivated, representing through *some form* of likeness), and indexical signs (causal, based on real connection). As mentioned in the previous chapter, Peirce further subdivided the iconic category into different kinds of likeness. Image icons are those that materially resemble that which they represent (Magnussen 2000: 196, Peirce cited in Bergman & Paavola 2003: np). Basic interpretations of the iconic category tend to be skewed towards image icons, suggesting a discernible similarity of form defines the category as a whole. However, there exist other types of motivated "likeness." Diagrams represent through more abstract correspondence, showing "the relations [. . .] of the parts of one thing by analogous relations to their own parts" (Peirce cited in Bergman & Paavola 2003: np). A schematic tree, for example, embodies the relationships between multiple branches and supporting trunk, without looking very much like a tree; a mathematical diagram similarly encodes the correlations between related items; and cartoon speed lines conceptually map out the flight path of a rapidly moving object. The third category, metaphors, "represent[s] the representative character of a representamen" (Peirce cited in Bergman & Paavola 2003: np). Metaphor icons work by a kind of parallelism of attributes, exemplified by the image (to avoid confusion I will refer to the different categories of icon fully as "image icons" or "metaphor icons" to keep these phrases distinct from "images" and "metaphors" in their more usual sense) denoting impact above (Fig. 7.1). This jagged shape metaphorically apes both the reverberation of sound and the sharp jolt that resonates from the site of the impact. Walker's term "emanata" (1980: 28) is apt: these shapes imply a shockwave emanating outwards.

There are, then, distinctions to be drawn between different types of motivation. These are often lost in comics criticism, which tends to use terms like "icon," "symbol," and "sign" synonymously. When the likes of McCloud and Raeburn speak, respectively, of "lines evolving to become symbols in their own right" (McCloud 2000: 2) and "cartoon language" as a "set of culturally engrained symbols" (Raeburn 2004: 7), they are quite justifiably noting the *conventionality* of comics' shorthand, but in

7.2 David Mazzucchelli, *Asterios Polyp* (New York: Pantheon, 2009), np.

doing so fail to acknowledge the nuanced degrees of motivation that distinguish these familiar signs from both imagistic pictures and arbitrary words. While conceding that certain of these signs may be symbols in the true sense, representing purely by arbitrary, conventionalized association, I maintain that visual images tend towards motivation. This motivation may not always be straightforward resemblance, but there is still a "relation of reason" (Peirce cited in Bergman & Paavola 2003: np) between signifier and signified. Such a logical connection is shared with realistic (or semi-realistic, in the case of cartoons) pictorial signs but not with the arbitrary signs of language, which are never deducible or interpretable in the way visual signs often are. This motivation is pertinent in any elucidation of how cartoon visual devises work and proves to be as relevant to the system's operations as is the impact of language's arbitrariness on users.

Asterios Polyp's use of the cartoon drawing style and comics medium is highly imaginative, and illustrates just what scope there is for *creating* visual signs as an alternative to using ready-made ones. Coinage in language is rare, as the arbitrary system depends on mutual agreement for its effectiveness, but visual forms can amply insinuate their own significance

7.3 David Mazzucchelli, *Asterios Polyp* (New York: Pantheon, 2009), np.

without recourse to established associations. Over the course of his text, Mazzucchelli aligns particular colors and drawing styles with particular characters, using this device to explore the waxing and waning of the central relationship. The first panel of Fig. 7.2 shows the eponymous Asterios with his girlfriend/wife/ex-wife Hana, each drawn in the markedly contrasting styles that periodically replace the prevailing aesthetic seen in Fig. 7.1. These drawing styles are motivated. The blunt, arrogant, coldly logical architecture professor is constructed of geometric shapes rendered in clean, blue outlines, his mathematical planes and angles unsoftened by any subtleties of shading. Hana, meanwhile, a meek and self-conscious artist, is presented in warmly pink, dense, and scratchy cross-hatching, with deepening patches of color filling in roundness and organic detail, where Asterios is clinical and mechanical.

These disparate styles speak volumes about the personality clash threatening to erupt within this partnership. However, though we can infer the aptness of these designated styles, they become a repeated standard across the text, the patterns of their emergence helping to institute their full significance. We come to recognize the meaning suggested by the fracturing into personalized styles based on our growing knowledge of what it implies: the device develops into a kind of "*langue* of the text." The varying line styles are used to explore both the distance between individuals and the potential for consciously bridging that detachment. When Asterios and Hana first meet, at a party populated with differently drawn people, they slowly take on each other's characteristics, becoming gradually tinged with shading or outlining until their respective styles are overlapping (Fig. 7.2). A later argument is heralded by a hot-pink circular border that seems to isolate Hana and stop her in her tracks, before she turns back to Asterios with the first angry flush of shading coloring her face—while a single blue line traces his profile, a stylistic portent of the looming row (Fig. 7.3). Across the next two panels, these antagonistic styles take over entirely from the standard aesthetic, and the significance of this creeping discrepancy is by now familiar and instantly readable. As the text progresses, we come to read the significance of this device based on knowledge of its previous appearances, yet it remains highly interpretable: the fluctuations between animosity and alliance are readily implied by the splintering and splicing of the differing drawing styles. Though the text may teach us to read this device, we nonetheless can deduce its meaning from its very first appearance. The consolidation of the convention does not undo the underlying motivation.

In acknowledging the potential "readability" of pictures, it is vital to be clear what this entails. Just as the label "icon" is often used in ways that obscure the distinctions between different types of motivation, so too "readability" can tend to be used somewhat figuratively, broadly applied to any act of decoding or interpretation. There is a distinction to be made between the readable structures comparable with language that can be found in certain images and the expressive, impressionistic structures within visual forms, which have no counterpart in language. Ronald Paulson charts a move, in the history of art, away from the Renaissance tradition that operated according to *topoi*, using widely recognized emblems not only to represent traditional mottos, but as "raw material" that can be used "in order to produce a total image that is more than the sum of its parts, that is independent, problematical, to be deciphered" (Paulson 1975: 14). This sort of iconography forms a visual lexicon that can be deployed in a variety of combinations: exemplary is Hogarth's portrait of Sir Francis Dashwood, which "wittily subverted a seventeenth-century type of hermit saint" by painting this "most notorious member of the rakish Hellfire Club" in the recognizable guise of an eremite, yet one practicing "highly blasphemous devotions" (Bindman 1981: 139). The result is an image whose significance is a readable—according to Paulson, *linguistic*—structure. The converse trend is elucidated through the characters of *Industry and Idleness*: Paulson avers that there is "something inherently [. . .] straight and unbending" in the industrious Goodchild's pose, which contrasts with "something servile, cringing, and dishonest in Idle's" (Paulson 1975: 64). These shapes are "only expressive in themselves" (Paulson 1975: 64), and work via a "psychological association, based on shape and form" (Paulson 1975: 85). Such expressive lines, like soft curves or sharp angles, are stimuli to which "*anyone* will respond in approximately the same way" (Paulson 1986: 86), and as such are structurally very different from the conventionalized, allusive symbols of established types.

The stylistic mantles draped so tellingly over key scenes throughout *Asterios Polyp* are comparably linguistically structured, but it would be a mistake to label them therefore *symbolic* (in the Peircean sense) since they are so palpably motivated. They function as metaphor icons, and it is their deployment in a variety of "explicit readable structures," rather than their growing recognizability within the text, that makes this device language-like. When creeping in to differentiate characters, as in Fig. 7.3, it denotes a growing animosity; when gradually overlapping, as in Fig. 7.2, it indicates the forging of unity and understanding; elsewhere, it spreads to a choice few of Asterios's students when he successfully conveys his way of thinking to them; and it is used to dramatize a dream, indicating focalization through one character's consciousness. Thus, these signs are deployed as part of readable structures, their recognizability allowing them to "say" a variety of different things. There remains, however, a degree of motivation to the actual drawing styles themselves, which are inherently characteristic of the personalities to which they are aligned. Their growing recognizability allows them to be deployed in various ways, signifying a variety of new meanings, but the conventionalization that enables this does not amount to their becoming arbitrary symbols.

As the phrase "*langue* of the text" may imply, Mazzucchelli's eloquent use of varied drawing styles does not draw on widely recognized *topoi*, but is a self-imposed pattern whose significance is created within this particular work. The emblematic tradition in art utilizes a lexicon of mythological symbols that have established, accepted meanings. Artists are not constrained to draw only from this lexicon, as speakers of language are, but like language it precedes them; they may choose not to employ traditional hieroglyphs, but they cannot alter the established

7.4 David Mazzucchelli, *Asterios Polyp* (New York: Pantheon, 2009), np.

associations. Mazzucchelli's lexicon is not entirely of his own making. The architecture professor is rendered a recognizable blueprint,
rendered in the conventionalized register of his profession. However,
though we may recognize this blueprint style, knowledge of its associations is not the sole source of its effectiveness. Even before they grow
familiar within the text, the teeming muddle of small, pink strokes and
punctilious regularity of bold even borders generate the sort of psychological responses Paulson identifies. The wider significance of the waxing
and waning device—particularly the implications of these styles creeping in, as in the upper right panels of Fig. 7.3, or of Asterios's students
appearing in the drawing style of their teacher—comes to signify what it
does through the use to which Mazzucchelli puts this device. He *institutes* this particular recognizable visual sign by reiterating it throughout
the text, and it does not rest on any wider established associations. A
"*langue* of the text," then, is no kind of *langue* at all. This association of
signifier and signified is established by, and need only function within,
this particular work. Its significance is a question of contextual utterance
not system, of *parole* not *langue*.

Asterios Polyp creates an extensive visual lexicon for itself. As in *Watchmen*, speech bubbles and script possess character-specific traits, and here
each character has slightly different lettering and balloon borders. Again
as in *Watchmen*, and like the stylistic device discussed above, these variations only grow into recognizable, conventional signs through the way
they are used in the text. It is the text itself that establishes their meaning.
Unlike the motivated character-specific drawing styles, script and balloon forms in *Asterios Polyp* are fairly arbitrary, and so could properly
be termed symbols. Readers enter into a mutual agreement that different scripts indicate different speakers, and this visual differentiation of

voices plays to the text's theme of isolated individual consciousnesses. However, it is possible to use this apparatus—or rather *make* it—so that it functions iconically, its form implying something of its meaning. We thus might infer from Hana's mother's jagged speech balloons a spikiness in her exchanges with her daughter, and certainly her disinterest is palpable in the way she *visually* talks over her (Fig. 7.4).

It has already been mentioned that the particular form of a given speech balloon conventionally indicates the manner in which it is spoken. I also conceded that such signs are one of the more convincing examples offered that the comics medium might be considered a language. However, in line with the clarifications presently at hand, I would hold that these signs are part of an optional lexicon of largely motivated signs, which is far from identical to verbal language. Outsize text in a jaggedly splayed balloon, or a tentative, porous, and indefinite outline respectively suggest a shout or whisper through a deducible "relation of reason." The speech balloon itself, too, so often held up as a conventionalized *symbol*, in fact works by a degree of metaphoric iconicity: the primal tail indicates from whence this bubble issues, and the closing off of its contents within a subframe signals that the graphic text is not present in quite the same way within the diegesis. Though we must approach speech balloons with the prior knowledge that they are not conventionally visible, diegetic objects (something the rest of a panel's content will strongly imply), once this is understood it is easy to deduce that the graphic text, emanating from a speaker's mouth, in fact represents spoken dialogue. Speech balloons have also been labeled indexical signs because they have an "existential link with [their] signified" (Miller 2007: 98), but this does not refute the metaphorical way in which they encode spoken words issuing from a character's mouth (the Peircean categories and sub-categories are not either/or designations, but a matter of proportion and degree [Magnussen 2000: 196]).

Admittedly, speech balloons are now highly conventionalized. They can be deployed in the kind of readable, linguistic structures described above, as tools that can convey new meanings: in Moore et al.'s *The League of Extraordinary Gentlemen* (2000) a supremely unnerving effect is created through the use of tailless speech balloons for Hawley Griffin whenever he is invisible, to signify the uncertainty of his whereabouts; Kevin Huizenga charmingly sends up the convention in a strip in which a recognizable speech balloon assumes the attributes of an image icon, floating up and away like a real balloon (2008: np). However, in developing from naturalized diegetic banners held by characters and scrolls issuing from hand

7.5 David Mazzucchelli, *Asterios Polyp* (New
York: Pantheon, 2009), np.

or mouth in medieval times (Carrier 2000: 37, Mitchell 2009: 117), the
modern speech balloon effectively encodes the implicit quotation marks
of these antecedent forms. Speech balloons are, then, potentially deducible and prove highly pliant to motivated modifications: twining tails and
merging bodies, for example, are used to emphasize the increasing affection in the divorced couple's conciliatory reminiscence (Fig. 7.5).

Speech balloons are part of comics' non-pictorial visual content, supporting apparatus (such as borders, titles, and other non-diegetic or compositional objects) whose form-specific shorthand proves conducive to
critical attempts to argue the medium is a language. However, though many
of these devices are standardized across the medium, they remain open to
the two key distinctions raised here. Firstly, though they may form a reus-
able lexicon, these signs are optional and highly flexible. Unlike the finite
signs of a constraining *langue*, they are open both to manipulation and
to being cast off entirely, and a new alternative created. Secondly, though
familiarity with these widely used signs allows them to be read based on
prior knowledge, many are nonetheless motivated; they can be worked out
based on their form and the context of their deployment, meaning prior
knowledge is *not always necessary* as it is with individual words. These
factors matter because they permit a level of inventiveness not confined to

7.6 David Mazzucchelli, *Asterios Polyp*
(New York: Pantheon, 2009), np (details
from two different pages).

combination (as in language) but at the level of individual signs—if indeed
we can speak of "individual signs" in such a heterogeneous system. The
potential for modifying conventional signs or creating new ones, which
readers can interpret deductively, allows for "infinite differentiation and
sensitivity" (Mitchell 1986: 70) in visual signification, which we have seen
the shared conventions of arbitrary language do not afford.

I do not deny that convention is heavily implicated in regulating visual
signification, but the issues of convention and interpretability sometimes
become entangled with those of arbitrariness and motivation in signifying,
and careful precision here is vital. As has already been acknowledged, even
realism depends upon culturally specific knowledge of the conventions
through which three-dimensional space is encoded onto a two-dimensional surface. Similarly, in insisting on the prevalence (if not ubiquity) of
motivation in images, I do not wish to steer into the mire of loaded terms
like "natural." Mitchell extensively documents the problematic privileging of naturalness that has informed the historical contest between words
and images (Mitchell 1986). Meanwhile, Hatfield protests against assumptions that images' motivation implies they are transparent, uncoded, and
"easy," compared to the complexity and abstraction of language (Hatfield
2005: 36). The relation of reason between signifier and signified may, of
course, be man-made and highly abstract: diagrams, for instance, require
a knowledge of the overarching mapping principle before the significance
of particular examples can be deductively worked out. But within comics

7.7 David Mazzucchelli, *Asterios Polyp* (New York: Pantheon, 2009), np (details from two different pages).

criticism, the issues of arbitrariness and abstraction are often confused. McCloud, for example, suggests that language is merely the next step on a spectrum of abstraction that runs from photorealism through pared-down schematization to verbal language, rather underplaying the break between the simplified yet motivated image of a face and the arbitrary signifier "FACE." Similarly, Isaac Cates's otherwise convincing exposition on diagrams in comics tends to synonymize increasing abstraction, rather than arbitrariness, with symbolism (Cates 2010). It is important to distinguish between modes of likeness, for realist images, schemata, and allegorical metaphor icons are all interpreted in different ways. But it is also vital to distinguish between these sometimes highly coded and abstracted relations of reason, and symbols proper, which are entirely arbitrary. It is the potential for deducibility that frees images from a constraining *langue* (though they may opt to draw on a recognizable lexicon), enabling the *creation* of visual signs, and affording a great deal of malleability.

The conventionalized shorthand that forms the cartoon lexicon is exemplary in proving extremely flexible. Stink lines, for example, are instantly recognizable, but easily transformed into a cipher of fuming anger by deploying the same lines in a different context (Fig. 7.6). We read both just as easily, because familiarity with the cartoon medium instructs us these wavering lines represent a metaphorical radiation. Though most commonly alluding to a specific kind of emanation, what these lines represent in a particular instance can be inferred from the surrounding information. Likewise, understanding the principle that maps these graphic marks onto their represented concepts allows us to read the rather similar bold, crimped lines emanating outwards from a recently punched arm and a band's sound system as, respectively, painful throbbing and reverberating sound waves (Fig. 7.7). The same forms in a different context could easily function as a literal resemblance to a halo of worms, but the context here cues us to the allegorical nature of this icon. The efficacy of the same form for suggesting very different ideas is testament to the malleability of these interpretive signs, whose context is heavily implicated in imbuing them with meaning. Of course, the material context of a particular usage affects the meaning of words too, but as the "heavy hill" example shows, when a word is imbued with new context-dependent meaning the utterance is permeated by an attendant sense of unorthodoxy in a way these visual forms are not. The forms themselves do not necessarily have a prior association in the way that words do and so are potentially far more flexible. They are open to *transformations* of meaning, where language can be augmented or shaped by its context, but without ever escaping its preordained significance entirely.

The above examples exemplify Walker's "emanata" signs. I have argued these are motivated, enabling readers to deduce the metaphoric radiation of invisible, but perceptible smell or of entirely intangible (indeed, subjective) throbbing pain, because these shapes encode a representative *aspect* of a signified, if not a visual characteristic. It could be argued that this aura of supple lines is merely a vague conventional symbol—that is, we recognize the *general* signification of emanation, with the context filling in the specific details. But in comics, standardized shorthand can be cast off entirely. It is, for example, a widespread practice to indicate flashbacks (or dreams, or imaginary scenes) using wavy panel borders. But Mazzucchelli creates an arresting, but still instantly decodable alternative. Hana's backstory is framed by a conversation between Asterios and Hana, but most of the information is delivered in the form of narration captions. These captions accompany photographs pasted onto a kind of scrapbook surface, whose hot pink pages (which assign them to Hana) peel back at the corners to reveal Hana and Asterios discussing the narrated history (Fig. 7.8). The significance of this composition is entirely inferred. The different diegetic layers are implied by the drawn-in turning pages, which, along with the photographs, invoke the artifacts of personal history—diaries, albums, letters, and the like. This is not a standardized device, but it mimics the effect of presenting a series of flashback scenes explicated by text. The point here is that there is no imperative to use comics' conventionalized signifying practices. The lexicon of repeatable signs is available,

7.8 David Mazzucchelli, *Asterios Polyp* (New York: Pantheon, 2009), np.

but visual motivation allows artists to formulate new signifying complexes that can be readily decoded even if they are not familiar. Where motivation enables deducibility, conventionalized signs become optional.

The three examples above raise questions about the extent to which images can be described in the same terms as the arbitrary units of language. Fig. 7.6 and 7.7 in particular preclude the possibility of breaking visual images down into "pictemes" or "syntactemes" (Hünig cited in Magnussen and Christiansen 2000: 12) that possess a preexistent signified, and correspond to language's minimal units. In the case of these "emanata," it is possible to delimit a group of marks or lines that correspond to a concept (throbbing pain; pulsating sound), but as soon as this set of graphic markings is isolated from the rest of the picture, it not only ceases to mean precisely what it did in that specific context, but potentially ceases to signify anything at all. Within a depiction of Asterios's face we can easily pick out the graphic marks that denote his eye or mouth, yet those lines cannot be called minimal significant units as they only convey meaning when viewed within the complex of graphic marks that make up his entire visage. They attach to no discernible signified when viewed alone, just as in the example Eco offers, cited previously, of a dot and semicircle that in one composition may elicit interpretation as a banana and grape seed and in another as a smile and eye. It is easy to conclude, from this, that the isolatable units of visual signification are polysemic, wherein "the meaning of the individual signs follows and is deduced from consideration of the [particular] collection of signs," while language is monosemic, and "the meaning of each sign is known prior to observation of the [particular] collection of signs" (Bertin 1983: 2).

This conclusion is in essence the same one that this chapter has already drawn: that in language, meanings are (relatively) fixed in advance, whereas in visual signification they are far more heavily dependent on context and open to deductive interpretation. However, the difficulty in finding stable minimal units in visual images raises a further issue: the artificiality with which these so-called units are picked out from within a complex image highlights the continuous nature of visual signification, in contrast to language's discreteness. The minimal units yielded by a particular picture are entirely dependent on its specific level of detail: even in the schematized image above we can discern Asterios's sardonically heavy, hooded eyelids, and in a highly detailed image might be able to isolate the forms of irises, pupils, eyelashes, etc. A particular collection of marks and lines in one painting may be identifiable with the signified "eye," but viewed amid a different set of graphic marks might either signify something else altogether, or form a part of a larger delimitation (e.g., blending into a patch of shading). The system is too variable for minimal units to be consistent across different pictorial styles, and the question is once again one of text, not system.

To reiterate Mitchell's parallel example from the introduction, "[a] particular spot of paint might be read as the highlight on Mona Lisa's nose, but that spot achieves its significance in the specific system of pictorial relations to which it belongs, not as a uniquely differentiated character that might be transferred to some other canvas" (Mitchell 1986: 66). That is to say, the *significant differences* in the visual system are themselves heavily dependent on context. Language is a discrete system comprised of a finite quantity of fixed characters: there is no functional midpoint between, say, *a* and *o*. Visual forms, on the other hand, cannot easily be quantified in terms of uniquely differentiated characters, and attempts to artificially delimit units along its gradations are rarely convincing. Kress and van Leeuwen offer cinematic shot-depths as an example, suggesting that "even though distance is, strictly speaking, a continuum, the 'language of film and television' has imposed a set of distinct cut-off points on this continuum, in the same way as languages impose cut-off points on the continuum of vowels we can produce" (Kress & van Leeuwen 1996: 122).

7.9 David Mazzucchelli, *Asterios Polyp* (New York: Pantheon, 2009), np.

This is of course mistaken, as there is no "distinct cut-off" that designates a particular depth as being definitively close-up, medium, or long, and all points between remain adequately functional—if potentially difficult to label. Value on a continuum is relative, admitting meaningful nuances where language recognizes only either/or distinctions. This "density" (Mitchell 1986: 66), the fact that every tiny alteration of each heterogeneous aspect of a visual form is potentially ripe with significance, proves to be as pertinent to visual images as the analysis of *Krazy Kat* showed minimal units to be to language.

Asterios Polyp is narrated by the eponymous character's stillborn twin, and Asterios describes feeling the ghostly shadow of this semi-present second self haunting him throughout his life, a sensation visualized through the use of schematic outlines (Fig. 7.9). These are identical *figures*, differentiated through facets other than their form: the one is a solid block of the same color used for the geometric rendering of Asterios, while the other is mere outline, a transparent superimposition, hazily present in the life of the living twin. Artificially selecting clusters of markings within these continuous contours that stand in for distinct body parts is unhelpful. Concentrating only on the lines that pick out these silhouettes affords no meaningful distinctions between the two, but plenty exist: color, transparency, outline, and overlapping all insinuate themselves as pertinent details in the constitution of these multifaceted signs. It is not merely the delimited objects, but the materials that carve each one out that invest these two outlines with their differential significance. These identical figures stand in for different signifieds ("Asterios"; "Ignazio"), but only because, when viewed together in this context, their dissimilar color, outlining, and block shading become differentiating characteristics, constituting these forms as distinct signs in this instance. In another context,

7.10 David Mazzucchelli, *Asterios Polyp* (New York: Pantheon, 2009), np.

7.11 David Mazzucchelli, *Asterios Polyp* (New York: Pantheon, 2009), np.

such as the dream sequence in which mime-like players don masks whose contours invoke "Asterios" and "Hana," the purple outline does not differentiate the familiar silhouette as a sign distinct from other outline versions of Asterios (Fig. 7.10). Material details are not relevant to the system of language: they may affect particular utterances, but the *system* does not distinguish between a blue letter and a black one, a large one and a small one. Such details are the tools of visual signification, and each heterogeneous material facet is potentially meaningful—and potentially differentiates otherwise like forms as distinct signs.

Form is just one aspect of visual signification, and to approach images as a set of isolatable markings standing in for concepts neglects the variegated nuances of which the system is capable. *Asterios Polyp*'s creative use of drawing style obviates this. Relenting after a fight, Hana is seen unmoving across four panels, essentially "fading out" of stylistic atomization (Fig. 7.11).

7.12 David Mazzucchelli, *Asterios Polyp* (New York: Pantheon, 2009), np, panels from two different pages.

Identifying groups of lines within these stylistically differentiated duplicate figures that signify "eye" or "mouth" tells us little, but though we can
perceive and talk about line style as an identifiable facet, it is not an isolatable unit in that its significance as a distinct element is bound up with its
particular deployment in this strip. This is what it means for a system to be
dense: "No mark may be isolated as a unique, distinctive character (like a
letter of an alphabet), nor can it be assigned a unique reference of 'compli-
ant.' Its meaning depends rather on its relations with all the other marks
in the dense, continuous field" (Mitchell 1986: 66). The pertinent distinctions on which differential meanings depend are, in visual signification,
context-specific, rather than instituted within an overarching, preexistent
system.

7.13 David Mazzucchelli, *Asterios Polyp* (New York: Pantheon, 2009), np.

Individual linguistic utterances, influenced as they are by their material context, are of course heterogeneous, but on the systemic level "language is homogenous in nature" (Saussure 1983: 14). Visual signification, on the other hand, is radically heterogeneous: functional differences within language boil down to distinctions between letters, while in visual signification multiple variables (two dimensions, size, value, texture, color, orientation, shape) collaborate in constituting any pictorial sign, and each of these facets is infinitely gradated. It is for this reason that it is difficult to conceive of minimal visual units that comply with the linguistic model, and also for this reason that visual *characteristics* can designate identical physical forms as differentiated signs, as in Fig. 7.9. Mazzucchelli exploits the heterogeneity of visual signification to great effect, imbuing a varying color palette with significance. As analysis of the text's personalized drawing styles has shown, certain colors are aligned with particular characters and these associations are used elsewhere in the text to great effect. For example, the main couple's personal territories, Asterios's New York apartment and Hana's studio, are subtly seasoned with the appropriate tones (Fig. 7.12). In these respectively cool and warm interiors, we also see intimations of the expressive lines that are exaggerated into each characters' individual drawing style.

Most notably, the story's various strands are each rendered in their own distinctive set of colors. Blue and purple are the dominant hues of Asterios's history and university life (as seen above). The homely hamlet of Apogee [sic], where the destitute and embittered Asterios undergoes his moral rehabilitation, is rendered in a hazy and unusual mixture of yellow and purple (Fig. 7.13). Softened shades of these contrasting colors, opposites on a traditional color wheel, are layered to create a slightly misty effect, perfectly redolent of the soothing, somewhat other-worldly quality of the town and its tranquilizing results. The dreamlike quality of the narrative thread concerned with Asterios's transformation is ratcheted up by the similar coloring of the fantasy (possibly dream) sequences in which Asterios encounters his dead twin. These episodes are likewise turned out in yellow and purple, but the colors here are much stronger, unrelieved by the gentle variations in shading seen in Apogee, with solid block colors boldly clashing within sparse compositions (Fig. 7.14). The link forged by this color palette is highly suggestive: there is a gentle eeriness in the tonal layering of contrastive colors in Apogee, which is more starkly alien in the fantasy sequences. Both provide a terrain for working through past strife, and the disquieting quality of the unusual color mixture is representative of the very real physical distance from familiar turf that provides Asterios with the clarity that drives the final, climactic reconciliation.

The final reunion itself is set apart from the previous tale through a distinct palette that uses colors not seen anywhere else in the text, such as a warm, orangey pink, beige tones, and khaki green (Fig. 7.6). Older and wiser, the characters are thus visually segregated from their past selves, and purged of the divisive blues and pinks that so often set them in opposition. There are no established dualisms at work in these panels. Instead the neutral but subtly warm tones provide hope for a fresh start, a "next chapter" whose narrative strand does not continually threaten to split into opposing camps. Colors themselves are surely pseudo-signs. Though some have argued they are inherently "'charged' with an expressive meaning" (Gombrich 1952: 326), they are rather one facet of a complex sign, taking their meaning from their deployment within a given picture rather than functioning as an isolatable unit. As put to use in this particular text, however, colors are adroitly imbued with a powerful significance, not transferable to other contexts but actually instituted here.

7.14 David Mazzucchelli, *Asterios Polyp* (New York: Pantheon, 2009), np.

The heterogeneity and continuity of visual signifiers logically stem from the system's motivation: signifiers respond to the flux of visual perception, and are thus themselves continuous and gradated, unlike language that imposes categorical divisions. To reiterate: insisting on the centrality of motivation is not a dismissal of the fact that visual signification is encoded, conventionalized, and often depends on prior knowledge of particular coding conventions. Indeed, it is an error of certain practitioner-theorists to view visual representation naively as a passive reflection of reality, somehow absolved of the "continual mediation of prose" (McCloud 2000: 39). It is as grave an error, however, to exaggerate the implications of conventionalization as meaning that visual signs are therefore *purely* conventional symbols bearing no correlation to their referent, as was suggested by comics progenitor Rodolphe Töpffer (1965: 6), and as is still argued by critics who see relative abstraction as a pathway towards arbitrary symbolism rather than a question of more abstruse relations of reason.

It has already been stated that even perspectival realism is a set of conventions, but Julian Hochberg stresses that, though these conventions did
indeed *develop* within the Western artistic tradition, they were not freely
invented, but rather discovered. In cultivating a realist style, the tradition
"discovered a stimulus that is equivalent in some way to the features by
which the visual system normally encodes the images of objects in the visual
field" (Hochberg 1972: 70). That is to say, there is real connection between
signifier and signified, though that relationship has indeed developed
into an instituted convention. Once a viewer is schooled in the manner in
which three dimensions map onto two, they can deductively interpret any
realist picture almost automatically. The same is true to a lesser extent for
other types of image, such as diagrams, which may require a different level
of knowledge but still enable us to interpret most individual signs once we
grasp the mapping principle of a particular mode. Words are very different as there is no underlying principle of correlation, and speakers have
to learn and remember each individual morpheme. It seems ironic that
so many critics elide the level of deductive interpretation that goes into
decoding motivated images, insistently overplaying interpretive involvement at the narrative level while at the level of the sign tending to posit
simplified cartoon signs as "diminishingly a matter a resembling" (Cates
2010: 26), and thus a matter of convention and knowledge. Comics, and
in particular cartoon shorthand, may rely less on straightforward resemblance, but they are not therefore necessarily symbolic and arbitrary like
language. Rather, we rely on some knowledge of the conventions that map
signifier to signified in order to interpret and deduce.

There is a partial truth to the statement that "[i]conic drawings [that
is, cartoons] are simplified to the point of being almost pure symbol,
with inessential or non-semantic visual elements abstracted away" (Cates
2010: 96). The mapping principle that underpins the cartoon drawing
style is indeed one of simplification. The extraneous details of realism are
abstracted away so that the remaining few key line strokes amplify what
Kress and van Leeuwen call the "criterial" (1996: 7–9) elements: the core
features that personify an object as belonging to a particular category of
objects. However, it is wrong to suggest this simplification transforms
motivated icons into arbitrary symbols. Taking the example of cartoon
facial expressions, evocable via a few line strokes and emphasized by Eisner as the stock in trade of comics "language" (Eisner 1985: 100–103), we
can see these signs are in fact more like diagrammatic icons than true symbols. Like most aspects of the "comicana" lexicon, expressions do not work

7.15 Schematic faces.

by a strict resemblance, being highly schematized, but are very persuasively redolent of mood through correlation rather than learned association. According to what has become known as "Töpffer's Law" (Gombrich
1952: 282), we are driven to not only recognize vaguely similar graphic
marks as faces, but to imbue those faces with character and expression
(Töpffer 1965: 11), and certainly the schematic faces below become highly
charged merely through the addition of eyebrow lines (Fig. 7.15).

Actual resemblance is here diminished to the vaguest similarity, yet
these prove highly evocative lines. However, it is not only familiarity with
drawing conventions that leads us to read these simplified lines as expressions. Human faces are all different but, crucially, they change in the same
ways when experiencing particular emotions. Facial expressions are "in
their native state [. . .] reflexes—a person's instinctive response, objecti-
fied, to a given emotional stimulus" (Wiese 1965: xxii). Cartooning may
encode these changes as the simplest of lines, but these lines correspond
to the real stimuli through which we intuitively recognize expressions, and
are thus motivated, if abstracted, signs. Thus, the standardized conventions of caricature Töpffer emphasized compare with Hochberg's account
of realism: they are "laws we do not make, but discover" (Wiese 1965: xxii).

Experiments have consistently shown that, when subjects are shown
a range of picture styles, they recognize simplified cartoons faster even
than photorealism (Hochberg 1972: 73–75, Medley 2010: 55). This does not
necessarily suggest images are recognized and read like words; rather they
encode simplified versions of real stimulus whose highly abstracted resemblance is discernible. Kress and van Leeuwen's description of representation via "criterial aspects" (1996: 7) is echoed by both Kunzle's description
of Töpffer's notion of "incomplete but 'essential' forms" (Kunzle 1990: 71)
and Gombrich's view of caricature working by amplifying one (or a few)
distinctive traits, which criterial features he calls "the mask" (Gombrich
1952: 11–13). The implication of these propositions is that cartoons work
by seizing on the key classifying features of a signified, enabling swift

decoding because all extraneous "non-semantic" detail is "abstracted away" leaving only the features that match the internalized schema besides which we identify categories of object. That is, as in any system, a visual sign "takes its meaning in a system of differences" (Mitchell 1986: 69) (though not oppositional, discontinuous differences, as in language), and cartoon faces work by encoding only those pertinent differences that characterize particular expressions. The complexities of individual muscle configurations are done away with, and only the criterial elements that identify particular moods included. Thus, in Fig. 7.15 the knitting of brows is diagrammatically encoded: the in-and-down linear forms evoke an angry aspect, suggesting a lowered, glowering forehead, while the in-and-up lines create a worried expression, implying a pensively puckered forehead. Only eyebrows, the most prominent part of these expressions, are required in order to imply the entire expression, which is effectively reduced to its single most pertinent "criterial" signifier. Facial expressions then are motivated just like other aspects of the cartoon lexicon. They may develop into familiar signs, as successive artists reuse the engaging shorthand discovered by others, but their effectiveness—the instantaneous efficacy Hochberg describes—is due to their amplification of characteristic details. The most schematized expressions are evocative precisely because we are already highly sensitized to human expressions, and recognize in these simplified forms an equivalent stimulus. Thus, contra McCloud's and Cates's suggestion that increasing abstraction is an automatic route towards arbitrariness and symbolism, requiring a greater degree of knowledge and interpretation on the part of the viewer, empirical evidence shows that reduction to core defining features in fact renders these abbreviated signs instantly decodable. Honing in on the criterial features that link signifier and signified creates a visual shorthand that we grasp more readily than either purely conventional words or realistic, but more complex and highly specific, visual modes.

Having already examined how the peculiarities of the linguistic system shape the literary effects it can achieve, I have striven here to not merely state the constitutional differences of visual signification, but to show that these differences are likewise relevant to how we process visual images. Motivated signs are potentially interpretable (though we may need prior knowledge of the correlative principle between signifier and signified) and this affords infinite possibilities for creating new signs, free from reliance on an obligatory and limited vocabulary that must necessarily be known in advance. It is thus that Mazzucchelli can instill such arresting significance into patterns of color and line style, allowing the inherent suggestiveness of expressive forms and inter-iconic contrasts to instruct his reader in the developing lexicon of his text. That readers can work out the significance of these signs does not render them simplistic, transparent, and easy, but highly flexible and infinitely sensitive, able to generate nuances of meaning that readers do not need to recognize in order to grasp but engage with interpretively. The relation of reason that connects signifier to signified may be highly conventionalized, but the deducibility of particular forms affords a greater scope for manipulating or even newly creating signs than is afforded by an arbitrary system that is constrained by a *langue*. The infinite nature of the visual system too means there is limitless possibility for creating new signs: unlike language's constitution in discrete units of the same type, visual signification's heterogeneous variables are infinitely gradated. These aspects of visual signification have here been shown to generate remarkable effects, and in order to understand the ways texts like *Asterios Polyp* work, it is vital to acknowledge the peculiar aspects of visual signification that enable these devices.

The perennial anxiety that acknowledging deducibility might reduce the status of visual signification next to the idealized linguistic system generates two key responses. Certain critics (such as Eisner, McCloud, Hatfield, and Harrison) posit some kind of visual *langue*, or at least a set of arbitrary symbols that we read in like manner, attempting to explain visual signification in a way that matches the model of language. Other critics (such as Kress, van Leeuwen, and Mitchell) query whether language is indeed constituted by a *langue/parole* division, challenging the original semiotic model in order to yield an adjusted version that can accommodate visual signification. The problem is the same: there proves to be something of a difficulty in describing, in any useful level of detail, a semiotic model that applies to both signifying systems equally. Such a model is necessarily a very general one ("signs stand in for concepts and are organized by codes and conventions"), and most of the critical attempts to describe a similar constitution of visual and verbal falter because they elide the specifics of one or both systems. This leads to questionable propositions, such as visual minimal units or motivated verbal signs. Kress and van Leeuwen, for example, suggest that because we use particular signs for particular reasons, language is motivated, confusing the purposeful selection of specific signs for specific utterances with a rational connection between signifier and signified (1996: 7–9).

Though semiotics is clearly a useful tool for approaching images, I would suggest that the problems outlined above stem from its basis on the linguistic system and specifically from the over-extension (or over-rigid extension) of that baseline model to other systems. Certainly, as already mentioned, while Saussure hypothesized a general science of signs based on his theories of language, even he questioned how far this science could account for non-arbitrary signs. Mitchell too suggests that the "friction between the properties of iconicity and the paradigms of language" (1994: 348, note 7) may render semiotics unsuitable for accounting for all aspects of visual signification entirely satisfactorily. There is a sense that "icons may lie partly outside the science of semiotics, that they may be 'other' to language, linked to instinct, the unconscious, the body, or other pre- or non-linguistic domains" (Mitchell 1994: 348, note 7). The attempt to unite language and images under the banner of a general science of signs propagates problematic overstatements of their equivalence, and while I would concur with Hochberg that "the concept of a 'language of vision' is not meaningless by any means," I would further agree that—*particularly* as used in comics criticism—this way of conceptualizing the visual "is sometimes used in a very misleading sense in drawing unjustified analogies between reading and pictorial perception" (1972: 66).

This is not intended to imply that the semiotics of visual signification cannot be meaningfully explored; indeed, it has here proved useful to consider the implications of continuity in contrast to minimal units, and of motivation besides arbitrariness. There do exist, however, aspects of visual signification not accounted for by the linguistic semiotic model, based as it is on a homogeneous system of arbitrary signs. An approach based on the linguistic model has here helped elucidate how a motivated, labile, continuous system can be deployed in ways that imaginatively institute new meanings, but that model does not wholly account for the expressive element of visual signification that enables these generative forms to be intuitively interpreted on first encounter. Thus, though semiotics provides a useful basis for approaching visual images, it does not address the slippery aspect of images' expressive aesthetics. The linguistic model may provide an entry point into analyzing the highly visual medium of comics, but additionally, "Comics have a specific visual means of expression – style – which the early comics semiology is unable to describe" (Christiansen & Magnussen 2000: 22). It is this largely unquantifiable, highly qualitative aspect of the visual that is considered in the next chapter.

Chapter Eight

Style, Expressivity, and Impressionistic Evaluation

Alongside narrative breakdown, panel composition, and page layout, Harvey identifies style, or "the highly individual way an artist handles pen or brush" (1996: 9), as the fourth of comics' graphic threads. He also notes that style is the "most illusive" (1996: 152) and hardest to account for of these elements. He states that "describing a style is about as far as criticism can legitimately go" because the expressiveness of a particular style is simply "too individual a matter to provide a basis for evaluation" (1996: 152). Drawing style is highly qualitative and impressionistic. It is "the visual result of an individual artist's use of the entire arsenal of graphic devices available" (Harvey 1996: 152), and is thus hard to quantify using a linguistic semiotic model based on a decomposable system of units. Mitchell warns that "semiotics, the very field which claims to be a 'general science of signs', encounters specific difficulties when it tries to describe the nature of images" (1986: 54). I would contend that it is particularly when "every mark, every modification, every curve or swelling of a line, every modification of texture or color is loaded with semantic potential" (Mitchell 1986: 67) that the often functionalist and content-focused way comics criticism has tended to invoke semiotics proves to be most inadequate. The tendency to approach comics' formal aspects with a linguistic model in mind frequently means that the expressive qualities of comics' artwork are neglected.

In aiming to address the aesthetic aspects of individual drawing styles, broader issues of "style"—the distinctive ways particular artists manipulate the medium as a whole—are rather sectioned off. In addressing the use an artist makes of the comics medium, we might consider the role and style of verbal text, narrative breakdown, and how devices like comics shorthand and layout are used, but my focus here is firmly on the aesthetic style of the artwork. It is generally seen as a trait of the comics fanboys to display a "devotion to artists" (Sabin 1993: 162), though it seems equally feasible that the reason academic critics pay limited attention to artwork is linked more to the reluctance to consider comics' constituent literary and artistic elements as separable. To study the pictures in their own right would be akin to analyzing the linguistic content on its own, running counter to the pervasive critical policy of positing the two elements as collapsing indissolubly into each other. Furthermore, as discussed in Chapter Four, it sometimes seems to be feared that acknowledging formal common ground with related, non-mixed media prevents comics being viewed as a distinct medium with its own specific properties and practices. The point argued here is not, of course, that looking at pictures and then looking at text can sufficiently account for a medium that interweaves the two in such a variety of ways, and has its own form-specific means for organizing narrative content. Rather, the aim is to show that, along with textual content, comics' artwork can be fruitfully examined in itself.

The methodologies of art history and fine art criticism, though they can only offer a partial account of the mixed medium, prove to be highly applicable to comics. These disciplines have not, however, had much significant input into what is otherwise a highly variegated multi-disciplinary field. The approach taken to the texts examined below draws on the standard practices of formalist art analysis in an attempt to bring these critical traditions into play. I aim to describe what Joshua Taylor calls the "expressive content" of artworks, which he defines as "the combined *effect* of subject matter and visual form" (Taylor 1957: 43–44; my emphasis). That is, it seeks to provide an alternative to the "[s]tandard readings, which privilege, in each image, the enunciable quality, [and thus] flatten the semantic richness of the image to profit from its immediate narrative function" (Groensteen 2006: 127). The readings that make up this chapter, instead of privileging content and representation, emphasize stylistic elements: line and brushwork, light and shadow, texture, mass, order, proportion, balance, and pattern, as well as figures and composition (Adams 1996: 2–13, Barnet 2011: 5–11). The aim throughout is to quantify the impact of these formal elements, going beyond *describing* pictures, and instead "connect[ing] effects with causes, thereby showing *how* the described object works" (Barnet 2011: 48). The close readings of pictures carried out here have less of a defined theoretical grounding than earlier readings have.[1] The application of formalist art criticism to comics, however, does have implications for comics theory: namely demonstrating that the practices and methodologies of art criticism are as valuable to the study of comics as the "literary" readings of theme and narrative that have to some extent dominated critical approaches to the form.

Some critics do attend to the impressionistic responses awakened by particular line styles, notably Harvey himself, a practitioner caught up in the inky materiality of comics production. However, such critics are relatively few in Anglophone circles,[2] and their analyses are rarely detailed or probing. Wolk is especially gifted at capturing the visceral expressiveness of particular ways of drawing, though his comments tend toward incisive summations rather than in-depth analyses. His description of the debt Marjane Satrapi's *Persepolis* displays to her teacher David B.'s *Epileptic* is striking: "Her deliberately flat, two-dimensional images are almost homages to B.'s fiercely squashed perspective and military-tapestry figures, but they're usually just simplified representations of real perceptions; they don't have B.'s scary mystery or sense of raging, overwhelming floods of imagination" (Wolk 2007: 145). Such a description is headily evocative for anyone familiar with these works, but it remains a deliberately pithy characterization rather than a thoughtful reflection on the various material means by which those tactile impressions are created. By exceeding the limits of such perceptive outlines and performing fuller formal analyses on comics' artwork element, we can see what art history's relative lack of interest in the medium has left out of an otherwise extremely variegated set of critical approaches.

Since one principal complaint of this project has been the over-literal extension of the semiotic model of language to other symbol systems and media, it would be obviously counterintuitive to import the practices of formal art criticism wholesale. Comics texts, made up of numerous panels arranged across multiple pages, require adjustments to be made to the framework through which analysts approach a single painting. Thus, a secondary aim of this chapter is to consider what differences should exist between a formal critique of a comics text as distinct from the sort of works traditionally examined as fine art. The texts utilized, Charles Burns's *Black Hole* and Hannah Berry's *Britten and Brülightly*, are each stylistically distinctive in markedly different ways. Each can be straightforwardly examined in the context of their particular drawing styles, considering how these relate to their respective content, but they can furthermore be used to showcase the elements of comics' formal repertoire that are not covered by a standard formal critique of a single painting. There are thus twin purposes at work here running in counterpart to Part One: I aim to demonstrate what is lost when we fail to attend to pictorial content in its own right—and to propose essential adjustments to the art historian's standard criteria of formal analysis in order to successfully reinvent this methodology for the new medium.

8.1 Charles Burns, *Black Hole* (London: Jonathan Cape, 2005), collected volume cover.

8.2 Charles Burns, *Black Hole* (London: Jonathan Cape, 2005), collected volume cover detail.

The first text, Charles Burns's *Black Hole*, is a plague-invasion-cum-teen-alienation horror story, about a sexually transmitted disease sweeping the youth population of a small suburban town. Those infected with "the bug," an obvious cipher for the Aids virus, sprout a variety of inhuman deformities (boils, a tail, a small second mouth at the base of the neck, a periodic shedding of the skin) and hide themselves in an outcast community in the woods where murderous tensions begin to surface. The spirit of the teen horror film genre, frequently mentioned in reviews of the work, is obvious in the content but tangibly felt in the drawing style as well. Wolk describes how Burns's artwork "warped the hip angularity of '50s and '60s illustration into twitchy deadpan confections of slightly off-kilter line and shadow, hinting at something rotten beneath their crisp surfaces" (2007: 54). The driving principle of the following analysis is to discover precisely what it is in these stark black-and-white woodcut-style pictures that makes this description so fitting.

There is, in some sense, a kind of plainness to the forms in Burns's drawings. They are "realistic," in the sense that they are not obviously exaggerated or caricatured, with simple, evenly portioned figures rendered in bold, smooth, blocky outlines (Fig. 8.1). But something sinister lurks in the shadows, largely inhabiting the feathery lines that fill in patches of shading. These lines function like hatching lines, though they are bolder than the quick, light strokes that would normally be labeled as such: solid, forking spines of black and white interlock to delimit areas of sheen or shadow. Wolk avers that everything in *Black Hole* is either concave or convex (2007: 247), and indeed every line here is curved and organic, though at the same time very precise and painstakingly neat. Nothing is uniformly straight. Instead, bristling fingers of black and white curve and taper, so that wherever highlight bleeds into shadow, the join resembles a frill of plant spines or insect feelers. Cates cites information design theorist Edmund Tufte as warning against "equal-width bands of black-and-white because of the 'after-image and vibration' or the 'shimmer' [. . .] that these graphic elements can cause" (2010: 98). It seems to be these even, tessellating tines that create in Burns's drawings a sense of something living, faintly palpitating, and thus an attendant impression of a kind of squirming movement in these neat barbs (Fig. 8.2).

A plethora of images showing sprouting tentacles and dramatically flowing, rolling lines amplifies the general impression of movement. Clouds, water, and smoke—and indeed nearly all carefully shadowed surfaces—are comprised of contours that seem to curl around the page in worming arcs (Fig. 8.3). These sprawling lines enlarge the sense of motion, so that those delicate hatching lines throb with a latent dynamism that threatens at any moment to flex and snake off like these more dramatic curves. Within these recurrent images of unfurling tendrils, those hatching lines are often literally elastically stretched out. The shedding of Chris's skin is particularly evocative of the gooey fluidity these lines suggest, stretching out like dough as it is torn away. The face that stares back from the discarded dermis is horribly mournful in its wilting limpness, mouth stretched into a

8.3 Charles Burns, *Black Hole* (London: Jonathan Cape, 2005), "SSSSSSSSSS," book 3, np.

sagging shriek (Fig. 8.4). Nuanced shading might not so effectively mag-
nify this seeping, sinuous quality in the way these stark and simple curves
do. Another of the infected, who appears to have developed a symmetrical
cleft palette, has a face scored with taut strokes that might either represent
wiry tendons or a downy pelt (Fig. 8.5). The effect is unnerving in its ambiguity, but this etched face is stylistically consistent with the hatching lines
that mark everything with shadows. On this character's face in particular,
these lines look sinewy and organic, like drawings of muscles in biology
textbooks—stringy, strained, and raw, represented with a level of precision that is, as one reviewer put it, "grotesquely meticulous" (Howe 2006:
np). The scrupulous evenness of the shading lines in these drawings is
somewhat at odds with the initial impression of rustic woodcuts that their

8.4 Charles Burns, *Black Hole* (London: Jonathan Cape, 2005), "Seeing Double," book 9, np; "SSSSSSSSSS," book 3, np.

8.5 Charles Burns, *Black Hole*
(London: Jonathan Cape, 2005),
"Rick the Dick,"
book 17, np.

heavily inked simplicity creates. Woodcuts are typically bold and simplistic, with ruggedly gouged outlines, and the almost mechanistic precision of these cleanly inked lacerations proves slightly unsettling.

Burns's text uses chiaroscuro, and his strictly monochromatic palette ramps up the drama inherent in the intense contrasting of light and shadow. A degree of subtlety is achieved through the *effect* of gradated shading, created by the interlocking hatching lines. However, stark jet black and bright white actually meet at precise and crisp borders. The hardness of such outlines was generally considered a drawback of earlier fifteenth-century chiaroscuro, mitigated by Leonardo's exploitation of

8.6 Charles Burns, *Black Hole* (London: Jonathan Cape, 2005), "Planet Xeno," book 2, np.

the *sfumato* style in which blurred edges melt mellowly into each other (Chilvers & Osborne 1997: 116, 320, 517). Here, the alienating harshness of the sharp black-and-white contrast is wholly appropriate to the drama and tension Burns seeks to convey. The surgical precision of the borders between black and white sits in unnerving contrast with the tapering curves of the shapes themselves, and it is this opposition that partly explains the palpable sense of unease and feeling of something at once alive and dead that hovers within these images.

The chiaroscuro and woodcut effects are made to serve the text's horror theme. In lighter panels, the plain, simplified realism of the drawings means everything looks benign, but in the vast majority of panels a thick, cloaking darkness, in which loom patches of illumination, produces a distinctly disquieting eeriness. The shadows replicate, in some ways, the unearthly effect of photo negatives, with figures picked out of blackness by slivers of highlighting. The sense of a single, often distant or muted, light source is tangible and has a ghostly, slightly distorting effect on everything it illuminates. The sheer amount of black ink makes any given panel or

8.7 Charles Burns, *Black Hole* (London: Jonathan Cape, 2005), "Bag Action," book 7, np.

page heavy and impenetrable, but it is not only this darkness that makes many compositions feel oppressive. Panels are often crowded with partially cropped figures and multiple panels squashed into tight page compositions. The pure black and white of the pictures can make the interframe space harder to discern, especially if narrow, and if figures that appear to spill over panel borders are buffered by other such figures in adjacent panels, so entire pages become obstructive masses of competing solid forms (Fig. 8.6). Additionally, the meticulous precision with which details are carved means that even expanses of open space are claustrophobically dense with sweeping curves, while the neat feathering that picks out slivers of highlights can often turn panels into heavy thickets of marks. In the woods especially, closely packed panels are teeming with tiny white blades and leaves, like so many multiplying microbes writhing across the page (Fig. 8.7).

Though a certain degree of subjectivity necessarily creeps into any analysis of this nature, the key task is to justify with formal evidence the claims that the artwork gives rise to the sensations it does. Using the art critic's checklist of formal properties (line, shape, composition, color, texture) we can come to understand just why Burns's artwork inspires the impressions Wolk describes. In summary, it is the drama and ominousness of chiaroscuro, along with the contrast between the crisp precision of the inking style and the organically curving shapes, which suggests something "off-kilter" in the shadows. Meanwhile the cold deadness of the severe monochrome mixed with the pulsating, worming sense of movement suggested by the bold "shimmering" hatching does indeed suggest "something rotten" beneath the surface. The impression created by the aesthetic style of the artwork infects the reader's experience of comics, and so it is vital that a theory of comics addresses this aspect of the form fully. The evocative yet superficial descriptions of drawing style that pepper the critical corpus are not sufficient and the scarcity of in-depth formal analyses of drawing style problematic. As suggested, this dearth perhaps stems from the broad unwillingness of art history to attend to comics, unlike the assortment of other disciplines such as visual studies, cultural theory, literature, politics, history, and childhood studies whose exponents make up the multidisciplinary field of comics theory. (This unwillingness is decried by James Elkins, who protests against the general insularity of art historians and suggests their focus on traditional High Art has been detrimental to the development of visual theory as a whole [2003].) The fact that few art historians are keen to get in on the comics game does not excuse the newer discipline from neglecting the pictorial aspect of comics texts, though it perhaps explains it. The aesthetics of drawing style produce stirring effects, flavoring the experience of reading and rendering it wholly necessary that critics try to account for the formal properties of comics' artwork, utilizing the formal analytical framework of art criticism in order to facilitate this.

The comparative text of this chapter, Hannah Berry's *Britten and Brülightly*, is very different in style but just as visually arresting as *Black Hole*. The first thing of note is that Berry's figures are markedly cartoonier than Burns's. Where he utilizes simplified but proportional line drawings, Berry chooses exaggeration, distorting features into subtle insinuations of character (Fig. 8.8). Depressive detective Fernandez Britten is gifted with a nose of Cyrano-esque proportions. It bears down heavily on the lower part of his face, pressing down on his small lowered mouth, and reproducing in its breadth the broadness of his jaw so that his whole face appears heavy, sagging, and burdened. His eyes are ringed with tired shadows that are thicker underneath, suggesting all his facial features are dragged downwards, slumping under the weight of his troubles. His client, Charlotte Maughton, has a chiseled bone structure, shapely and expressively curling lips, and languorously lidded eyes, giving her an austere glacial beauty that suits her role as the aggrieved victim who is at once coolly poised and

8.8 Hannah Berry, *Britten and Brülightly*, (London: Jonathan Cape, 2008), np.

vulnerably brittle. Her suspect mother's permanently narrowed eyes and drawn, pinched features aptly make her shrewd, mean, and cold where her daughter is sculpted and striking. The recourse to caricature is entirely suited to this more humorous text, whose wisecrack-laden, noirish dialogue is mixed with elements of outright whimsy (Britten's detective partner, Stewart Brülightly, is a teabag). The text's humor can, admittedly, be rather dark, but the exaggerated cartooning style is in keeping with the pitch of this generally droller work.

Britten and Brülightly plays up contrasts of light and shadow in a comparable manner to *Black Hole*, though without the dramatic, cloaking density of darkness that that text employs. Light is rarely bright in Berry's text, and is instead a kind of negatively defined presence, only serving to show how everything else in the pictures is draped in dreary grey shadows. Indeed, in watercolor, the lighter areas are those that allow the whiteness of the paper to show through the paint, so the actual brushwork serves to layer on deepening gradations of murkiness. The subtlety of the water-color medium's modulations of tonal value allows the palest of washes to fill in sunken areas on a pallid face, with filmy suffusions of paint creating understated patches of gloom. The consistency of light/dark values and color palettes across whole pages and double spreads infuses these areas with a kind of washed-out dullness. All the colors used are of low saturation, tending towards grey and brown, and this, along with the lack of variation in hue and value that persists across the reader's peripheral vision, produces a drained feeling, giving the book a certain faded weariness (Fig. 8.13, 8.14, and 8.15).

Despite the exaggeration of its cartoon distortions, then, Berry's is a softer, more restrained text, tending to dejected, yet mildly off-beat melancholy where *Black Hole* is intense, sinister, and menacing. The subdued colors and diminished tonal variation afforded by the watercolor medium are assisted by the brushwork style itself, which contributes to making this a gentler (if still rather bleak) text. The translucent strokes are not smoothly blended, but form washy layers with slightly uneven borders so that individual brushstrokes are often perceptible. While we might suppose that invisible blending would create a softer smoothness, the delicately transparent, rough-edged quality of the brushwork gives the pictures a hazy, textured warmth. This texture and the reedy black outlining stop the pictures short of wispy ethereality, but their effect remains more temperate than the hard edges and stark blocks of *Black Hole*.

To hark back to the perennial concern with the fitness of semiotics for visual art that has been somewhat shelved in this chapter in pursuit of an alternative, I want to consider Kress and van Leeuwen's assertion that individual brushstrokes are themselves semiotic units (1996: 215–16). Objections to this assertion have already been made through the previous chapter's contention that discrete units cannot be picked out of complex visual forms; for though they may be *isolatable forms*, they are not *meaningful* units in their own right. Kress and van Leeuwen sidestep this objection by explaining that they "wanted to" (1996: 215) characterize semiotic systems as being other than homogenous systems of meaningful units of the same type; that is, they classify brushstrokes as semiotic units by redefining what a semiotic unit is. Certainly it is important to consider how pictorial elements like brushstrokes function within a larger work, but it seems a logical contortion to label them as fulfilling a certain function while being forced to re-describe that function in order to make the label appropriate. Applying terms, the definitions of which are specifically fitted to the symbol system of language, to aspects of other systems that demonstrably do not mimic the position occupied by the linguistic unit, only serves to obscure the issues. I have already extensively outlined the difficulties of positing artificially isolated visual forms and marks as discrete units, and demonstrated the error of denying the relevance of language's constitution in such units. This issue is raised again here in order to stress that this chapter's approach—visual-based rather than language-based, and treating brushstrokes as expressive features not symbolic or emblematic units—is more fruitful and more revealing than dubious assertions that a representation of an eye is the equivalent of a morpheme or a brushstroke the same as a phoneme.

In posing a more fitting methodology for approaching the pictorial aspect of comics, it remains as necessary to acknowledge the limitations of this transfer as when the linguistically based semiotic model is attached to visual media. Though useful, the framework for formally analyzing individual paintings necessarily requires some adjustment in order to apply it successfully to a medium that is decomposable into discrete narrative units. Individual panels may be examined on the same terms as a single composition, but we additionally need to consider how that panel fits into the larger arrangements of the page and whole work. Furthermore, it is not possible to analyze every single panel in a text with the same thoroughness that is warranted by a singly bordered work. It is therefore necessary to select, as we might when analyzing the formal makeup of a film's shots, arrangements that are either recurrent, conspicuous, or dramatically prominent. Chiefly, in transferring the art historian's scheme of formal analysis to comics, we need to bear in mind the new medium's inherent multiplicity.

Much more than a complex image with multiple elements, comics' narratives are subdivided into interdependent yet discrete narrative units (panels). These are dissimilar to language's minimal units, as they are in themselves compounds of complex pictorial representation and text, but they are also very different from the continuous two-dimensional composition of a picture because they are spliced into larger whole (pages) on which they partially depend for their relational meaning. Formal analysis of the multiframe artwork, then, needs to consider both the levels of panel and page spread (and, indeed, entire work), and the various interrelations across and between these different levels—a subject examined in semiotic terms in the final chapter. It must also bear in mind the reader's progression through the text and the formal compositional effects that arise from a linear narrative movement. What follows is less a comprehensive checklist of the various devices available (which are of course limitless, not fixed in advance, and interpretable like most visual signs), but rather a survey of the particular formal devices used in the two texts considered here, intended as exemplars of the sort of formal mechanisms a multiframe narrative work can produce.

It has already been shown how panels in *Black Hole* are densely packed with a multitude of small marks picking out many forms, and how the packing of many such panels onto a page intensifies the oppressive closeness of the text. The proximity of panels, along with the way in which

8.9 Charles Burns, *Black Hole* (London: Jonathan Cape, 2005), "Racing Towards Something," book 4, np (details from two different pages).

the monochromatic pictures compromise the clarity of the interframe space, further serves to disorientate readers as we move across the page. In numerous episodes, characters in conversation are laid out in panels so that we see half of their face (or the back of their head), with an adjacent panel showing half of their interlocutor and the partial views of the different characters aligned over the interframe space (Fig. 8.9). This creates a kind of split-panel effect that encourages the eye to fuse the two halves into a single image, making it difficult to take in the transition and grasp who we are looking at in any given panel. The device is used several times, though most sustainedly in a conversation between Chris and Rob. The wavy border lines that frame this (flashback) episode easily cohere with

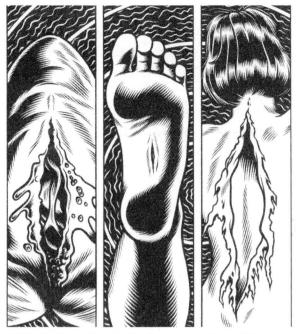

8.10 Charles Burns, *Black Hole* (London: Jonathan Cape, 2005), "Biology 101," book 1, np.

the curving lines of the pictures, and so are even less prominent than the usual narrow but rigid interframe boundaries, and this assists in enabling the mental splicing of these bisected faces. This conjoining disturbs our reading, momentarily bewildering our conceptualization of these panels as traditional (or realist) progressive moments and contributing to the creeping uncertainty and unearthliness that the entire text inspires. The larger formal composition, as much as the aesthetic impact of particular panels, thus plays its part in affecting the reader's experience of moving through the text.

Black Hole is additionally laden with motifs. There is an obvious link between the text's sexual content and its persistent images of tears and fissures: the opening biology-class dissection of a frog, Chris's cut foot and shedding skin (Fig. 8.10), and Rob's second mouth are just some of the numerous suggestive orifices created in the text. Again, the drawing style itself, with the curved lacerations of its hatching and fluidly curling forms, echoes these vaginal openings. The effect created even by the gnarled bark of a tree or ripples on water, if we look at the slivers of highlighting that

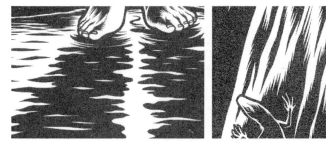

8.11 Charles Burns, *Black Hole* (London: Jonathan Cape, 2005), "Racing Towards Something," book 4, np; "Lizard Queen," book 13, np.

construct these textures, replicate these allusive openings (Fig. 8.11). Comics' particular usage of recurring forms and compositions has already been addressed in Chapter Five. However, the ways that naturalized objects are suggestively shaped in this text, and the manner in which Burns's drawing technique itself complements that suggestiveness, are both aspects of artwork style which it is the business of formal analysis to explicate.

The formal aspects that emerge within *Britten and Brülightly*'s progressing narrative in many ways overlap with cinematic practices—perhaps appropriately given its film noir trappings. The text is firstly noteworthy for the ways that panels frame particular scenes. The salience of framing in comics begs an association, as already mentioned, with the analysis of cinema shots, as much as painting. However, in approaching panel framing as analogous to shot framing we must, as ever, bear in mind the pertinent distinctions between them. As mentioned earlier, comics printed, static nature yields narratives broken down into a staggered chain of key representations, experienced differently to film's mimetic flow of action. This point should caution us to think differently about the punctuation offered by cinema's cuts or edits compared with panel gaps. The simplified and often cartoonishly exaggerated drawing styles of comics mean that "the comic book aesthetic projects unreality" (Versaci 2008: 1) and, compared with a live action film, staginess, stylization, and artificiality will consequently be judged differently within this medium. Nonetheless, the film theorist's approach to formal analysis is usefully borne in mind when reshaping the framework of fine art to suit the narrative medium of comics. As in both of these other media, the angles and depth of viewpoint and the form, proximity, and spacing of figures all need to be considered.

The sequence where Britten is confronted by a gunman proves to be a revealing example. This gunman receives classic action-shot treatment

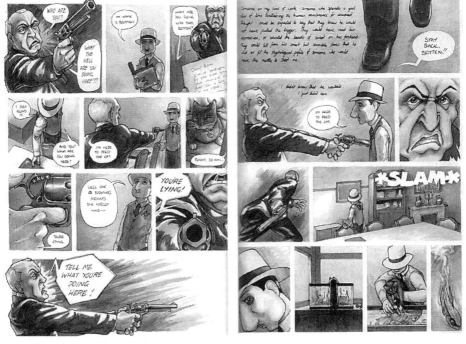

8.12 Hannah Berry, *Britten and Brülightly*, (London: Jonathan Cape, 2008), np.

(Fig. 8.12). He is largely in close-up, with some extreme shots of both his face and gun, the latter of which often points aggressively out at the reader, even violating the border of the first panel. The vantage point from which he is seen swings dynamically from panel to panel: we look at him front and side, peer over his shoulder, and from a lowered viewpoint watch him sprint away. The shifts in depth and angle give these panels a dramatic vigor, which is heightened by the halo of sweeping brushstrokes that fill in the background, fanning out from his figure and following the thrust of its action. The depictions of Britten are oddly devoid of activity. He is seen mostly in middle distance, framed by stagnant space, and primarily from the same position but for one rather unnatural shot that peers down on him from a spectator-like position overhead, a strangely removed and indifferent angle. In the second, fifth, and eighth panels of the first page, his figure is nearly aligned, grouped by the eye into a staid mass running down the page. His stance too is rather dormant, slightly slumped, and weirdly free of any taut anxiety. The gunman himself is stiffened with panic. In the panel in which both

8.13 Hannah Berry, *Britten and Brülightly*, (London: Jonathan Cape, 2008), np.

figures appear, he rears backwards slightly, as if retreating, while his gun is propelled forcefully forwards, his figure forming two straight, strong trajectories (Fig. 8.13). Meanwhile, Britten is meek, stooped, and rather disinterested. Interestingly in this panel, there is even a difference in the background wash that frames each figure, a subtle corona of agitated lines radiating out from the gunman while the space around Britten is as smoothly blank and muted as he is himself. The characterization of Britten as deadpan and dejected to the point of inertia is powerfully realized through such framing.

The printed text's use of light is similarly analogous to the capabilities of cinema, yet adapted to better exploit the specific mechanics of the comics form. It has already been mentioned how light and color are frequently consistent across page spreads. This harmonization of the double-page is dramatically exploited twice within the narrative, when the reader turns the page and enters into a glaringly different state of illumination. In the first of these episodes, Britten falls asleep in an all-night cafe and the reader unwittingly follows him into what turns out to be a dream in which he breaks into a darkened office building. That we have drifted into a dream is sublimely revealed when the detective, leafing through a blunderingly labeled file of incriminating evidence, puts on the hat he lost in a previous endeavor—then, as both he and the reader realize the continuity error this represents, a waitress appears at his side proffering a full English breakfast. The realization is dextrously timed to coincide with the last panel on the spread, so that the reader turns the page and, along with the

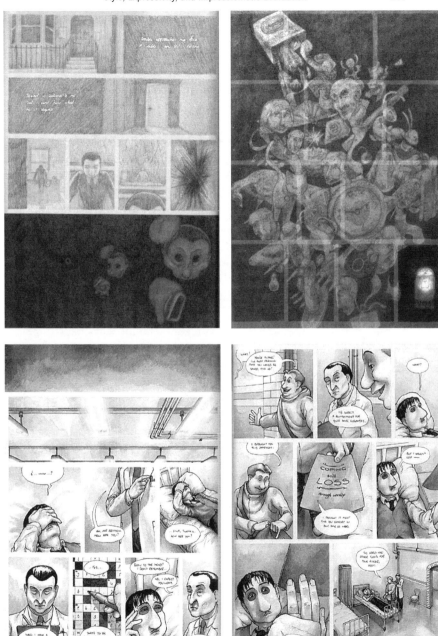

8.14 Hannah Berry, *Britten and Brülightly*, (London: Jonathan Cape, 2008), np.

bleary detective, awakens into the pasty, pale light of arriving dawn that streaks the subsequent double spread.

The second time this trick is played, the contrast between consecutive spreads is perhaps even more jarring. The grainy despondency of pencil drawings and the darkness of a full-page montage of images tumbling through Britten's concussed mind, after being knocked unconscious, give way overleaf to a hospital fluorescently lit with a sickly green tint (Fig. 8.14). Far more than a contrast between two adjacent panels, the shift in lighting between whole page spreads has an immersive effect, akin to that which might be experienced in a darkened cinema lit only by the light from the screen. By enveloping the reader's gaze first in grim darkness and then in comparable luminosity, the shift from gloom to brightness crowds the peripheral vision, and is *felt* as much as comprehended.

This chapter has striven to conduct a formal analysis that concentrates on these texts' pictorial styles alone. These examinations must be acknowledged to be somewhat subjective in nature. For Harvey, "evaluation based upon style becomes largely a matter of personal taste" (1979: 649), and it might be claimed that a degree of personal engagement is an inevitable feature of formal analysis. Indeed, as mentioned, for Barnet such impressionistic descriptions only become analytical in nature provided they explicate formal causes for the subjective effects described, which I have been cautious to include here. The explicit purpose of this exercise has been to propose art history as another source discipline for comics theorists and, in demonstrating the fruitfulness of formal analysis, to implicitly argue for a move away from the "linguistic turn" of contemporary thought (Mitchell 1994: 14) in which Anglophone comics criticism has been so heavily implicated that has seen visual images and the comics form itself habitually discussed in terms of linguistic structures. My determination to concentrate on form, rather than content, has led to a quite deliberate abandonment of the features of these comics' layouts that obviously serve narrative, rather than aesthetic, ends. It is of course difficult to strictly maintain this distinction as, as I have been arguing, aesthetic impressions feed into our understanding of a narrative. For example, the washy, shadowy watercolors of Berry's text serve to augment the leadenly grey, despondent atmosphere clouding the depressive Britten. Similarly, the hard, boldly edged curves and dense black of Burns's artwork are unsettling, seeming to palpitate and suggest something sinister lurking in the shadows, thus working as a cipher of the insidious bug and the stalked/stalking infected hiding in the woods. But there are many aspects of formal arrangement that have been avoided

8.15 Charles Burns, *Black Hole* (London: Jonathan Cape, 2005),
"Bag Action," book 4, np.

here, such as the breakdown of action and ways flashbacks or other parallel
strands are compositionally spliced. These aspects are more the preserve of
an analysis of *narrative* and though, as ever, there will be some form-specific devices, these are better explicated by current narrative theory than
by structural models.

It is worth taking a brief detour here to explain this distinction more
fully, as a concern with the improper blurring of boundaries is a recurrent
issue in this book, and this particular topic will inform the next chapter.
The sorts of compositional features that do not come under the banner
of a formal analysis of artwork (as opposed to an analysis of the unified
hybrid text and/or its narrative devices) are exemplified by two instances

8.16 Hannah Berry, *Britten and Brülightly*, (London: Jonathan Cape, 2008), np.

of narrative splicing found in these texts. *Black Hole* undertakes a fusion of parallel rows of panels into a single strand, so that the upper halves house a flashback-cum-fantasy inner monologue (wavily bordered) and the lower halves depict the here-and-now (straight-edged) in which this is pondered (Fig. 8.15). Such a layout obviously dramatizes the way this imagined sequence peripherally hovers over the character's consciousness, with the fusion of the two threads into a single row of panels suggesting both their simultaneity and the way these thoughts invade or cloud reality.

Berry utilizes a similarly noteworthy page composition for the episode in which Britten finally cracks his case. A dramatic staircase sprint is squeezed into a narrow, page-height column of panels, pressurized by their tight confinement at the edge of the spread, while a montage explaining his realization floods expansively over the central space (Fig. 8.16). Here too the implications are clear: Britten's mind is crowded with the sudden sprawling understanding of the truth, which squeezes his mad dash (up a staircase, encoded in the tall column of panels) to the margins of his awareness. This column also runs to the very edges of the page, while the main spread retains a slight border at top and bottom, thus subtly apportioning these two distinct narrative levels different spatial territories, though they share the same page plane. These compositional tricks are issues of *narrative*, rather than formal, strategy. The narrative devices of the comics medium are, of course, of great interest to any theory of comics, but crucially, unlike expressive line-work, arrangements such as these *have no value in themselves* but only in relation to the content that they organize. The concern of this chapter has been with the semantic values of visual form in its own right and it is this, separated as far as possible from content, which is the proper preserve of the formal analytical framework. In general, issues of narrative have been shelved here because a consistent attempt has been made throughout to distinguish between the central issue of formal structure and issues of story or narrative. Secondarily, though, there are fewer objections to be leveled against critical approaches to comics' specific narrative practices, for this scholarly niche exhibits a more conscientious crossover with established narrative theory (as is summarized in—and indeed exemplified by—a recent article by Derik Badman [2010]).

Mitchell characterizes a move away from the "linguistic turn" in critical thought as a "realisation that [. . .] visual experience or 'visual literacy' might not be fully explicable on the model of textuality" (1994: 16). Having previously argued against the ways a linguistic framework is applied to both visual signification and the comics medium, the obvious illustrative exercise of analyzing pictures through the framework of art criticism has ably demonstrated that this approach is better attuned to aspects of aesthetic style than the language-based semiotic approach. This analysis of how drawing style inflects our experience of a narrative text has demonstrated two things: firstly, it has made the case that comics critics should attend to pictures in themselves, just as we should analyze the formal properties of linguistic content; secondly, implicitly, it has exposed a further flaw in the language metaphor, in that this paradigm does not provide any way of examining these expressive aspects of visual art. We have here, then, another discipline that should be, but as yet has rarely been, inculcated into the field of comics criticism. The framework for formal analysis of paintings of course requires modifying in this transfer in order to account for the inherent multiplicity of the segmented narrative medium. Comics theory cannot simply be built by splicing together pieces of other critical disciplines, but, provided they are invoked with due care, and adjusted to take media specificity into account, they can be utilized as an initial grounding for understanding particular aspects of the form. Conscientious and cautious use of related theory can and should at least closely inform the development of specialized comics theory.

The conclusions made here, therefore, feed into the overarching conclusions to which this book has continually been working. The primary of these is that the focus on literature is a mistake, and that this is just one discipline, and not even the best, that can usefully inform comics theory, alongside visual theory, narrative theory, film criticism, and of course art criticism. This chapter also calls for more rigor in applying these disciplines to the new medium, avoiding vague generalities in favor of a scrupulous acknowledgment of the differences between media and therefore the mutable efficacy of the established frameworks. Having been habitually suspicious of the diverse and incautious claims made for comics' uniqueness, the argument made here is essentially that we should acknowledge crossovers with other disciplines, yet without importing the entirety of their structural models wholesale. We must pay due attention to relevant differences and consider what variation of the existing models is required in order for them to usefully inform and develop comics theory. What is unique about comics is not any particular one of the range of textual, visual, hybridizing, or narrative practices that animate it, equivalents of which can be found in a range of other media, but rather the particular combination of these aspects that coalesce in the comics form. The comics form occupies a unique point in the Venn diagram of media practices, and any fully developed theory of the form must reflect that fact.

Chapter Nine

Composition
Continuity, Demarcation, and Nesting

The final aspect of the formal framework set forth here considers composition in comics, namely the ways in which the form integrates individuated panels into a larger whole. Doing so involves a certain resurrection of issues touched on in Chapter Five, addressing the relationships between panels' contents and their frames, and also between those panels and the larger totalities of page and entire work, focusing on the page as a semantic unit. As mentioned earlier, Groensteen proposes the "multiframe" as the basis for understanding layout, a conceptualization based on "the reduction of images to their frame, either their outline or, especially, the feature that delimits it. Thus, it allows us to imagine a contentless comic, 'cleansed' of its iconic and verbal contents, and constructed as a finished series of supporting frames" (Groensteen 2006: 24). A given text's multiframe comprises its total page space, subdivided as it is into multiple panels and supporting margins. This chapter explores the idea that "the strip, the page, the double page, and the album are nested multiframes" (Groensteen 2006: 148), proposing that it is the relationships between, not only these nested layers, but also their contents, that provides the basis for understanding composition in comics.

To begin with something of a concession, it should be noted here that there is some value in comparing the way panels are embedded within a larger text to the system of language. Panel frames are meaningful only as part of a system of differences, as already stated. The value of the panel as a visual unit (as distinct from the significance of its story information) depends on its relation to other panels within the work and placement within the work's multiframe: a panel is judged large or small, regular or irregular, emphatic or unobtrusive relative to the standards established within a particular text (depending too, of course, on the degree of standardization a particular text employs). Thus, the value of a particular panel or page layout is constituted within the individual work. Panels assume meaning according to a localized "*langue* of the text" rather than as part of a system consistent across the entire medium. There also exist more fixed compositional values, such as the emphatic narrative weight lent to the "initial, central, and terminal positions" within a page's sequence (Groensteen 2006: 29–30), which likewise are imbued with significance through their relative position within a page's multiframe.

It should be noted that page composition is less widely theorized among Anglophone scholars, who tend to privilege the sequence over the page (Cohn 2008: 2), and for this reason this chapter does not concern itself with a specific, engrained problem as other sections have done. Generally, composition is most incisively described by the pioneering practitioner-critics. Although, as has been stated, unquestioning acceptance of this vital groundwork has preserved certain theoretical errors within the field, it nevertheless provides a valuable mine of perceptive close readings. Harvey in particular decomposes page and panel compositions in ways that are highly instructive, and the ensuing analyses, if not directly relying on dissections of the particular examples he offers, certainly follow his lead in their overall approach. This chapter also makes use of two useful critical frameworks: Benoît Peeters's handy taxonomy of compositional types, and Evelyn Goldsmith's method of evaluating the readability of images, the latter of which is used to slightly amend the former.

The schema Peeters proposes first assesses the relative autonomy or interdependence of narrative content and composition, and then examines which of the two factors dominates. Thus, both the autonomous and interdependent categories are split into two subcategories, one in which narrative is the dominant force and one in which composition is paramount. In Peeters's conventional type of layout, narrative is the primary concern and is conveyed through an autonomous, self-effacing default grid. That is to say, this type of layout is conventional insofar as the grid is a norm invoked in service of conveying narrative information, and not used for what its form in itself contributes. There is no relationship between the story content and the multiframe; the latter is merely utilized as a platform for the former. Barry's standardized four-panel strip is of this type, the regular layout little implicated in aesthetically emphasizing or assisting the narrative content. The decorative type also entails independence of narrative and layout, but here an intricate and elaborate page design serves its own aesthetic ends, rather than supporting the narrative. Primary concern is for the page as a visual unit and narrative breakdown is subordinated to it. Story information is fitted into this totality rather than the page being designed to complement narrative content.

The subdivision of the interdependent category Peeters proposes is slightly odd. The rhetorical type is characterized by "an expressivity of the panel or the page in relation to the narrated action" (Peeters 2007: np). This aptly describes, for example, Adrian Veidt's fight scene in *Watchmen* (see Chapter Five, Fig. 5.8) and the brick-ascension *Krazy Kat* strip (see Chapter Six, Fig. 6.11), in which frame dimensions mimic or reflect the action within. However, the productive type works by a similar correspondence between layout and content, but here "it is the organisation of the page which seems to dictate the narrative" (Peeters 2007: np). Peeters cites as evidence Winsor McCay's recurrent use of a "staircase" format in *Little Nemo in Slumberland* to argue that layout precedes and inspires story. That is, in the rhetorical type a layout is constructed around a story, so as to complement its action, while in the productive type a layout is constructed and then a story invented which responds to that layout. The question of correlation between layout and content is a pertinent one, but the issue of whether a given layout inspired a story that would fit into it or was designed around a ready-conceived story seems not only impossible to decide after the fact, but also not particularly illuminating even if such a classification is possible. This chapter will propose that a more relevant distinction might be drawn between layouts that correlate to *narrative* content and those in which *formal* content is drawn into play. The question becomes one of whether the layout corresponds to the semantic information of the story content, or whether it is the physical shapes of the figured pictorial content that interacts with the multiframe, a distinction that will be fleshed out via various examples. In dealing with the motivated visual system, of course, form and significance themselves are often correlated, but the differing degrees to which formal and story content are drawn into play can be clarified through the second analytical framework utilized here.

Goldsmith, in seeking to evaluate the functional readability of images, proposes a framework to assess how easily core information can be extracted. Approaching images as communicative tools used to illuminate text and assist understanding in educative settings, Goldsmith shares in the assumption of numerous comics scholars, and of the visual grammarians Kress and van Leeuwen, that the purpose of images is to "make their message maximally understandable in a particular context" (Kress & van Leeuwen 1996: 13). However, as the example used to illustrate Goldsmith's framework will show, this schema does not demand that images be reduced to functional vessels for story information. Goldsmith identifies three semiotic levels on which we engage with pictures:

9.1 Jason, *The Left Bank Gang* (Seattle: Fantagraphics, 2006), np.

the syntactic (to do with our ability to identify separable physical forms within an image, though not necessarily to recognize what they represent); the semantic (relating to our ability to identify the signifieds represented by those forms); and the pragmatic (to do with our interpretation of the represented object and our understanding of its wider significance in its particular context) (Goldsmith 1984). In relation to the proposed adjustment of Peeters's schema, this chapter will go on to propose distinguishing between types of layout/content interdependence on the basis of whether it is the formal content of panels (that is the physical forms within them, Goldsmith's syntactic level) or our conception of the represented narrative information (that is the interpretive, or semantic and pragmatic levels) that is drawn into interaction. Goldsmith's framework has wider uses, however, enabling us to consider how we mine comics' pictorial compositions for their narrative information, though without necessarily assuming that the only purpose of these pictures is to "smuggle your idea" through to the viewer. In the example above, from Jason's *The Left Bank Gang*, this framework actually helps explain how a vital clue is deliberately obscured from the reader.

In this panel, the crux of the tale—a duplicate bag of loot—is scrupulously included, but the composition prevents all but the most conscientious of readers from spotting it (Fig. 9.1). This is achieved in part through what Goldsmith calls syntactic emphasis, or the way areas of a picture are highlighted through the arrangement of figures and their physical characteristics. The first bag is centrally positioned, framed by a ring of figures occupying this focal area, and stands in front of a jagged, yellow curve that stands out from the predominant red-brown tones and draws the eye along its arc towards this bag. The image also employs semantic emphasis, that is to say, recognizing what these objects represent lends further prominence to certain ones. We recognize the bright yellow shape as fire, dangerous, and our attention is drawn to this dramatically accentuated area and so to the bag just in front of it. On the pragmatic level—the level of active interpretation of an image's wider significance, on which we might differentiate general human (or here anthropomorphized) figures (always *semantically* important) from recognized main characters in a given text—at this point in the text we are only aware of a single bag and of the standing character's later possession of it. Thus, the reader hurrying through this ingeniously plotted, pacy heist tale is simply not attentive to the second bag, once we have found the prominently displayed single bag we expect to see. The second bag is artfully obscured through its lower syntactic emphasis, confined as it is to the picture's edge. It is also subsumed into a (syntactic) semi-circle of peripheral clutter, which includes the (semantically unimportant) chair, sideboard, and dark corner that delimits the room. Formally, we are discouraged from lingering here, and thus the game is not given away. In his analysis of Hogarth's *Harlot's Progress*, Paulson expounds on the ways visual forms direct the gaze around these teeming, complex, very *readable* pictures (1975: 40–45), and Goldsmith's schema provides a useful tool for examining how even seemingly simple compositions can control the way we consume their content—not necessarily to make them as blandly functional as possible, but, as here, to deliberately obscure a vital piece of information. The above analysis shows, contra-McCloud, how visual images do actively mediate their message.

These two frameworks prove highly useful in explicating the approach to composition that this chapter puts forward. It is also informed by the idea of nesting, mentioned above, and aims to draw together a composite, slightly adjusted conceptualization of the page, the panel, and their iconic contents as nested units, clearly demarcated but drawn into collaborative play within the continuous surface of the page. Where theorists do attempt to quantify comics as a system built from discrete building blocks comparable with language, they frequently pose either the panel or the page as the pertinent unit of this system (Abbott 1986: 156, De Haven 2005: 180). Groensteen explicitly rejects the idea that "the study of comics, like that of every other semiotic system, must pass through a decomposition into constitutive elementary units" (2006: 2), refuting the assumption that the model of language is paradigmatic of all systems of signification. A key contention of this chapter is that the units of page and panel provide a vital basis for understanding comics, but that these units are manifestly not "elementary units." The impossibility of identifying minimally significant visual units has already been asserted, and though the comics form is clearly delimited into separable, bordered segments such as the page and panel, crucially these are not *minimal* units. Panels are complex, multi-elemental units and there is never a point at which we can no longer break down those elements into smaller constituent pieces, for this exercise leads us to the continuous, heterogeneous, semantically dense iconic content itself.

While Groensteen acknowledges that "page layout does not operate on empty panels, but must take into account their contents" (2006: 92), he nevertheless asserts that "entering inside the frame, in order to dissect the image by counting the iconic or plastic elements that compose the image, then studying the methods of articulation for these elements [. . .] does not lead to any significantly advanced theory" (2006: 4). He advocates an "approach from on high" (2006: 5), emphasizing the contentless schema and level of the entire work's multiframe over the contents of individual panels nested within that multiframe. However, this chapter will demonstrate that the formal content of panels plays an essential role in constructing the page or double page as a totalized image. The minimal unit debate, which Groensteen dismisses as "useless" (2006: 3), rather requires reframing in order to make it applicable to comics, for demarcated units are the crux of the comics system even if they are different in nature to language's minimal, arbitrary morphemes. We are presented again with the need for a conscientious readjustment of the available critical model in order to make it applicable to comics. Once more, the semiotic language model cannot be imported wholesale without the poor fit between its and comics' constitutive units leading to an impoverishing vagueness of the source theory. Instead, we must attend to how comics' units systematically combine into a larger whole, while remaining alert to the implications of those units' density and the fact they can be decomposed into smaller constituent elements.

In service of providing a fuller account of the compositional practices of comics, the layout of figures within individual panels provides an apt starting point (though it is one to which Groensteen explicitly objects). Of course, as has been asserted throughout, comics are distinguished as a medium by the multiplicity and simultaneity of their constituent panels, and much of what can be said about intra-panel layout crosses over with the film theorist's approach to a shot that has been touched on in previous chapters. As mentioned then, film terminology pervades comics criticism despite a common reluctance to cite that medium as comics' closest structural relative. By working outwards from the panel, we begin to encounter the features specific to the medium: the variability of panel frames and their relative value within the work; and the participation of both frames and contents in creating the larger image of the page and double page. Ultimately, comics composition must be understood in terms of the systematic relationships between its nested layers of contents, frame, page, double-page, and entire text, always attentive to both the smaller units' valuation and place within the whole, and the larger units' constitution in the smaller.

As previously demonstrated, individual panels may be approached much as we would a film shot or painting. The full-page panel by Eisner below (Fig. 9.2) justifies his reputation as a virtuoso formal stylist (Harvey 1996: 29, Barrier 1988: 197–98). Most of the page is a murky wash, with the prison-like grille of a sewer grate that lets in daylight from the street above reflected in a mirror-image patch of sun on the ground beneath. Each shape functions as a sort of sub-panel, housing the pictorial contents illuminated within it. The viewer's vantage point is level with the drain, and the buildings outside rise dramatically above us. The picture's emphasis is on the lighter patch of ground and detailed close-up objects scattered there, while the skyline is obscured by the dark lines of the grille. The imposing majesty of the city is, however, subtly heightened by the contrasting perspective planes employed here. The rising buildings' lines converge to a vanishing point toward the top of the page, while the grille that sits just above the reader's eye level converges toward its furthest edge, which sits *downward* on the page plane. Thus, this window onto the world above ground forms a trapezium that opens exaltingly upwards and outwards, aggrandizing the towering cityscape it frames. This "splash page," an opening gambit that became Eisner's trademark (Harvey 1996: 70), primarily aims at establishing mood; because it is designed as a single, full-page image, the splash page particularly lends itself to detailed

9.2 Will Eisner, *New York: Life in the Big City*
(New York: Norton, 2006), p. 15.

compositional analysis, but the potential for doing this exists within individual panels too.

Frank Miller's *The Dark Knight Returns*, a formally impressive Batman revision that helped initiate the wider interest in comics as a serious
medium that sprang up in the 1980s (Sabin 1993: 87), also makes interesting use of full-page panels in several depictions of the superhero. The
foreshortened perspective of these dynamic action shots (Fig. 9.3) gives us
a truncated Batman of resounding bulk, his broad, solid figure crowding
each composition, palpably heavy with the "weight of age" (Miller 1986:
1.1) that burdens Miller's fifty-five year old, semi-retired reboot of the
character. There is, however, a further aspect of these panels that amplifies the dramatic showcasing of this burly figure, and it lies in the very fact
they are full-page pictures. The text is based around a four-by-four panel
grid, and when this gives way to such expansive images a certain sense of
drama is created. There is little story information to be gleaned from these
sprawling, exhibitionist drawings, but their grand size, in relation to the
text's established standard, invites the reader to linger over this imposing
display of physicality. Compositions such as these can only be understood
through their relationship to the text's standardized multiframe, for their
particular impact lies in the way they differ from it. Their value as semantic units is thus dependent on their position within the system of the text.

9.3 Frank Miller, *The Dark Knight Returns* (London: Titan Books, 1986).

9.4 Frank Miller, *The Dark Knight Returns* (London: Titan Books, 1986), book 3, p. 5.

In addition to this differential constitution of large and small units within a particular work, panel compositions differ from film and painting through their incorporation of visual elements that are not part of the iconic picture. The inclusion of speech bubbles, narration subframes, and sound effects makes panels multimodal, though assessing these elements' place within a composition is largely a natural extension of the deconstruction of a film shot or single picture. For example, in the two panels above (Fig. 9.4), the action of the collapsing staircase is traced by the two

9.5 Lynda Barry, "Imagination Stoppers," *Salon*, 2004, http://www.salon.com/life/comics/barry/2004/09/10/imagination_stoppers [accessed 30 May 2008].

lexias that turn corners to plummet down the panel and recede, visually mimicking the diminishing crash of the staircase and scream of the tumbling victim. Of course, pictorial composition too can marshal isolatable forms in ways that draw the reader's eye around the painting, and the way these lexias elicit the reader's gaze is similar to the construction of reading pathways described in Chapter Six. The position of lexias and the frames that contain them can, however, also have more symbolic significance.

In "Imagination Stoppers" (Fig. 9.5), Barry complicates her usual four-panel structure. The first two panels are irregularly subdivided into narration frames, diegetic scenes, and mock-up representations of the eerie hypothetical situations that are the object of Freddie's imaginative game. The final two panels, in which the irrepressible Marlys interrupts with suggestions whose gruesomeness contravenes Freddie's stipulation that the scenarios should "weird ya" but not actually "freak ya," are each uniformly split into two diegetic scenes. Marlys's scenarios are never pictorially shown and are verbalized only through her speech balloons rather than by narration text. This is extremely telling. The narration subframes and imaginary pictures remain the exclusive domain of the game as it is meant to be played. That these panel elements disappear shows how the more vociferous character manages to shut down the game, edging out the two more reserved characters' imaginings. However, she fails to force them to accept her grisly scenarios as legitimate, and is thus excluded from the game's designated territory. There is an even more concrete significance to the placement of speech balloons within the diegetic scenes. Freddie and Arna initially face each other across uninterrupted picture space, their speech balloons confined to opposite corners of their subframe. Marlys at first offers comment from the side, but her speech balloons start to intrude between her and the other characters, gradually crowding and overlapping until they create a solid barrier that bisects the picture and isolates Marlys from her interlocutors. By the final subframe, she is not only visually cut off from Arna and Freddie, but figured within a blacked-in background as if occupying a different scene altogether. Chapter Two dwelt on the ways language often acts as a barrier to communication in Barry's strips, and this is figured visually through the internal arrangement of these intra-panel subframes and way content is apportioned across them.

Implicit in the analysis above is the fact that the panel unit is not minimal. It can be broken down into smaller elements, whose mode, positioning, and content interact in ways that generate further meaning. The consistent presentation of particular kinds of semantic content (such as the imaginary situations here) in certain areas and through certain modes (pictures and narration for Freddie and Arna; speech bubbles for Marlys) assumes an interpretable significance. These clearly demarcated panels can be broken down into smaller meaningful units, which together add up to create a complex, multi-sign *text* rather than an elemental sign comparable with a minimal morpheme. If the panel is to be fruitfully compared to an element of language, it would have to be the sentence, which is itself already a dense and structured compound. It takes the duration of this four-panel strip to establish the significance of this placement of content, but as much as they plug into the larger totality, these panels are themselves made up of smaller, isolatable, internal units of their own, which

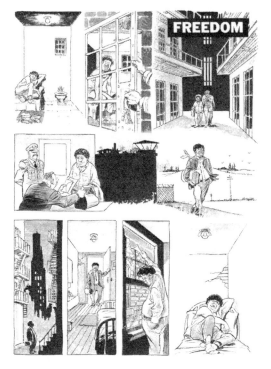

9.6 Will Eisner, *New York: Life in the Big City* (London: Norton, 2006), p. 112.

are instrumental in constituting the positional values that give the whole piece its meaning.

This sort of interpretable significance of placement is also possible at the level of the multiframe, as is neatly demonstrated by Eisner's one-page strip "Freedom" (Fig. 9.6). The repetition of the first image in the final panel offers the obvious suggestion that the protagonist has simply swapped one form of imprisonment for another. However, by bookending the strip this way, this repeated scene effectively recaptures the reader's gaze at the terminal point on their habituated rightward-downward progression across the page. It is notable that in the first version of this scene the character nestles against the left wall with a darkened ceiling buffering the upper edge of the page, while in the second instance he is against the right with the bed forming a baseline perspective plane level with the strip's edge. The compositional differences between these panels create inverted orthogonal barriers that effectively bound the strip—a decisive and highly suggestive compositional "penning in." The aforementioned narrative weight of these initial and terminal positions is open to a varied exploitation. For example, artists may time their delivery of narrative information to spread suspenseful pauses or create dramatic reveals at these junctures (as does Berry, in those dramatic treatments of light seen in Figs. 8.14 and 8.15 in the previous chapter). Here, these barriers achieve both a unity and finality that would be compromised if the strip did not so neatly occupy a full single page in this way. The strip also cannily uses three tall, constrictively narrow, and firmly bordered panels to suggest, after the more expansive preceding panels and particularly the open, unbordered walk away from prison, that the city itself might be *more* confining—though the repeated grids of the prison windows and doors seem to counter this suggestion. There is something slightly ominous too about the way the page pivots round the dark silhouette of the prison, in the inherently focal central position. Utilizing both the intrinsic values of page location and frames whose significance (narrow, expansive) is constituted within this composition, the strip marries both elements to its story content, forging interpretable links between narrative information and both framing and layout.

The relationship between layout and content in the above strip is largely confined to the semantic and pragmatic levels of Goldsmith's framework. The relative sense of confinement and openness is interpreted according to what we recognize the iconic content to signify. On the syntactic level, the buffers at the opening and closing right angles are implicated in creating the sense of containment that is also pertinent to the semantic/pragmatic narrative level. There are, however, much stronger ways in which the syntactic level (formal contents, rather than the conceptual idea of the story) can actively participate in constituting the page as an image, along with the panel borders that frame those contents. The page below (Fig. 9.7) achieves much of its drama from Miller's abandonment of his four-by-four grid for seven page-width slices that mimic the frantic, uncontrolled slaloming of a skidding car. The effect of these frames, however, is exponentially heightened by the inclusion within them of *syntactic*-level elements that also work toward emphasizing this streaking across the page: the elongated bands created by the various sound effects, along with the theatrically whipped-out cape, cause the eye to slash repeatedly across the whole page. These bold, horizontal forms are simultaneously visible within the page. The physical shapes contained within the panels solidly amplify both the sweeping panel frames and the pragmatic level concept of the swerving car, which those frames also play to. In a composition such

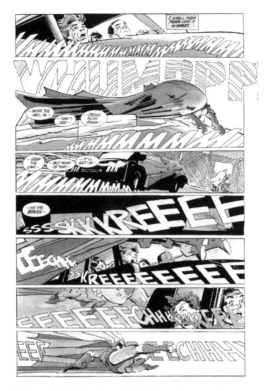

9.7 Frank Miller, *The Dark Knight Returns* (London: Titan
Books, 1986), book 1, p. 27.

as this, the contentless multiframe gives a necessarily incomplete account
of the page as a total image with iconic forms within panels as distinct
from their narrative significance, very much involved in the construction
of that whole image. As we would expect from a motivated system, it is not
only the layout, but the iconic contents themselves that can be rhetorically
expressive of the narrative information.

As discussed in Chapter Five, the comics form has great scope for framing scenes in ways that showcase action, a device dependent on reciprocal play with the content itself. In the composition below the tiny figure
falling down the darkened shaft (eerily "lit" with piercing bat screeches
that rise out of the depths) is further dramatized by forging a panel that
is itself a plunging, dark tunnel down the page (Fig. 9.8). Our recognition
of this panel as long and narrow once again largely depends on the work's
standard grid. To some extent, a page-height panel is unlikely to appear

9.8 Frank Miller, *The Dark Knight Returns* (London: Titan
Books, 1986), book 1, p. 10.

anything but "tall," but this tallness would carry far less weight within a
multiframe comprising panels of similar proportions. The significance of
the panel's dimensions is also, in part, constituted through its productive
relationship to its content. As discussed in Chapter Five, there is a certain tendency among comics critics to imply there is an inherent narrative value to certain panel dimensions, with, for example, narrower panels
necessarily speeding up action. However, as was demonstrated through
the analysis of narrative breakdown in *Watchmen*, we cannot really deter-
mine the narrative implications of panel shape separately from the content that reciprocally defines the frame's significance. Here, for example,
this particular panel is long, narrow, and yawning, not only relative to the
other panels, but because of the large amount of black space and tiny figure plummeting on a downward trajectory. If instead this panel framed,
say, a cramped and close-up sliver of a character peeking round a curtain

(see for example Chapter Six, Fig. 6.4), a similar frame would connote cloaking confinement, concentrated intensity, and taut stasis, its largeness adding a very different stripe of drama. The narrative impact of a particular panel's formal dimensions, then, is due as much to its narrative content as to the relative position of those panels within the larger composition. Nested contents, as well as the nesting of panels within a multiframe, must be taken into account.

The above page is also noteworthy for its extension of the first and last panels all the way to the page's edges. These panels bookend the composition, and this apparent extension over page borders is suggestive of the way this formative experience bleeds out and infects Bruce Wayne's later life. It is also significant that the gaping tunnel buffets against the top of the page, as if its distant opening is out of reach off the page's edge, lost to the character hurtling towards its bottom. The final panel, in extending off the page's edge, inversely suggests the bottomless depths that lurk beyond. The interframe space is a constitutive part of this page's design unit. Not just a background vessel housing and demarcating panels, the interframe space can be made to participate in the larger composition, as, for example, when characters are shown vigorously bursting panel borders and spilling over into this space, or in the previously mentioned *Dream of the Rarebit Fiend* strip where a spurned lover gradually rips up the panels, hard content disintegrating until this white space is all that remains. In this respect, layout is comparable to painting in that every discernible element, every facet of every mark, or line, or area of white, is an integral part of the continuous, motivated whole. Clearly, comics layouts are not precisely continuous in the way that iconic pictures have been shown to be, delimited as they are into separable, internal units. However, the semantic density of those complex panels, which can themselves be broken down into smaller and smaller internal forms that are continuous and never finally minimal, means comics layouts operate more in accordance with the visual semiotic model elucidated here than with the discrete, doubly articulated language system with its finite pool of discrete, minimal units.

The involvement of syntactic panel content (physical, rather than conceptual) in the constitution of the larger composition is even more evident in the exemplary Eisner strip below (Fig. 9.9). The panels here, as far as they can be labeled as such, *are* the content. Towering building planes burst through jutting alley floors to become ground-level walls, their continuous surfaces seemingly unbroken wholes, though we judge their represented location to be wholly different. According to Goldsmith's

9.9 Will Eisner, *New York: Life in the Big City* (London: Norton, 2006), p. 104.

evaluative framework, location is another visual factor like emphasis: with these walls, we *semantically* locate them within different scenes at different heights and angles, depending on which part of them we are looking at and what their proximate content is. However, because of the apparent continuity of the outlines that bound them, these planes have a *syntactic* unity—that is, we identify them as unified pictorial figures, though we recognize they signify several different objects in several different scenes. Eisner's ability to pull off this contradiction between semiotic levels without confusing the reader is testimony to his mastery of the form. What this content-reliant construction generates is a feeling of the city's alleyways, loomed over, jostled, and boxed in by close-packed high-rises in which the sermonizing figure performs on a protruding stage that overhangs the scene below.

Having begun with the interior of panels, this discussion has inevitably been led outwards into considering the whole page as an integrated

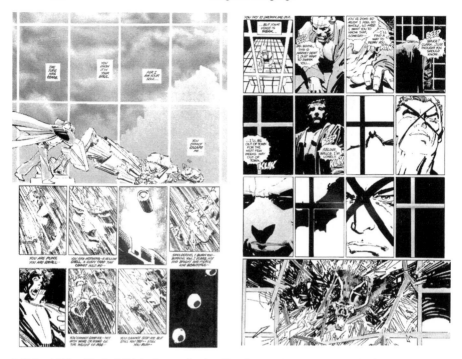

9.10 Frank Miller, *The Dark Knight Returns* (London: Titan Books, 1986), book 1, pp. 17–18.

composition through demonstrating how these delimited images are drawn into reciprocal play with both their frames and the larger multiframe. This movement is essentially retraced throughout the remainder of this discussion, which explicitly considers the page as a cohesive image, but is equally inescapably led into quantifying that whole in terms of the formal (syntactic) and narrative (semantic, pragmatic) contents of its nested, internal elements. The value of frames and precise effects of contents depend on their place within the larger schema of the text, and likewise those composite wholes are palpably reliant on their separable constituent elements, not only on the borders that constitute the multiframe but the concomitant iconic contents too.

The four-by-four grid of *The Dark Knight Returns* operates much as *Watchmen's*, subdividing and clustering into alternative configurations expressive of content. It is tempting to label this sort of gridding, which attains a kind of transparency through habituation, as conventional according to Peeters's typology. However, Peeters notes that this very regularity, when "radicalized" (2007: np), assumes significance. The fastidious uniformity of *Metronome*, for example, demonstrates that regular grid-ding need not have the "neutral" (Peeters 2007: np) relationship to story content that properly characterizes this type. Miller's standardized grid is not obviously correlated to any aspect of the narrative, but it is periodically drawn into play with (indeed *by*) the panel contents. In the first page above (Fig. 9.10), the latticed lines extend to the page's edges in the form of panes in a vast window, foregrounding the underlying page pattern. In the second, the self-reflexive presence of non-synchronous grid patterns within panels, either aligned, angled, or sized differently to the page's grid, provides an uneasy undercurrent through the off-kilter shadowing of that pattern, which builds to a bat crashing through that paned window (whose frames symbolically appear as crucifixes within the panels' pictures) and destroying the grid that has been subtly disturbed from within. Thus, the grid receives a kind of echo from within the panels that constitute it, their contents actively transforming it from an easily read vessel for narrative information into the *content* of a complex visual unit.

Karasik and Mazzucchelli's *City of Glass* adaptation utilizes its three-by-three pattern in a similarly strategic way. As in Miller's text, this grid is referenced by nested grids that appear within panels in various forms. Its neatest trick, however, is in the climatic disintegration of this layout, with the hitherto orderly grid growing distorted and uneven, panels beginning to drift about the page, as the protagonist loses his grip on reality. The multiframe of the page or double page, like the panels within it, derives its compositional significance from its relationship to the established pattern of the text in which it is nested. However, the significance of this collapsing regularity is also interpreted in relation to the story information it delivers. The disintegration of the multiframe is differentially evaluated besides the preceding regularity, but only assumes its connotations of instability, collapse, and disorder when interpretively sutured with the story content (in another story, this crumbling uniformity might connote freedom or escape). There is a mutual exchange between narrative content and page composition that those critics cited here, Harvey, Peeters, and Groensteen, all acknowledge. However, the extent to which visual forms within panels also participate in constituting the page as a meaningful semantic totality is not often clearly distinguished from this more open and interpretable relationship, and it is this distinction I wish to firmly establish here.

The difference between the involvement of narrative and formal content in composition, between the semantic/pragmatic and syntactic levels of Goldsmith's framework, can be further clarified with reference to the

9.11 Winsor McCay, *Dream of the Rarebit Fiend: The Saturdays* (West Carrollton: Checker Book Publishing Group, 2006), p. 150.

following strip from *Dream of the Rarebit Fiend* (Fig. 9.11). In the main, the outline of the multiframe interacts with story content, though there is additionally some interplay with syntactic-level iconic forms. Panel height fluctuates regularly, creating an uneven and disorientating reading pathway whose choppiness is redolent of the confusion of the sleeper who intermittently wakes from a series of bewildering dreams. The repetitive reemergence from a series of non-sequitur dream scenes is encoded into this succession of unsettling leaps and troughs, and the layout caters more to the experience of reading the sequence than to the page as a visual totality. The oscillating grid notably stands out within the notional multiframe of the entire serial strip, but for the most part there are few nested levels drawn overtly into play here. The varied panels are read in relation to each other and implicitly in relation to the ongoing body of work, while the experience of moving through this muddled sequence inferentially connects with the general story content. There is, however, some use made of the syntactic semiotic level through the repeated image of the sleeper in bed in the squashed panels here. This is not a question of a repeated motif. The image occurs periodically, always peripherally visible at regular junctures across the continuous page, which is punctuated by this visual assonance in the same way the scattered dreams are repeatedly punctured by a return to wakefulness.

The "all at once" aspect of comics' simultaneous panels has already been discussed in relation to the disruptions of linear narrative progression that

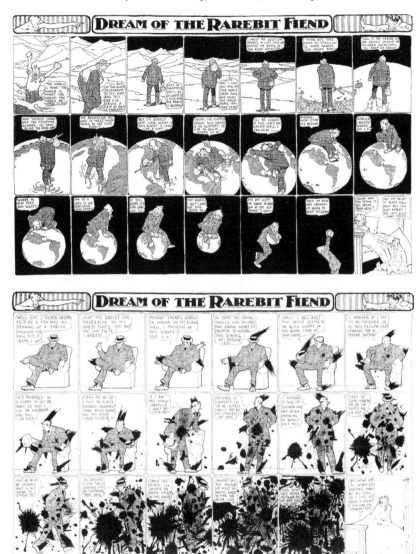

9.12 Winsor McCay, *Dream of the Rarebit Fiend: The Saturdays* (West Carrollton: Checker Book Publishing Group, 2006), p. 63; p. 27.

occur when split panels create larger wholes from contiguous panels. This device bears resemblance to the practice of drawing formal contents into play within the visual unit of the page. The example above demonstrates how contents can be brought into productive play within a composition on two distinct levels. On the narrative, semantic/pragmatic level the regular resizing of panel dimensions creates an uneven and disorientating reading pathway that speaks to the *idea* of bewilderingly unsettled sleep. On the formal, syntactic level the repetition of the sleeper in bed *embodies* the return to waking reality that punctuates the perplexing muddle of dreamscapes. Current theorizations of narrative/layout relations do not always make this distinction explicit. Furthermore, the involvement of formal contents in constituting a page composition particularly demonstrates that this larger visual unit cannot be adequately understood as a complex network of delimiting frames. The formal contents housed within those frames are always simultaneously visible "all at once" on the continuous page surface, and play a role in constituting those units' value within a composition.

Two further examples from McCay's strip show that the co-presence on the page plane of formal contents can create continuous totalities while exploiting our tacit understanding that these co-existent elements read as a sequential narrative. In both strips above (Fig. 9.12) the composition inscribes a sense of escalation through the progressive intensification of a certain physical feature, all peripherally visible at once on the continuous surface of the page. In the first strip, a steadily shrinking globe leaves its sole inhabitant awkwardly perched on and finally desperately clinging to its diminishing surface. Across the first row there is a consistent stripe of black as the horizon lowers and rounds off, and the dark space beyond strengthens into an ever-more substantial presence beside the waning white band of the earth. In the second row, the palpably continuous caterpillar-chain of globes continues to trail off, while in the third the black space gradually comes to dominate each panel. The second strip, which hinges on a metafictional acknowledgment from its central character of the artist who draws him, works by much the same device, occasional blots and smears worsening till the bottom of the page is an indistinct splatter of ink. These examples depend upon a conception of the page space as an advancing narrative, but the presence of all parts at once within the unified composition means we perceive it less as the one-at-a-time words in prose or shots in film, and more as a cohesive expanse whose narrative development is inscribed across the continuous page, in both cases as black insistently crowds out white.

The participation of the iconic contents of panels in page compositions can in some cases more radically override panel boundaries. Visual forms can appear to traverse the page, effectively laid over the organizing grid. In this section from *The Dark Knight Returns* shapes within adjoining panels

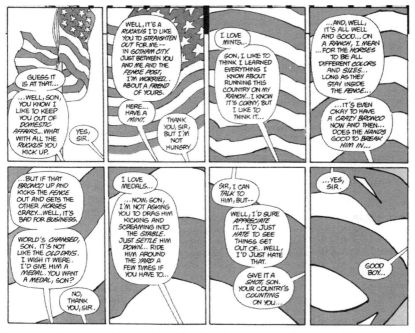

9.13 Frank Miller, *The Dark Knight Returns* (London: Titan Books, 1986), book 2, p. 28.

coalesce to form nuanced continuities that persist across rows of panels
in a manner not dissimilar to split panels (Fig. 9.13). (Here, as in the strips
above, this continuity flows across rows, but there is no bar to its working vertically or diagonally.) As a rather veiled conversation introduces a
plan to quell the chaos arising from Batman's return from retirement, the
"camera" zooms in on an American flag, whose undulating stripes loosely
merge over panel boundaries. In the penultimate panel, white is replaced
with yellow, and in the last the camera pulls back slightly to reveal the
S emblem of Superman—recast in Miller's text as a dutiful government
stooge charged with reining in the renegade Batman. The merging of these
red and white waves in some sense mimics the smooth continuity of a film
zoom that is usually implicit in comics' discontinuous panels, but more
than this it is suggestive of the way Superman is woven into the institution of the American state in Miller's text. Superman, more so than the
"decadent, reactionary, vampiric" (Sandbrook 2011: 34) Batman, is the
archetypal American superhero, a powerful symbolic figure in himself.
Here, he is the tool of a shady administration, and the way the stripes of
the flapping flag merge into the curve of his insignia is suggestive of this

association. That these flowing lines do not exactly match implies a certain discord, both within the country itself, whose iconic stripes also falter over panel divisions, and between superhero and government.

Once again, the operation of the composition above differs from an arthrological visual echo between the forms of flag stripes and insignia, which could occur between dispersed, non-contiguous panels. These shapes actually segue into each other to create thickening bands across the width of the page. There is a palpable shift with the replacement of white with yellow, which is underscored by the speech balloons. When we look onto the red-and-white of the flag, the speech balloon tails of both interlocutors point downwards to where they stand below it, but this changes with the shift to the red-and-yellow emblem in which panels one speaker's balloons have tails pointing upwards while the other's point off to the side: the different placement of the speakers in relation to the background indicates that our gaze has been repositioned. This neatly clarifies the shift, without disrupting the formal continuity that ties these two symbols, emblem and flag, into uneasy complicity. In this particular example, the underlying multiframe all but ceases to be a pertinent measure of the page composition. It is formal content—syntactic-level visual figures—that constitutes the visual unit of the page.

In stressing the possibility of formal contents participating in the larger unit of the page, I am of course not arguing that this is always or predominantly the way that composition is constructed in comics. Rather, the aim is to point out that the suggestion that analysis concentrates on frame is rather limiting, and there is a pertinent distinction to be made as to whether it is primarily formal or narrative content that is drawn into reciprocal play with the multiframe. The generic approach to layout put forth here does not assign to a particular element the status of basic, fundamental unit, but instead attends to all the various nested layers and the particular relationships that exist between them in a given composition. Though, in a given work, not all of these layers may be drawn into productive play, they potentially include: the text's grid and the relationship of particular pages and panels to it and to each other; formal contents, and their correlation with their individual frame, the larger multiframe and, as the later examples here showed, formal contents in other panels on the page; narrative information and the way this plugs into the individual frame and composite multiframe. We might even say, in the motivated visual system, that narrative information is essentially a nested layer "within" formal content since the two are potentially linked, and a layout that exploits formal content is almost certainly playing to story content too.

Admittedly, there are ways in which composition in comics compares with language. Like any semiotic system, meaning depends on differential relationships, and individual panels are imbued with a significance dependent on their place within a larger system. However, their values are constructed within the bounds of individual texts and are often additionally imbued with significance through their content. Composition is a system of motivated forms whose significance is often interpretable in ways arbitrary language is not. The implication of all elements in constructing meaning within the motivated and semantically dense system of comics layout means its operations can be understood as much—if not more so—according to the model of visual signification that this book has sought to distinguish from the linguistic model. The linguistic model is of relevance here, insofar as composition can in part be understood as a system that combines discrete units that are differentially defined. Crucially, however, those units are not minimal, and in dissecting how comics combine these units into larger, integrated wholes we have to acknowledge the continuousness, motivation, relative autonomy, and semantic density that characterizes those demarcated units. Theorizing comics' composition according to semiotic models ultimately exposes a kind of tension between the discreteness of its constituent elements and the continuousness of those elements themselves, always already complex compounds. Because of this, the debate around pertinent units is "useless" only insofar as it attempts to identify a single type of *minimal* unit. Each unit, each layer, is constituted by what is inside it as much as by where it fits into a text's multiframe. For this reason, given the multitude of nested layers and their co-presence on the continuous page surface, Groensteen's analogy of the reverse Russian doll seems a highly apt one (2006)—although crucially, this is an infinite Russian doll, one whose nested innards are always visible "all at once," and whose innermost layer is never finally reached.

Conclusion

The preceding arguments have sought to expose the problems inherent in many of the stock assertions that are widely made about the formal makeup of comics. These prevailing assumptions have become engrained as the basis for understanding this hybrid medium in formal terms and the use that it makes of the visual and verbal signifying modes. It has been shown throughout that the resultant formal critical framework corresponds to defensive preoccupations with the supposed superior status of language and literature and has less to do with the evidence provided by comics texts themselves. I have ascribed this problem in part to a degree of critical insularity, which has seen the development of a critical discourse that is often very attentive to its own self-perpetuated ideas, but somewhat less attuned to the established theories and disciplines that could usefully illuminate the commonly propagated notions around comics formal structures.

In bringing to light the shortcomings of these defensively motivated critical standpoints, the aim has not been by any means to cast aside all aspects of the current formal model, but rather to amend it. Careful application of the relevant semiotic theory destabilizes the accepted wisdom regarding the negligible differences between words and images, and challenges the overextension of a generalized linguistic model to a diverse range of visual signifying practices. The corrections and caveats this exercise gives rise to, when applied to a range of comics through detailed close readings, empirically demonstrate the shortcomings of the dominant theory for accounting for what actually goes on within the pages of the texts themselves. Thus, this book is not only a challenge to the established patterns of defensive formal criticism, but an attempt to provide a modified conceptual framework in which a firmer relationship with wider critical discourses, and greater precision, takes the place of the perceived need to bolster comics to the privileged position of literature and the visual mode in general to the supposedly elevated level of language.

Throughout, a skepticism has been maintained regarding the routine reach toward literature as the appropriate medium for comparison with comics. It has been continually suggested that the form has as much—if not more—in common with the narrative medium of cinema, as well as the field of visual art, as it does with literature. I concur with Bart Beaty (writing in critical exchange with Hatfield on the *Comics Reporter* website) that "we have to sacrifice too much specificity in order to regard comics as a literary form," and in doing so "los[e] all sense of what the term means" (2005: np). Hatfield's rejoinder is that he wishes to expand the very notion of what literature can be, which does not seem to respond to the issue of what the term usefully describes if it is so expanded. His response still begs the question: "If literary studies is going to incorporate art exhibitions, have we reached the end of literature as a useful concept?" (Beaty 2005: np). Such a conception of literariness becomes so broad as to be meaningless, providing no practical means of engaging with the variegated forms to which it would refer. Accordingly, I have advocated a new way of evaluating the literary qualities of the comics form, one that does not counter-intuitively align narrative with prose fiction or concentrate on thematic content at the expense of media-specific formalism.

The first section here demonstrated that the language-focused close-reading tools of literary criticism can be usefully brought to bear on comics, both in terms of the quality of the writing itself and its particular deployment within the fragmentary comics form. It should be cautioned, however, that this will only be fruitful to the extent that a particular text works to exploit the literary potential of its textual content. I do not advocate literary writing as a hard and fast evaluative criterion of *all* comics: a given text is not necessarily poor just because its writing is mediocre; it is simply not a literary comic. Indeed, something I have tried to expunge from the amended critical model is a notion that the words, pictures, or their degree of blending are always present in every text in a generalizable way, or that we can automatically judge a comic as being better if word and image interact in certain ways, or worse if its sense is heavily dependent on text. These various aspects of the form are points of entry for a formal analysis of a given text, but we cannot decide in advance that certain word-image balances are always superior or more fundamentally "comicsy" than others independent of the specific ways in which they are put to work in individual texts.

Admittedly, for an argument that hinges on questioning the assumption that comics are a kind of literature, this book has been heavily skewed towards language. This tactic deliberately aims at challenging the bias away from language and verbal content, too frequently sidelined for defensive reasons, and at correcting the over-general understanding of the linguistic semiotic model that allows comics and visual signification to be described loosely in its terms, while eliding the specificities of the form and its twin semiotic modes. Primarily, though, this focus on language has sought to problematize the prevalent notions of what it means for a comic to be literary. I have aimed to prove that language can, potentially, be integral within comics, and that it is this use of language and not the telling of a story that renders some comics, potentially, literary. I have also had some recourse to the formal analytical approach of the art critic, a line of exploration that has more universal application than that of literary criticism. Whatever use is made of verbal text, there will always be present visual qualities—aspects of design, composition, line character—which can be fruitfully examined, and which there is some risk of neglecting if we continue to assert that comics are literature (read "narratives") and that iconic images can be understood wholly in terms of a linguistic model.

The main thrust of this book has, of course, been to show that both visual signification in general (whether it is aspects of iconic pictures, conventionalized comics shorthand, or the supportive apparatus of borders, frames, and whitespace) and the comics medium (including its panel-units, its articulation of narrative information, and its arrangement of content across its segmented, simultaneous surface) work in ways that are very much distinct from the model of verbal language. I have striven to demonstrate not only that these differences exist but, following Mitchell, to address the more pertinent question of "what difference do the differences (and similarities) make?" (Mitchell 2009: 116). The preceding chapters have shown exactly why it matters that visual and verbal work in different ways. Our understanding of the comics form is dependent on acknowledging these differences. In order to comprehend how the language games of Herriman and Barry work, we need to grasp the principles of double-articulation, arbitrariness, and the distinction between *langue* and *parole* that govern how we make meaning from language. Similarly, to appreciate how speech bubbles, speed lines, and the like signify the way they do, we must recognize their underlying motivation, interpretability, and consequent malleability, even in the face of their conventionalization. We need also to understand the implications of their radical heterogeneity and density in order to realize how the flexibility of motivated signs and their relative lack of constraint by a *langue* enables many of the effects generated by comics' diverse iconic shorthand. The principles of syntactic and semantic density too, the constitution of every mark, line, and visual trace within the context of a specific complex of relations, open the way to explaining the nuanced aesthetic effects of drawing style, which the linguistic model provides little means for exploring.

The medium itself also needs to be understood via a sign model altered to account for the features of visual signification. The question of the separation of *langue* and *parole* allows us to separate visual and verbal even when the former is heavily implicated in the concretization of a linguistic sign in a particular instance of usage. The co-presence of panels on the page also complicates the equation of sequential narrative progression with syntagmatic linguistic relations. This book has worked to challenge the way that the form's broad tendency toward linear narrative progression across chains of panels has solidified into a nebulous and over-expansive definition of comics as "sequential art." If language can be understood as articulations within a flux of sound that we learn to map on to differentiations in the flux of experience (leaving aside the issue of which precedes or enables the other), then we can see at once that comics' transitioning panels cannot be viewed in the same way: "in an instant of perception, linear systems communicate only in a single sound or sign" (Bertin 1983: 3), but comics' panels, even when they are to be read in straightforward linear sequence, are already rich and complex collections of signs, very different to the single sound or minimal sign that the language user is dealt strictly one at a time. Additionally, these complex, non-minimal signs are drawn into play with spatially continuous but non-consecutive panel-units, making two-dimensional, and not linear one-dimensional, spacing the most pertinent feature of comics narratives.

It has been acknowledged that there are valid points of comparison between the structural model of language and the systematic integration of smaller units into the coherent whole of the comics page. Panels, in terms of their size, shape, and internal makeup, are signs constituted through their relationship to and place within a system of other panels. But it has also been shown that those key points of difference, non-minimalism and motivation, once again prove to be instrumental in defining these composite units and explaining how they signify. The relevance of these differences between visual signification and language is not, as so many comics critics seem driven to think, a question of establishing (or challenging) the communicative efficacy of images beside the hallowed benchmark of the verbal. As Eco says, "When we analyze a literary work we do not discuss the virtues or defects of the medium of writing" (2002: np). There is simply no need to explain that images are as valid as text. There is, however, a need to examine the uses to which comics artists put words, pictures, and the visual devices of the form. This is something that can only be done effectively with a clear and precise acknowledgement of the structural differences between the various signifying practices involved, for they generate meaning in different ways. It is these differences and their implications for how we read and process comics, rather than any question of whether one set of signifying practices is somehow inherently better than another, with which formalist criticism of comics should be most concerned.

As well as an interest in the differences made by the differences between words and images, this book has finally been concerned with why these differences matter for comics criticism in particular. They matter because, despite the field's exponential growth over the past couple of decades, comics criticism is still a burgeoning rather than established field of scholarship. This nascence accounts for the demonstrable pressure critics feel to argue for the seriousness of comics and their study. But this imperative is not ill served by the sometimes woolly, vague, and conceptually unsophisticated way that broader theory—semiotics in particular—has regularly been treated. Given the cultural history of comics as a low status form, it can be no surprise there has been a widespread "concern with the legitimacy of the field" (Beaty 2007: 206), but the defensive strategy of simply pleading that the art form and its study not be dismissed is a false move. As Wolk says, "Demanding (and wishing for) a place at the table of high culture is an admission that you don't have one; the way you get a place at the table of high culture is to pull up a chair and say something interesting" (2007: 64). The most effective strategy against any persistent dismissal of the form is not to insist on the worth of images or the comics medium, but to lead by example, producing criticism that is careful, thorough, and sophisticated in its approach. Charges that there exists "something of a dearth of serious criticism of comics" (Meskin 2009: 221) still persist. This is something of an exaggeration: reams of meticulous, thoughtful, and conceptually accurate work on comics are out there, but nevertheless a streak of theoretical weakness remains that critics are not always sufficiently conscientious about challenging—particularly where formal models are concerned. The differences between words and images particularly matter for comics critics, because when they are denied it is generally done via over-generalization, defensive dismissal, and incautious recycling of hypotheses that were never grounded in a proper understanding of the related theoretical frameworks in the first place. To reframe Mitchell's question "what difference do the differences [. . .] make?," for comics critics they make the difference between precise and imprecise theory, between serious scholarship and academic laxity. Too many of the tenets generated during the field's awkward adolescence are still being asserted as it emerges into maturity, and a key aim of this book has been to attempt to draw a line under these persistent problematic convictions.

I am not, of course, advocating that as academic scholars of this art form we should dismiss the rich vein of practitioner criticism that many of these notions first stemmed from. Though the field's traditional attentiveness to the wisdom of comics' creators might bring to mind Claes Oldenburg's remark that "anyone who listens to an artist talk should have his eyes examined" (cited in Barnet 2011: 96), this would be going rather too far in a critical field that largely owes its genesis to practitioners and other non-scholarly enthusiasts. We do, however, need to be vigilant about theoretical shortcomings, wherever these exist. It would be outrageous to suggest that all practitioner criticism is error-prone and that it can never hold its own beside academically ratified scholarship. But it is the duty of academics to acknowledge conceptual problems when they do arise, and not to deferentially recite poor theory out of a fear that such acknowledgments entail participating in the kind of snobbery that has for so long kept comics out of the academy altogether. This occasional reluctance to take on the recognized practices of scholarly discourse at the risk of colluding in its perceived exclusivity and elitism represents a rather ironic distortion of the defensiveness about the academy's traditional lack of respect for the form. Instead of commanding that respect through theoretically sound study of comics that takes itself precisely as seriously as it asks to be taken, there has sometimes been an unwillingness to essentially "gentrify" a field that has hitherto been very much open and democratic. But it is this attitude that has yielded the exceedingly patchy field we now have, so democratic and inclusive it risks failing to discern between good and bad criticism. While it is something of an exaggeration to suggest that there is still a "dearth" of serious comics criticism, it is true that the theoretically sophisticated criticism that exists is too rarely distinguished from the theoretically inadequate, and this remains a particular problem for formalist conceptions. Following Elkins's call to arms for the field of visual studies, as a general addendum to the specific issues raised in this book, I hope comics scholarship continues to develop into a field that is "denser with theories and strategies, more reflective about its own history, warier of existing visual theories, more attentive to neighboring and distant disciplines, more vigilant about its own sense of visuality, less predictable in its politics, and less routine in its choice of subjects" (2003: 65).

As comics criticism continues to strengthen its presence within the academy, it becomes ever more urgent that this kind of properly thoughtful scholarly criticism becomes the norm, not the exception, for if the seriousness of the field really does need defending, this can be the only viable strategy.

Notes

Introduction

1. Art Spiegelman, speaking to Tom Gatti, refers to "those early painted-glass comics that were used in churches to tell the superhero story of that guy who could walk on water" (2008: np).

2. Eco was writing in 1972 but is cited in illustration of a situation that has not changed.

3. This tendency is on the wane among Francophone critics, who are turning to the visual arts as the most apposite comparator (Beaty 2007: 7), a tradition that the Anglophone field has thus far rather neglected as a useful model.

4. The assertion that "comics are a language" is near universal, and the phrase "the language of comics" has effectively been canonized. See: Kunzle 1990: 371, Sabin 1996: 8, McCloud 2000: 1, Christiansen 2000: 109, Raeburn 2004: 22, Chute & DeKoven 2006: 768, Versaci 2007: 187, Bartual 2010: 83, Ball & Kuhlman 2010: p. xvii; and of course the twin titles of Saraceni's (2000) and Varnum & Gibbons's (2001) *The Language of Comics*.

5. For example, comics grammar is variously characterized as: panel gaps (McCloud 1993: 67, Chute 2008: 455); the specific sequential arrangement of panels (Peeters 2007: np); as panel *borders* and word balloons (Raeburn 2004: 22); as individual pages (being the "crucial units of comics grammar") (Chute 2009: 340); as "the multipage booklet story form" (Harvey Kurtzman cited in Harvey 1996: 66); and, rather expansively, as the rendering of elements in the frame, arrangement of inner images, and relationships to the rest of the sequence (Eisner 1985: 39).

Chapter One

1. A more extensive summary of these attempts is given in Chapter Seven, in which their inherent problems are fully demonstrated.

2. Unleavened maize bread; presumably what "korn poems" is meant to evoke.

Chapter Two

1. To adopt Gene Kannenberg's term: "I use *lexia* to describe a distinct textual division in a graphic, not grammatical sense: a block of text which is designed to be

read/viewed as a single unit, usually (although not always) a smaller sub-unit in a larger structure such as a panel or page" (Kannenberg 2001: 178).

2. In the sense of being "ostentatious, exaggerated, affected, theatrical" (OED), suggesting a "banality, mediocrity, artifice, ostentation, etc. so extreme as to amuse or have a perversely sophisticated appeal" (Webster's).

Chapter Three

1. For example: the mental suturing of narrative ellipsis afforded by panel gaps, sometimes termed "closure" (McCloud 1993: 92); as a consequence of this, the participation required of the reader (McCloud 2000: 3); its reciprocal mixture of word and image (Hatfield 2005: xii); sequentiality (Beaty 2007: 77). All these effects have parallels in other forms, and several will be examined in greater detail in due course.

2. "Commutation" is given by the OED as "the action or process of commuting a judicial sentence or a legal obligation or entitlement"; the word "commute" (meaning either to reduce a sentence, as above, or latterly but perhaps now primarily "to travel some distance between one's home and place of work on a regular basis") "derives from *commutation ticket*, the US terms for a season ticket (because the daily fare is commuted to a single payment)." Eisner attempts to take the word "commute" and create from it a word that means something like "commute-ing-ness," or perhaps "commuting needs"—unfortunately landing on a word that already exists and means something else.

3. The name is possibly a reference to the obscure literary figure Joseph Joubert, whose legacy includes not a single work published in his lifetime, but a huge volume of writing in the form of diaries containing philosophical musings, literary criticism, and contemporary observances—though little chronicling his own life. This rather resonates with the fictional Joubert's dramatizing redaction of his neighbor Gemma's diary.

4. An inverse effect is seen in Joubert's guileless purification of the term "cottaging," which rewrites that phrase in a much more innocent and artless way (Fig. 3.4).

Chapter Four

1. See also: Pratt 2009: 107, Chute & DeKoven 2006: 769, Harvey 1996: 3, Hatfield 2005: 36, Meskin 2007: 378.

2. See also: Kannenberg 2001: 176, Sabin 1993: 9, Whitlock 2006: 969.

3. For the former, see: Cohn 2005: 237, Chute & DeKoven 2006: 769, Harvey 1996: 3. For the latter, see: McCloud 1993: 92, Whitlock 2006: 969, Sabin 1993: 9.

4. This chapter cannot go by without including the caveat that, of course, comics do not always utilize verbal text. I do not intend this reference to the form's mixed nature to suggest that silent comics are in fact some other form, nor would most critics insist

on the inclusion of words along with images as a definitive criterion (though Harvey appears to do so [2001: 75]).

5. Sabin himself does not explicate exactly what these terms might refer to in comics. In addition to the divergent characterizations of "grammar" cited in the introduction, attempts have been made to designate visual forms as a vocabulary (McCloud 1993: 67, Whitlock 2006: 968) (though such forms are infinite, and not necessarily repeated, unlike language's finite pool of repeatable signifiers); to liken cartoon figures and "speed lines and shock waves and their ilk" respectively to nouns and verbs (Raeburn 2004: 22); and, more convincingly, to ascribe comics' linguistic nature to the syntax of its sequential panels (Cohn 2005: 237).

6. Harvey claims the form emerged when expository captions disappeared and incorporated speech balloons emerged (Harvey 1996: 107–9); Carrier too distinguishes the comics form from eighteenth-century broadsheets and older forms of strip narrative by the inclusion of speech balloons within the picture space (2000: 4); and Ann Miller notes that the device is frequently cited as criterial in arguments over the form's genesis (Miller 2007: 16).

Chapter Five

1. This configuration is actually more complex than this: following the reading protocol, we first see the familiar bird, recognizable as part of the picture. It seems to wheel into the distance over an emerging landscape backdrop in the upper row, which aligns with the background in the lower row. However, in the leftmost vertical pair of panels, the bird appears rather too low and too close to be part of a split scene and seems rather artificially to hover in un-located space (as in the frozen picture). Thus, the bird seems to escape from its picture as it slowly calibrates with the perspective of the background across the top row, peeling away and soaring over the hills as the couple themselves steadily move away from the confines of the city.

Chapter Six

1. Chute's own position on this prevalent practice is not entirely clear. In the earlier publication she appears to affirm that comics "might be defined" as a form that "register[s] temporality spatially" (2008: 452), but seems warier of this avowal in the later text, reporting that "'time as space' is a description we hear again and again from theorists" (2009: 342) in a way that seems to distance her from this viewpoint.

2. There is not room here to adequately engage with the ways readers negotiate a reading pathway through multiple speech balloons, though I would suggest these too are processed by testing possibilities and deducing an appropriate order as much by following hard and fast rules, which some critics have been wont to suggest is the case (Khordoc 2001).

Chapter Seven

1. See for example: Koch (1971), Hünig (1974), Oomen (1975), Kloepfer (1977) (cited in Christiansen & Magunussen 2000: 12–13); and Gauthier (1976) (cited in Groensteen 2006: 3).

Chapter Eight

1. The primers cited in clarifying this approach (alongside such other handy "formalist art criticism 101" guides as Henry Sayre's *Writing About Art* [2008], Mary Acton's *Learning to Look at Paintings* [1997], Nadeije Laneyrie-Dagen's *How to Read Paintings* [2004]) are not woven into the ensuing discussion in any extensive way, describing as they do an established basic approach to appraising pictures' formal features, rather than more specialized or specific slant on theorizing visual art.

2. As footnoted in the introduction, viewing comics as visual art objects, rather than literary ones, is more the norm within European circles (Beaty 2007: 7), though Groensteen's objections to the information-focused functionalism of Francophone scholarship suggests this has not always been the case.

Bibliography

21 Grams, dir. Alejandro González Iñárritu. Focus Features. 2003

Abbott, Lawrence L., "Comic Art: Characteristics and Potentialities of a Narrative Medium." *Journal of Popular Culture*. 19.4 (1986): 155–76.

Adams, Laurie Schneider. *The Methodologies of Art: An Introduction* (London: Westview Press, 1996).

Addams, Charles. *Happily Ever After: A Collection of Cartoons to Chill the Heart of Your Loved One* (London: Simon and Schuster, 2006).

Aijmer, Karen. *Conversational Routines in English: Convention and Creativity* (London: Longman, 1996).

Ashford, Daisy. *The Young Visiters* [1919] (London: Chatto & Windus, 2003).

Atkinson, Paul, "The Graphic Novel as Metafiction." *Studies in Comics*. 1.1 (2010): 107–25.

Auster, Paul. *The Invention of Solitude* (London: Faber and Faber, 1988a).

———. *The New York Trilogy* (London: Faber and Faber, 1988b).

Auster, Paul, Paul Karasik and David Mazzucchelli. *City of Glass* (London: Faber and Faber, 2004).

Badman, Derik A. "Talking, Thinking, and Seeing in Pictures: Narration, Focalisation, and Ocularisation in Comics Narratives." *International Journal of Comic Art*, 12.2/3 (2010): 91–111.

Baetens, Jan. "Revealing Traces: A New Theory of Graphic Enunciation," in *The Language of Comics: Word and Image*, ed. by Robin Varnum and Christina Gibbons (Jackson: University of Mississippi Press, 2001), pp. 145–55.

———. "*The New Media Reader* review," *Image & Narrative*, 4.1 (2003), http://www.imageandnarrative.be/inarchive/graphicnovel/wardripfruin_montfort.htm [accessed 1 November 2008].

Ball, David M. and Martha B. Kuhlman (eds.). *The Comics of Chris Ware: Drawing Is a Way of Thinking* (Jackson: University Press of Mississippi, 2010).

———. "Intro: Chris Ware and the 'Cult of Difficulty,'" in *The Comics of Chris Ware: Drawing Is a Way of Thinking*, David M. Ball, and Martha B. Kuhlman (eds.) (Jackson: University Press of Mississippi, 2010), pp. ix–xxiii.

Barnet, Sylvan. *A Short Guide to Writing About Art*, 11th edn. (London: Pearson, 2011).

Barrier, Michael. "Comics Master: The Art and Spirit of Will Eisner," *Print*, 42.6 (1988): 197–98.

Barry, Lynda. *Come Over, Come Over* (New York: Harper Perennial, 1990).

———. *The Freddie Stories* (Seattle: Sasquatch 1999).

———. *The! Greatest! Of! Marlys!* (Seattle: Sasquatch, 2000).

———. "Generosity," *Salon*, 2001, http://www.salon.com/life/comics/2001/09/07/lynda7 [accessed 30 May 2008].

———. *One! Hundred! Demons!* (Seattle: Sasquatch Books, 2002a).

———. "Means He Likes You." *Marlys Magazine*, 2002b, www.marlysmagazine.com/421 .htm [accessed 18 March 2007].

———. "Hot Curler." *Salon*, 2002c, http://www.salon.com/life/comics/2002/11/22/hot_ curler [accessed 30 May 2008].

———. "Zombie Girl." *Salon*, 2002d, http://www.salon.com/life/comics/2002/11/15/ zombie_girl [accessed 30 May 2008].

———. "Boomeranged." *Salon*, 2002e, http://www.salon.com/life/comics/2002/10/04/ lynda_boomerang [accessed 30 May 2008].

———. "Drastic Action." *Salon*, 2002f, http://www.salon.com/life/comics/2002/03/21/ lynda31 [accessed 30 May 2008].

———. "Trick Answers." *Salon*, 2003a, http://www.salon.com/life/comics/2003/08/26/ lynda [accessed 30 May 2008].

———. "Sudden Dance Party." *Marlys Magazine*, 2003b, www.marlysmagazine.com/659 .htm [accessed 18 March 2007].

———. "Imagination Stoppers." *Salon*, 2004, http://www.salon.com/life/comics/ barry/2004/09/10/imagination_stoppers [accessed 30 May 2008].

———. "Mood Ring Cycle." *Marlys Magazine*, 2005a, www.marlysmagazine.com/874 .htm [accessed 18 March 2007].

———. "Take Me Back." *Marlys Magazine*, 2005b, www.marlysmagazine.com/991.htm [accessed 18 March 2007].

———. "Too Creative." *Marlys Magazine*, 2007a, www.marlysmagazine.com/517.htm [accessed 18 March 2007].

———. "Summer Love Showdown." *Marlys Magazine*, 2007b, www.marlysmagazine .com/562.htm [accessed 18 March 2007].

———. "Things I Can See From Here." *Marlys Magazine*, 2007c, www.marlysmagazine .com/243.htm [accessed 18 March 2007].

Barthes, Roland, *Elements of Semiology*, trans. by Annette Lavers, and Colin Smith (London: Jonathan Cape, 1967a).

———. *Writing Degree Zero*, trans. by Annette Lavers, and Colin Smith (London: Jonathan Cape, 1967b).

Bartual, Roberto. "William Hogarth's *A Harlot's Progress*: the Beginnings of a Purely Pictographic Sequential Language." *Studies in Comics*, 1.1 (2010): 83–105.

Beaty, Bart. "The Search for Comics Exceptionalism." *Comics Journal*, 211 (1999): 67–72.

———. *Unpopular Culture: Transforming the European Comic Book in the 1990s* (Toronto: University of Toronto Press, 2007).

———. "Autobiography as Authenticity." in *A Comics Studies Reader*, ed. by Jeet Heer and Kent Worcester (Jackson: University Press of Mississippi, 2009), pp. 226–35.

Beaty, Bart, and Charles Hatfield. "Let's You and Him Fight: Alternative Comics –
An Emerging Literature," online discussion. *Comics Reporter*, 2005, http://www
.comicsreporter.com/index.php/briefings/commentary/3370/ [accessed 11 June 2011].

Bennett, Tamryn. "Towards Comics Poetry," unpublished conference paper presented
at *Fractured Words, Broken Images*, Lancaster University, 2010, http://www
.tamrynbennett.com/wp-content/uploads/2011/03/Tamryn-Bennett-Luminary
-submission-Towards-Comics-Poetry-web-1.pdf [accessed 11 June 2011].

Bergman, Mats and Sami Paavola (eds.). *The Commens Dictionary of Peirce's Terms:
Peirce's Terminology in His Own Words*, 2003. www.helsinki.fi/science/commens/
dictionary.html [accessed 17 January 2011].

Beronä, David. "Pictures Speak in Comics Without Words: Pictorial Principles in the
Work of Milt Gross, Hendrik Dorgathen, Eric Drooker and Peter Kuper," in *The
Language of Comics: Word and Image*, ed. by Robin Varnum and Christina Gibbons
(Jackson: University of Mississippi Press, 2001), pp. 19–39.

Berry, Hannah. *Britten and Brülightly* (London: Jonathan Cape, 2008).

Bertin, Jacques. *Semiology of Graphics: Diagrams, Networks, Maps*, trans. by William J.
Berg (Madison: University of Wisconsin Press, 1983).

Bindman, David. *Hogarth* (London: Thames and Hudson, 1981).

Brunetti, Ivan (ed.). *An Anthology of Graphic Fiction, Cartoons, and True Stories* (New
Haven: Yale University Press, 2006).

Burns, Charles. *Black Hole* (London: Jonathan Cape, 2005).

Butler, Judith. *Gender Trouble: Feminism and the Subversion of Identity* (London:
Routledge, 1990).

———. *The Psychic Life of Power: Theories in Subjection* (Stanford: Stanford University
Press, 1997).

———. "Performativity's Social Magic," in *Bordieu: A Critical Reader*, ed. by Richard
Shusterman (Oxford: Blackwells, 1999).

Carrier, David. *The Aesthetics of Comics* (Pennsylvania: The Pennsylvania State
University Press, 2000).

Cates, Isaac. "Comics and the Grammar of Diagrams," in *The Comics of Chris Ware:
Drawing Is a Way of Thinking*, ed. by David M. Ball and Martha B. Kuhlman
(Jackson: University Press of Mississippi, 2010), pp. 90–104.

Christiansen, Hans-Christian, and Anne Magnussen (eds.), *Comics and Culture:
Analytical and Theoretical Approaches to Comics* (Copenhagen: Museum
Tusculanum Press, 2000).

———. "Introduction," in *Comics and Culture: Analytical and Theoretical Approaches to
Comics*, ed. by Hans-Christian Christiansen and Anne Magnussen, pp. 7–25.

Christiansen, Hans-Christian. "Comics and Film: A Narrative Perspective," in *Comics
and Culture: Analytical and Theoretical Approaches to Comics*, ed. by Hans-
Christian Christiansen and Anne Magnussen, pp. 107–21.

Chilvers, Ian and Harold Osborne. *The Oxford Dictionary of Art* (Oxford: Oxford
University Press, 2004).

Chute, Hilary. "Decoding Comics." *Modern Fiction Studies*, 52.4 (2006): 1,014–27.

———. "Comics as Literature? Reading Graphic Narrative." *PMLA*, 123:2 (2008): 452–65.

———. "History and Graphic Representation in Maus," in *A Comics Studies Reader*, ed. by Jeet Heer and Kent Worcester (Jackson: University Press of Mississippi, 2009), pp. 340–62.

Chute, Hilary, and Marianne DeKoven. "Introduction: Graphic Narrative." *Modern Fiction Studies*, 52.4 (2006): 768–82.

Cioffi, Frank L. "Disturbing Comics: The Disjunction of Words and Image in the Comics of Andrzej Mleczko, Ben Katchor, R. Crumb, and Art Spiegelman," in *The Language of Comics: Word and Image*, ed. by Robin Varnum and Christina Gibbons (Jackson: University of Mississippi Press, 2001), pp. 97–122.

Cohn, Neil. "Un-Defining 'Comics': Separating the Cultural from the Structural in 'Comics,'" *International Journal of Comic Art*, 7.2 (2005): 236–48.

———. "A Visual Lexicon." *Public Journal of Semiotics*, 1.1 (2007): 35–56.

———. "Navigating Comics: Reading strategies of page layouts." *Emaki Productions*, 2008, http://www.emaki.net/essays/pagelayouts.pdf [accessed: 17 August 2010, no longer available].

———. "The Limits of Time and Transitions: Challenges to Theories of Sequential Image Comprehension." *Studies in Comics*, 1.1 (2010): 127–47.

Culler, Jonathan. *The Pursuit of Signs: Semiotics, Literature, Deconstruction* (London: Routledge & Kegan Paul, 1981).

Cwiklik, Greg. "Understanding the Real Problem." *Comics Journal*, 211 (1999): 62–66.

Dalwood, Dexter. *Sharon Tate's House*, painting, 1998.

De Haven, Tom. "The Master's Hand," in *Masters of American Comics*, ed. by John Carlin, Paul Karasik, Brian Walker (Los Angeles: Hammer Museum, 2005), pp. 177–84.

De Luca, Gianni. *Hamlet*, trans. by Barbara Graille (Paris: Les Humanoïdes Associés, 1980).

De Saussure, Ferdinand. *Course in General Linguistics*, trans. by Roy Harris (London: Duckworth, 1983).

"Dexter Dalwood," in *Saatchi Gallery*, nd, http://www.saatchi-gallery.co.uk/artists/dexter_dalwood.htm [accessed 29 May 2009].

Di Liddo, Annalisa. *Alan Moore: Comics as Performance, Fiction as Scalpel* (Jackson: University Press of Mississippi, 2009).

Eco, Umberto. *A Theory of Semiotics* (Bloomington: Indiana, 1976).

———. "Four Ways of Talking About Comics," trans. by Levana Taylor, *Comics Voyeur*, 2002, http://comicsvoyeur.blogspot.com/2008/10/eco-on-comics.html [accessed 19 June 2009].

Eisner, Will. *Comics and Sequential Art* (Florida: Poorhouse Press, 1985).

———. *New York: Life in the Big City* (London: Norton, 2006a).

———. *The Contract with God Trilogy: Life on Dropsie Avenue* (New York: Norton, 2006b).

Elkins, James. *Visual Studies: A Skeptical Introduction* (London: Routledge, 2003).

"Erector Spinae: muscles of the back," illustration, *Encyclopaedia Britannica*, 2008, http://www.britannica.com/EBchecked/topic/191213/erector-spinae [accessed 20 June 2011].

Forsdick, Charles, Laurence Grove, Libbie McQuillan (eds.). *The Francophone Bande Desinée* (New York: Editions Rodopi B.V., 2005).

Foucault, Michel. *This Is Not a Pipe*, trans. by James Harkness, illustrations by Rene Magritte (Berkeley: University of California Press, 1983).

Garland, Nicholas. "The emptiness at the heart of snobbery." *Telegraph Online*, 27 November 1999, Culture section, http://www.telegraph.co.uk/culture/4719144/The-emptiness-at-the-heart-of-snobbery.html [accessed 22 May 2011].

Gatti, Tom. "Exclusive interview with Art Spiegelman." *Times Online*, 21 December 2008, Art & Entertainment section.

Genette, Gerard. *Fiction and Diction*, trans. by Catherine Porter (Ithaca: Cornell University Press, 1993).

Goldsmith, Evelyn. *Research into Illustration: an approach and a review* (Cambridge: Cambridge University Press, 1984).

Gombrich, E. H. *Art and Illusion: A Study in the Psychology of Pictorial Representation* (London: Phaidon, 1952).

Gombrich, E. H., Julian Hochberg, and Max Black. *Art, Perception, and Reality* (Baltimore: John Hopkins University Press, 1972).

"Good Grief." *Arrested Development*. Fox Broadcasting Company, Season 2, Episode 4 [aired 5 December 2004].

Gravett, Paul. "De Luca and Hamlet: Thinking Outside the Box." *European Comic Art*, 1.1 (2008): 21–35.

Groensteen, Thierry. *The System of Comics*, trans. by Bart Beaty and Nick Nguyen (Jackson: University of Mississippi Press, 2006).

———. "A Few Words About *The System of Comics* and More." *European Comic Art*, 1.1 (2008): 87–93.

———. "Why Comics Are Still In Search of Cultural Legitimization?" trans. by Shirley Smolderen, in *A Comics Studies Reader*, ed. by Jeet Heer and Kent Worcester (Jackson: University Press of Mississippi, 2009a), pp. 3–13.

———. "The Impossible Definition," in *A Comics Studies Reader*, ed. by Jeet Heer and Kent Worcester (Jackson: University Press of Mississippi, 2009b), pp. 124–31.

Gross, Sabine. "The Word Turned Image: Reading Pattern Poems." *Poetics Today*, 18.1 (1997): 15–32.

Harrison, Randall P. *The Cartoon: Communication to the Quick* (London: Sage Publications, 1981).

Harvey, Robert C. "The Aesthetics of the Comic Strip." *Journal of Popular Culture*, 12.4 (1979): 640–52.

———. *The Art of the Comic Book: An Aesthetic History* (Jackson: University of Mississippi Press, 1996).

———. "Comedy at the Juncture of Word and Image: The Emergence of the Modern Magazine Gag Cartoon Reveals the Vital Blend," in *The Language of Comics: Word and Image*, ed. by Robin Varnum and Christina Gibbons (Jackson: University of Mississippi Press, 2001), pp. 75–96.

———. "How Comics Came To Be," in *A Comics Studies Reader*, ed. by Jeet Heer and Kent Worcester (Jackson: University Press of Mississippi, 2009), pp. 25–45.

Hatfield, Charles. *Alternative Comics: An Emerging Literature* (Jackson: University Press of Mississippi, 2005).

———. "An Art of Tensions," in *A Comics Studies Reader*, ed. by Jeet Heer and Kent Worcester (Jackson: University Press of Mississippi, 2009), pp. 132–48.

Heer, Jeet. "Kat Got Your Tongue: Where George Herriman's Language Came From," in George Herriman, *Krazy & Ignatz: 1941–1942*, ed. by Bill Blackbeard (Seattle: Fantagraphics, 2008), pp. 7–9.

Heer, Jeet, and Kent Worcester (eds.). *A Comics Studies Reader* (Jackson: University Press of Mississippi, 2009).

———. "Introduction," in *A Comics Studies Reader*, ed. by Jeet Heer and Kent Worcester (Jackson: University Press of Mississippi, 2009), pp. xi–xiv.

Herriman, George. *Krazy & Ignatz: 1925–1926*, ed. by Bill Blackbeard (Seattle: Fantagraphics, 2002).

———. *Krazy & Ignatz: 1937–1938*, ed. by Bill Blackbeard (Seattle: Fantagraphics, 2006).

———. *Krazy & Ignatz: 1939–1940*, ed. by Bill Blackbeard (Seattle: Fantagraphics, 2007).

———. *Krazy & Ignatz: 1941–1942*, ed. by Bill Blackbeard (Seattle: Fantagraphics, 2008).

———. *Krazy and Ignatz: 1919–1921*, ed. by Bill Blackbeard (Seattle: Fantagraphics, 2011).

Hochberg, Julian, "The Representation of Things and People," E. H. Gombrich, Julian Hochberg, and Max Black (eds.). *Art, Perception, and Reality* (Baltimore: John Hopkins University Press, 1972), pp. 47–94.

Horrocks, Dylan. "Inventing Comics: Scott McCloud's Definition of Comics." *Hicksville*, 2001, www.hicksville.co.nz/Inventing%20Comics.htm [accessed: 29 September 2009].

Howe, Justin. "*Black Hole*: Review." *Strange Horizons*, 2006, http://www.strange horizons.com/reviews/2006/06/black_hol.shtml [accessed: 7 March 2011].

Huizenga, Kevin. "Balloon." *Kramers Ergot #7* (Oakland: Buenaventura Press, 2000).

Iser, Wolfgang. "The Reading Process: A Phenomenological Approach," trans. by Catherine Macksey and Richard Macksey, in *Reader Response Criticism: From Formalism to Post-Structuralism*, ed. by Jane Tompkins (Baltimore: John Hopkins University Press, 1980), pp. 50–69.

Jason. *The Left Bank Gang* (Seattle: Fantagraphics, 2006)

Kannenberg, Gene. "The Comics of Chris Ware: Text, Image, and Visual Narrative Strategies," in *The Language of Comics: Word and Image*, ed. by Robin Varnum and Christina Gibbons (Jackson: University of Mississippi Press, 2001), pp. 174–98.

Khordoc, Catherine. "The Comic Book's Soundtrack: Visual Sound Effects in *Asterix*," in *The Language of Comics: Word and Image*, ed. by Robin Varnum and Christina Gibbons (Jackson: University of Mississippi Press, 2001), pp. 156–73.

Kitching, Gavin. *The Trouble With Theory: The Educational Costs of Postmodernism* (Pennsylvania: Pennsylvania State University Press, 2008).

Køhlert, Frederik Byrn. "Review of Contemporary Comics: A Symposium." *International Journal of Comic Art*, 12.2/3 (2010): 684–87.

Kress, Gunther, and Theo van Leeuwen. *Reading Images: The Grammar of Visual Design* (London: Routledge, 1996).

Kunzle, David. *The History of the Comic Strip: The Early Comic Strip: Narrative Strips and Picture Stories in the European Broadsheet from c. 1450 to 1825* (Berkeley: University of California Press, 1973).

———. *The History of the Comic Strip: The Nineteenth Century* (Berkeley: University of California Press, 1990).

———. "The Voices of Silence: Willette, Steinlen and the Introduction of the Silent Strip in the *Chat Noir*, with a German Coda," in *The Language of Comics: Word and Image*, ed. by Robin Varnum and Christina Gibbons (Jackson: University of Mississippi Press, 2001), pp. 3–18.

———. "Rodolphe Töpffer's Aesthetic Revolution" in *A Comics Studies Reader*, ed. by Jeet Heer and Kent Worcester (Jackson: University Press of Mississippi, 2009), pp. 17–24.

Lecercle, Jean-Jacque. *Philosophy Through the Looking-Glass: Language, Nonsense, Desire* (London: Hutchinson, 1985).

Lefèvre, Pascal. "Intertwining Verbal and Visual Elements in Printed Narratives for Adults." *Studies in Comics*, 1.1 (2010): 35–52.

Lent, John A. "The Winding, Pot-Holed Road of Comic Art Scholarship." *Studies in Comics*, 1.1 (2010): 7–33.

Levinson, Jerrold. *Music, Art, and Metaphysics* (Ithaca, Cornell University Press, 1990).

Lewis, A. David. "The Shape of Comic Book Reading." *Studies in Comics*, 1.1 (2010): 71–81.

Lichtenstein, Roy. *Sweet Dreams, Baby!*, painting, 1965

Lombard, Matthew, John A. Lent, Linda Greenwood and Asli Tunc. "A Framework for Studying Comic Art." *International Journal of Comic Art* 1.1 (1999): 17–32.

Magnussen, Anne. "The Semiotics of C. S. Peirce as a Theoretical Framework for the Understanding of Comics," in *Comics and Culture: Analytical and Theoretical Approaches to Comics*, ed. by Hans-Christian Christiansen and Anne Magnussen, pp. 193–207.

Mathieu, Marc-Antoine. *Le Processus* (Paris: Guy Delcourt Productions, 1993).

Mazzucchelli, David. *Asterios Polyp* (New York: Pantheon, 2009).

McCay, Winsor. *Dream of the Rarebit Fiend: The Saturdays* (West Carrollton: Checker Book Publishing Group, 2006).

McCay, Winsor. *Little Sammy Sneeze* (Palo Alto: Sunday Press Books, 2007).

McCloud, Scott. *Understanding Comics: The Invisible Art* (New York: Kitchen Sink Press, 1993).

———. "Round and Round with Scott McCloud: Interview by Robert C. Harvey." *Comics Journal*, 179 (1995): 52–81.

———. *Reinventing Comics: How Imagination and Technology Are Revolutionizing an Art Form* (New York: Perennial, 2000).

McQuillan, Libbie. "Introduction," in *The Francophone Bande Dessinée*, ed. by Charles Forsdick, Laurence Grove, Libbie McQuillan (New York: Editions Rodopi B.V., 2005), pp. 7–13.

Medley, Stuart. "Discerning pictures: how we look at and understand images in comics." *Studies in Comics*, 1.1 (2010): 53–70.

Memento, 2000, dir. Christopher Nolan, Summit Entertainment

Meskin, Aaron. "Defining Comics?" *Journal of Aesthetics and Art Criticism*, 64.4 (2007): 369–79.

———. "Comics as Literature?" *British Journal of Aesthetics*, 49.3 (2009): 219–39.

Miller, Ann. *Reading Bande Dessinée: Critical Approaches to French-language Comic Strip* (Bristol: Intellect Books, 2007).

Miller, Frank. *Batman: The Dark Knight Returns* (London: Titan Books, 1986).

Mitchell, W. J. T. *Iconology: Image, Text, Ideology* (Chicago: University of Chicago Press, 1986).

———. *Picture Theory: Essays on Verbal and Visual Representation* (Chicago: University of Chicago Press, 1994).

———. "Beyond Comparison," in *A Comics Studies Reader*, ed. by Jeet Heer and Kent Worcester (Jackson: University Press of Mississippi, 2009), pp. 116–23.

Moore, Alan, and David Lloyd. *V for Vendetta* (New York: Vertigo 1990).

Moore, Alan, Dave Gibbons and John Higgins. *Watchmen* (New York: DC Comics, 1995).

Moore, Alan, and Eddie Campbell. *From Hell: Being a Melodrama in Sixteen Parts* (London: Knockabout Comics, 2000).

Moore, Alan, Kevin O'Neill, Ben Dimagmaliw and Bill Oakley. *The League of Extraordinary Gentlemen: Volume One* (La Jolla: America's Best Comics, 2000).

Paulson, Ronald. *Emblem and Expression: Meaning in English Art of the Eighteenth Century* (Massachusetts: Harvard University Press, 1975).

Peeters, Benoît. "Four Conceptions of the Page," trans. by Jesse Cohn, *ImageText*, 3.3 (2007): np, http://www.english.ufl.edu/imagetext/archives/v3_3/peeters/ [accessed 17 March 2010].

Petersen, Robert S. "The Acoustics of Manga," in *A Comics Studies Reader*, ed. by Jeet Heer and Kent Worcester (Jackson: University Press of Mississippi, 2009), pp. 163–71.

Pinker, Steven. *The Language Instinct: The New Science of Language and Mind*, 1994. http://www.scribd.com/doc/10213245/Steven-Pinker-The-Language-Instinct [accessed 31 January 2010].

Pratt, Henry John. "Narrative in Comics." *The Journal of Aesthetics and Art Criticism*, 67.1 (2009): 107–17.

Raeburn, Daniel. *Chris Ware* (London: Laurence King Publishing Ltd., 2004).

Rifas, Leonard. "Is Dis a System?" *Comics Journal*, 284 (2007): 99–100.

Rommens, Aarnoud. "*The Language of Comics* review." *Image & Narrative*, 2.2 (2002), http://www.imageandnarrative.be/inarchive/gender/aarnoudrommens.htm [accessed 15 January 2009].

Round, Julia. "Visual Perspective and Narrative Voice in Comics: Redefining Literary Terminology." *International Journal of Comic Art*, 9.2 (2007): 316–29.

Sabin, Roger. *Adult Comics: An Introduction* (London: Routledge, 1993).

——. *Comics, Comix & Graphic Novels* (London: Phaidon Press, 1996).

Sandbrook, Dominic. "*Supergods: Our World in the Age of the Superhero* by Grant Morrison." *Sunday Times*, 3 July 2011, Culture section.

Saraceni, Mario. *The Language of Comics* (London: Routledge, 2000).

Screech, Matthew. "Jean Giraud/Moebius: Nouveau Réalisme and Science Fiction," in *The Francophone Bande Dessinée*, ed. by Charles Forsdick, Laurence Grove, Libbie McQuillan (New York: Editions Rodopi B.V., 2005), pp. 97–113.

Searle, Ronald. *The Terror of St. Trinian's and Other Drawings* (London: Penguin Classics, 2000).

Simmonds, Posy. *Gemma Bovery* (London: Jonathan Cape, 2001).

——. *Tamara Drewe* (London: Jonathan Cape, 2007).

Tallis, Raymond. *Not Saussure: A Critique of Post-Saussurean Literary Theory* (New York: St. Martin's Press, 1995).

Tanaka, Veronique [Bryan Talbot]. *Metronome* (New York: NBM Publishing, 2008).

Taylor, Joshua C. *Learning to Look: A Handbook for the Visual Arts* (Chicago: University of Chicago Press, 1957).

Thought Bubble Homepage, nd, http://thoughtbubblefestival.wordpress.com/about/ [accessed 8 October 2011].

Töpffer, Rodolphe. "Essay on Physiognomy," in *Enter the Comics*, trans. and ed. by E. Wiese (Lincoln: University of Nebraska Press, 1965).

Troutman, Phillip. "The Discourse of Comics Scholarship: A Rhetorical Analysis of Research Article Introductions." *International Journal of Comic Art*, 12.2/3 (2010): 432–44.

Varnum, Robin, and Christina Gibbons, eds. *The Language of Comics: Word and Image* (Jackson: University of Mississippi Press, 2001).

——. "Introduction," in *The Language of Comics: Word and Image*, ed. by Robin Varnum and Christina Gibbons (Jackson: University of Mississippi Press, 2001), pp. ix–xix.

Versaci, Rocco. *This Book Contains Graphic Language: Comics as Literature* (London: Continuum, 2008).

Walker, Mort. *The Lexicon of Comicana* (Lincoln: iUniverse.com, Inc., 1980).

Walsh, Richard. "The Narrative Imagination Across Media." *Modern Fiction Studies*, 52.4 (2006): 855–68.

Ware, Chris. "Big Tex." *Acme Novelty Library Number 7* (Seattle: Fantagraphics, 1996), p. 28.

——. *Jimmy Corrigan: The Smartest Kid on Earth* (London: Jonathan Cape, 2001).

———. *Quimby the Mouse* (London: Jonathan Cape, 2003).

———. *Acme Novelty Library Number 16* (Chicago: Acme Novelty Library, 2005).

———. *Acme Novelty Library Number 18* (Chicago: Acme Novelty Library, 2007).

White, Curtis. *The Spirit of Disobedience: Resisting the Charms of Fake Politics, Mindless Consumption, and the Culture of Total Work* (Sausalito: PoliPointPress, 2007).

Whitlock, Gillian. "Autographics: The Seeing 'I' of the Comics." *MFS*, 52.4 (2006): 965–79.

Wiese, Ellen. *Enter: The Comics* (Lincoln: University of Nebraska Press, 1965).

Witek, Joseph. "American Comics Criticism and the Problem of Dual Address." *International Journal of Comic Art*, 10.1 (2008): 218–225.

———. "The Arrow and the Grid," in *A Comics Studies Reader*, ed. by Jeet Heer and Kent Worcester (Jackson: University Press of Mississippi, 2009), pp. 149–56.

Wolk, Douglas. *Reading Comics: How Graphic Novels Work and What They Mean* (Cambridge, Massachusetts: De Capo Press, 2007).

Index

Page numbers in **bold** indicate an
illustration.

accent, 34–35
accented pronunciation, 32, 35–36
Acme Novelty Library Number 7, **144**
Acme Novelty Library Number 16, **152**
Acme Novelty Library Number 18, **148**,
   158, **160**
Addams, Charles, 84–87, **85**, **86**, 89
adjusting the model of language, 13, 171
"All Different," **42**
alliteration, 20, 28, 32–34, 62
Anglophone: academia, 3; scholarship, 3,
   170, 222
approximate, 28–29, 34
arbitrariness, 10–11, 169, 171, 174, 181–82,
   194, 196, 248
arbitrary constituent units, 9
arbitrary minimal units. *See* minimal
   units: arbitrary
arbitrary signs, 43, 137, 170, 174, 182,
   196
arbitrary symbol, 150, 177, 191–92, 195
arbitrary system, 174, 195
arbitrary words, 9, 174
Arrested Development, 99
art form. *See* form: art
arthrology, 109–10, 127–29, 134, 140–41
Asterios Polyp, 169, 171–96, **172**, **174**, **175**,
   178, **180**, **182**, **184**, **186**, **187**, **188**, **189**,
   191
Auster, Paul, 90–96, **91**, **93**, **94**, **96**, **101**,
   105

B., David, 199
"Bag Action," **205**, **217**
Barry, Lynda, 41–58, **42**, **51**, 62, 65, 78,
   222, 230–31, **230**, 248
Barthes, Roland, 8, 29, 78, 104
Batman, 228, 243
Berry, Hannah, 199, 206–7, **207**, 212–19,
   213, **214**, **215**, **218**, 233
"Big Tex," 143–45, **144**
"Biology 101," **211**
Black Freighter, The, 136
Black Hole, 199–214, **200**, **202**, **203**, **204**,
   205, **210**, **211**, **212**, 217–18, **217**
Bovery, Gemma, 68–69, 71–72, 74–76,
   254
Britten and Brülightly, 199, 206–18, **207**,
   213, **214**, **215**, **218**
Building Stories, 151, 154, 157
Burns, Charles, 199–206, **200**, **202**, **203**,
   204, **205**, **210**, **211**, **212**, 216–17, **217**
Butler, Judith, 53–56

Carrier, David, 89, 100–102, 255
Carroll, Lewis, 21–22, 37
cartoons, 65, 85–87, 89–90, 169–71,
   173–74, 182, 192, 194, 207, 255
chiaroscuro, 203–4, 206
childhood, 94, 96, 147, 206
City of Glass, 90–96, **91**, **93**, **94**, **96**,
   101–2, **101**, 104–5, **105**, 239
Coconino County, 33, 38
Cohn, Neil, 42, 109–10, 117–18, 124–29,
   124, **125**, 133–34, 139–41, 149, 153, 156,
   160, 169

267